洞月亮

CAVE MOON PRESS

YAKIMA 中 WASHINGTON

2018

Alfredo Arreguín's World of Wonders

Critical Perspectives

Editors: Lauro Flores and Doug Johnson

洞月亮
CAVE MOON PRESS
Y A K I M A 中 W A S H I N G T O N

© Copyright 2018, Cave Moon Press
All rights reserved by each contributing scholar. All pieces used with permission.
Artwork by: Alfredo Arreguín
Front cover image by Alfredo Arreguín
Cover design by Doug Johnson
Copy Editing by Lisa Alvarado and Lauros Flores
Interior design: Doug Johnson

ISBN: 978-0692137567

Alfredo Arreguín's World of Wonders

Critical Perspectives

Acknowledgments

Tess Gallagher, "Viva La Vida" was first published in honor of the Alfredo Arreguín's exhibit of same title, which toured throughout United States in 1992.

Raymond Carver, "Menudo" was first published in *Where I'm Calling From* by Raymond Carver, 1988.

Raymond Carver, "What you Need for Painting" was first published in *All of Us* by Raymond Carver, 1996, gratefully used with the permission of Tess Gallagher.

Peter Rodriguez, "Alfredo Arreguín" was first published in *AMERICAS Magazine* by Peter Rodriguez, 1984.

Rigoberto González, "Papalotzin and the Monarchs: A Bilingual Tale of Breaking Down Walls" was first published in *Teaching Tolerance Magazine* 30 (Fall, 2006).

Jose Felipe Herrera, "alfredo pinta pinta" (from *Clay Dragons,* 2014) was first published in *A Arreguín: Correspondencias,* Marquand Books, 2015.

Jose Felipe Herrera, "TASMANO" (from *Tasmano Notebook,* 2014) was first published in *A Arreguín: Correspondencias,* Marquand Books, 2015.

Lauro Flores, "The Eyes of Arreguín" was first published in *Alfredo Arreguín: Patterns of Dreams and Nature* 2002/2007. University of Washington Press.

Lawrence Matsuda, "Finding Morelia, Michoacan de Ocampo" was first published in *A Cold Wind From Idaho,* Black Lawrence Press, 2010.

Lawrence Matsuda, "Rose City Vacation (Excerpt)" was first published in *Boogie Woogie Crisscross* MadHat Press, 2016.

Linda Hodges, for help and support with images in the book at Linda Hodge Gallery, Seattle Washington.

Lisa Alvarado for her help in copy editing the English in the book.

Lauro Flores for his help in copy editing the Spanish in the book.

Table of Contents

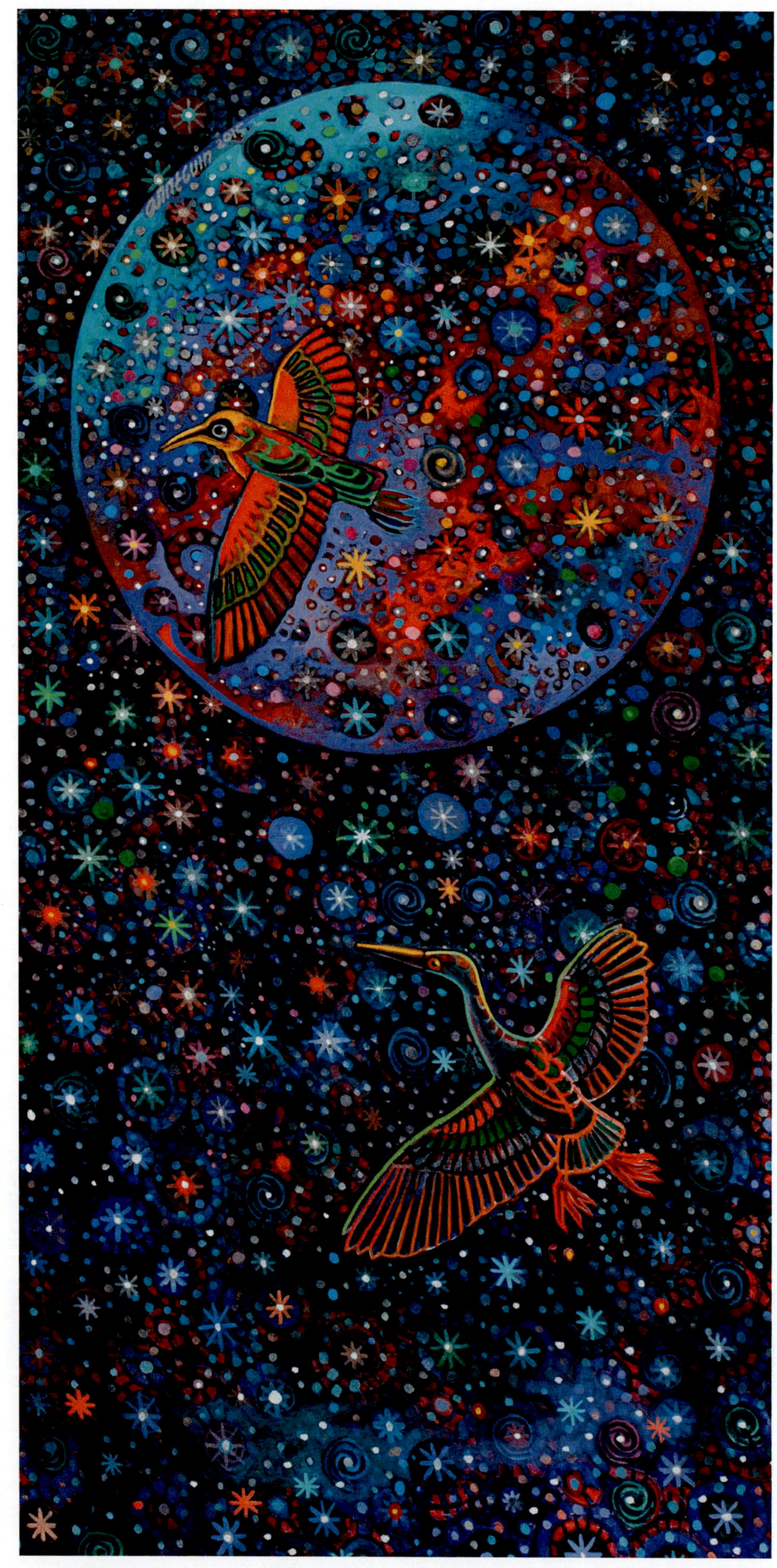

Under the Stars. 2015, 48 × 24, collection of the artist

Lauro Flores

Párvulo viaje

(Sueño de Las Canoas)

¿Aún recuerdas, mi querido Alfredo,
aquel verde paraje recogido
en un cerro, reclinado en sus faldas?
¿Aún perdura en tu alma el recuerdo
de tu párvulo viaje por las pardas
laderas de aquel volcán dormido?

Las Canoas, rancho remoto, vecino
del viejo cerro, allí donde moraron
mis ancestros, y a donde un claro día
tu abuelo, los rieles del destino,
un intrépido tren de cercanías
y tres nobles arrieros te llevaron.

En aquella recóndita colina,
descubriste el ocote por vez primera,
y viste el vuelo errante de la golondrina;
allí sentiste, también por vez primera,
el aroma del bosque, de la primavera,
y el porfiado perfume de la trementina.

Allí contaste las fulgentes estrellas,
contemplaste el Arado y el Pequeño Cazo,
hasta que las voces aquellas,
moduladas en su sorda armonía,
y el abarcinado ronroneo del gato
te cerraron los ojos hasta el otro día.

Childhood Trip

(Dream of Las Canoas)

Do you still remember, dear Alfredo,
that secluded green place nestled
atop a mountain, reclined on its foothills?
Do you still preserve the memory
of your first childhood trip over the grayish
slopes of the sleeping volcano?

Las Canoas, remote village near
the old hill where my ancestors settled,
the place where, on a clear day,
your grandfather, destiny's rails,
an intrepid short-distance train
and three noble mule drivers took you.

On that concealed hillside,
you discovered kindling for the first time,
and saw the meandering flight of the swallow;
there, you felt, also for the first time,
the fragrance of the woods and spring,
and the persistent perfume of pine resin.

There, you counted the resplendent stars;
you gazed at the Big Dipper and the Little Dipper
until those droning voices,
modulated into muffled harmony,
and the brindled purring of the cat
finally closed your eyes until the following day.

Tess Gallagher

Viva La Vida

A bridge of forest and jungle connects my thirty-year friendship with Alfredo Arreguín, and it is visible in Arreguín's painting and the spiritual climate of my poems.

Rain and vegetable abundance. Wildlife, the unseen and unseeable. The great tall darkness with its chinks of light—that sense of mystery and beauty were early gifts to our psyches—a poet and a painter meeting, linked by rain forests thousands of miles apart. Alfredo Arreguín had come as a youth to respect and love the rain forests of the state of Guerrero, Mexico while working on a dam there, while I had been raised in logging camps near the Olympic Peninsula rain forest.

At the beginning of our friendship in the early 60's in Seattle Alfredo Arreguín was rather the *enfant terrible* and I was simply the infant, a kid literally from the sticks. It was a ragged, Bohemian group we formed with Alfredo at the center-gigantically unpredictable, maniacally jovial or swirling like liquid fire around us, scorching us with insults and insights by turn.

We welcomed each other's stories, inspired, tested and argued with each other, viewed and listened to our early attempts at art in those days one biographer has called "The Blue Moon Period," after the bar we frequented near the University of Washington where were students, the same bar where the Pulitzer Prize winning poet-teacher, Theodore Roethke, drank in the afternoons wearing his bedroom slippers.

I'm grateful that this mutuality of art and friendship allows me now to turn my art of words toward Arreguín's rare gift in these wild, sacred grottoes—to say things perhaps no one else can. As a poet, I can mention Arreguín next to the name of Federico García Lorca, the great Spanish poet, for Arreguín too is a lyric-narrative poet whose Miltonic range hints its hell by implication because it so gloriously gives its vision of paradise on earth. But Lorca says it best:

> "I came into this world with eyes
> and I'll leave without them."

For this is what Arreguín celebrates first of all—the ability of our eyes to feast. His palpitations of color and light and arrested movement awaken our subliminal vision, which belongs to metaphor. His paintings seem to force our entire being to experience its livingness as an insatiable yearning and questing of the eyes. Before one of his jungles we become freshly aware of the tactile sensuality of our reaching, its sighted caressing. We feel our curiousity leading

us forward, experience its pleasure in color and pattern and in the overlapping discernable animal and human shapes emerging from the density. It is this very density itself which insures a non-linear reading of these paintings, for the eye must leap, must search, even lose itself, since the narrative is airborne and lyrical. That is why I speak of Lorca and not Gabriel García Márquez.

If Lorca developed the notion of "Deep Song" from the ballads of the Andalusian gypsies, Arreguín has invented a form of "deep painting"—emotional and sensual, splashed with the sapphire water of his dreams of a world in harmony. These paintings are his answer to an era during which rupture has been the ruling climate in art, yielding now perhaps to an age of convergences, of dialogue.

We are mightily instructed and delighted by the way everything holds and supports everything else in his paintings, by the interdependence and dynamic implosion of life at every corner of his canvases, the inextricable relationships of plant-to-animal-to human life.

I call Arreguín's paintings "deep" in their psychic and spiritual capacities, but also as I am aware of their physical composition through accrued detail and daily meditative revision. Like Matisse who was a tireless worker, Arreguín goes to his canvas early and works sustained long hours. Someone said of Mary Cassatt that she was also an architect in each of her paintings, and I think the same may be said of Arreguín whose keen sense of design and ongoing awareness of architecture are evident, especially in the pyramidal shapes of his madonnas, but also in the sophisticated handling of framing within the canvas.

Since I've been visiting Arreguín's studios these many years I've had occasion to see paintings in their early stages metamorphose Into the encyclopedic catalogue of impulse and intent so rich with nanging, sinuous tendrils in their final result. For every finished painting, literally dozens of paintings have disappeared under Arreguín's brush as he embellished and explored his canvas with the meticulous care of a cell biologist.

In *Chaos* James Gleick describes "forms in nature--not visible forms, but shapes embedded in the fabric of motion—waiting to be revealed." It is this excitement in Arreguín—of revealed form still clinging to its instant of being arrested from its mystery—that so engages me. The poet John Ashbery's line, "Wonder that confronts its own wonder" comes to mind.

Much has been said to place Arreguín historically at the head of a movement in the early 1970's called "Pattern and Design" and more recently "Pattern Painting." I admit to feeling these categories are as superficial, as the term "minimalist," when applied to the stories of Raymond Carver, my late husband and a close friend of Arreguín's. Such categories are often a robbery of genius, reductive for their attempt to roll the artist onto the skein of lazy attentions. The complex iconography of Arreguín's patterns don't separate out from the surfaces of his paintings, but remain integral aggregations clustered to meaning, as if they were spontaneous electrical discharges from the artist's mind to his brush. Even his ornaments are like waves washing the shore of our sight clean.

Having mentioned Raymond Carver, I want to recall having introduced him to Alfredo and his wife, the painter Susan Lytle, in 1980. while they were still living in their humble but glad cottage on N.E. 15th Street. I'd known them through the 70's, and Ray ultimately wrote a portrait in his story *Menudo* of Alfredo in that house as he fictionally prepares this Mexican New Year's dish with tripe. Ray appreciated Alfredo's story of personal struggle as an artist, so close to his own, in which the silent entry on both their chronicles was "the family subsists at the poverty level." Alfredo's choice against university teaching meant that the family, which included their daughter Leslie by then, lived precariously from the sale of one painting to the next. Yet what a sense of abundance and thanksgiving and celebration persisted in that household of artists! I took my out-of-town friends there as I might have taken them to a monument. Raymond Carver and I, as two writers collaborating and making a life together, were inspired by their dedication—Alfredo Arreguín and Susan Lytle—each artist stationed at opposite ends of the small dining room cum living room cum entryway with a scarred, plank table the central element of furniture, painting day in and day out.

It was no accident of recognition when Lytle began (in the early 1970's) to read biographies of the Mexican painter, Frida Kahlo, as ballast to her own life with Arreguín. Lytle, like Kahlo, continued her art while companioning a painter nearly twenty years her senior, whose creative genius has received international recognition. One of the personal metaphors behind Arreguín's Kahlo series may be the acknowledgement of Lytle's many unspoken gifts to his work, especially in pieces such as his *Echo Kahlo* in which Kahlo (as metaphor for Lytle) is embedded in a vortex of jungle effusion.

Certainly Arreguín had his own early connections to Kahlo. He attended the National Preparatory School in México City, where Kahlo first met Diego Rivera, the great Mexican muralist whom she later married. Alfredo and his playmates bounced balls against the mural Rivera had painted years earlier. Add to this a shared fidelity to Mexican Indian life and folk art, and his attraction to Kahlo gains dimension. Kahlo represents an image of maverick self-making in the ace of extremities of physical pain and societal strictures. Perhaps this is why she has become a popular icon of the 90's. But Arreguín was painting her in 1978 long before her recent popularity. He reinvests her image with its essential solitude which, in *Cuarto Kahlo,* has the viewer scanning the foliage for the fourth Kahlo who is stitched upside down into the tapestry of water. Frida's explanation for having painted herself so often was: "because I was so often alone." As we search for her in this painting we add ourselves to an elusive embrace by the jungle that all but reabsorbs her.

Arreguín's patterns are taken from Colonial Mexican art, Baroque church facades, decorative Pre-Colombian art, animal and floral motifs of ceramic work from Tlaquepaque, as well as Islamic architecture, Indian Tantric painting, Eastern, and Near Eastern sources as diverse as the stenciled kimono or the intricately chased sword hilt. The dialogue of these patterns causes all history to become one instantaneous present, what the great Mexican poet Octavio Paz has called an *eternal now.*

The *eternal now* seems to be the time of Arreguín's paintings, even though we know his madonnas—*Madona Afro-Latina* (1989). with here upturned palms in and the sad expression of *Nuestra Señora de La Selva* communicate a timely plea for the threatened jungle behind them.

Arreguín's fierce *Nuestra Señora de Cuzco* intensifies the guardianship role of the madonnas. She seems primordial, agressively adorned, full of warnings and omens despite the floral design of her mantel and the medicinal lily in her left hand. Her face is painted for battle and camouflage at once.

In *Sacrificio na Amazonia* 1989. Arreguín pays direct homage to Mendes, the Brazilian rubber harvester martyred on Dec. 22, 1988 for his defense of the Amazon jungle. The face of Mendes loom broodingly, impervious to death, released into his full spiritual potential as the abiding conscience and guardian of the rainforest.

Although the immediate imperative of protecting these rare plant and animal preserves does accentuate the impact of these paintings, something beyond environmental mandates will cause them to endure as works of art. As with the poetry I admire, productive reticence keeps Arreguín's work from entirely yielding usefulness. In them we experience the undeniable unity of living organisms. We seem to sense the invisible templates behind growth itself.

Arreguín's hypnotic meditations assume their most sustained vision in the triptych *Sueño(Dream: Eve Before Adam),* 1992. He painted these lush panels over a period of seven months, whereas most of his larger paintings have taken four to eight weeks. One doesn't look at these paintings, one *gazes*—is made to fix the eyes in a steady, prolonged attention as it to enter what Neruda describes as "the great silence when grass was born."

Especially in this triptych, I am aware of how pattern induces a certain state of tranquility, a spiritual balance in which it is possible again to believe in what is before us, against that readiness of irony to collapse the ideal—this Eden which is an invention our imaginations move to sustain. Arreguín has made the jungle paradise more real than life. It has enough excess to be true-this sinless, effulgence of breasts and butterflies, parrots and red berries, baboons and iguana, tendrils and primordial eyes emerging from indigo leaves.

Octavio Paz reminds us that physics perceives matter to be neither a substance nor a thing, but "a relation."Arreguín's intense desire for relation makes the direct assault on the nervous system, which real painting is—what Francis Bacon calls "the mysterious and continuous struggle with chance." We feel nature's ability to perpetually invent and erase or subvert that invention.

The ambition of painting at times to defy its very stillness is present in *Siete Leguas* named for Emiliano Zapata's magical horse which Alfredo painted for the cover of *The Lover of Horses*, my first book of short stories. After Zapata was ambushed, and killed, in the Mexican Revolution of 1910, his horse made its escape into the mountains and became a metaphor for Zapata's indomitable spirit, since the horse is said to have travelled seven leagues back to the revolutionary forces without Zapata. The horizontal band of what appear to be variations on American Indian designs at the horse's legs seems to give velocity and power so the mosaic of horse speeds away from us, even as it plunges steadily in place. Susan Lytle read my title story aloud, as Alfredo painted and I believe his eye and hand captured the gypsy flavor of freedom and animal spirit power there.

I know of no better way to free my painter friend from these attempts to describe what he does than to quote again from Lorca in the conversation of the Lieutenant Colonel of the Civil Guard with the Gypsy:

Lt. Colonel: Where were you?

Gypsy: On the bridge over the rivers.

Lt. Colonel: Over what rivers?

Gypsy: Over all the rivers.

Lt. Colonel: What were you doing there?

Gypsy: Building a tower of cinnamon .

Perhaps this then is the ultimate gift of the poet to the painter: to restore the painter's freedom to build the tower of cinnamon, to paint those images which compel his art beyond reason and reality, in this case Alfredo Arreguín's invincible *Yes* to life.

Doug Johnson

Writers Celebrate Alfredo

"You listen to me. Listen to what I say, man. I'm your family now," Alfredo said. (*Menudo* by Raymond Carver, 1988)

When you experience the art of Alfredo Arreguín you quietly understand that the human family has hope. Alfredo, as a true master, uses a specific niche to tap into the universality our experience. He offers peace and hope with his special way of viewing the world. As a constant friend of poets and writers, he has enriched and inspired many an article, story and poem. This book compiles perspectives, stories and poems for Alfredo to return the favor.

A note about the structure and book design. This is an unconventional book because it blends so many different types of writing. Like Alfredo's paintings it has its own rhythm. Each section starts with poetry and a short story. Then it is followed by non-fiction prose either offering personal anecdotes or scholarly commentary on Alfredo's place in the canon of the art world. The sections are interspersed with Alfredo's paintings. Occasionally, there are images internal to articles where the writers is making some specific comments. There also is an intermingling of English and Spanish. When the authors and poets offered translations, they were utilized. Images are sometimes placed on the horizontal to enjoy as much of the artwork as possible. Hopefully, the entire design emulates the dream world he transports people into as they view his paintings.

Like Alfredo, this book is unique for a scholarly anthology. Instead of like-minded scholars speaking to a theory or figure in history, this anthology is full of scholars from different schools. The vessel shapes the contents, and formatting the written word shapes a scholar's world after their years of training. It shapes their perspectives on the life and work of Alfredo. This book, celebrates his life. More than spotting the formatting, the hope is that the human family will notice the readers, writers, and Alfredo are all at a party celebrating his life and work.

It is a rare gift from the universe for a person to recognize their talent, hone it, and offer it to the world over decades and decades. Alfredo is a rare person to have recognized his gift. Although people have tried to label Alfredo as belonging to a certain school of Pattern Painters, he has remained uniquely his own, not accepting the labels of the art world. We all want to say we are unique, but it is part of the human condition to seek the protection of the herd. An art label offers the safety of the herd. Alfredo, however, launched into the risky and competitive world of oil painting and invented his own unique, visual vocabulary. We are all grateful for this leap of love and faith in his ability. He has freed us all to seek our own version of the world. He has proven that it is in the description of a phenomenon, whether about politics or nature that we determine the outcome. Looking at it differently challenges the *status quo*. Looking at it differently soothes a troubled mind. From children to professors in universities, we all "get it" when we look at his paintings.

The unique thing about Alfredo is that from being honored with pieces in the Smithsonian, to winning the OHTLI Award (The highest honor from the Mexican government) to being given the keys to the city of Morelia (an honor shared only with Pope Francis), his kind humility in his day to day life can lend some people to discount how great his art remains for the Americas. He welcomes people into the conversation and helps us all "get it" with his self-effacing grace.

I am eternally grateful to Alfredo and Susan for acting as mentors on this part of my journey. A great deal of gratitude also goes to Lauro Flores, for his guidance and acting as the co-editor of this anthology. He gave the community the seminal scholarship on Alfredo in his book, *Alfredo Arreguín: Patterns of Dreams and Nature* (2002/2007) University of Washington Press, and inspired the idea for this work.

We hope you enjoy the celebration. We hope you enjoy the party.

Doug Johnson Ph.D.
Cave Moon Press

Raymond Carver

What You Need for Painting
from a letter by Renoir

PALETTE:
Flake white
Chrome yellow
Naples yellow
Yellow ochre
Raw umber
Venetian red
French vermilion
Madder lake
Rose madder
Cobalt blue
Ultramarine blue
Emerald green
Ivory black
Raw sienna
Viridian green
White lead

DON'T FORGET:
Palette knife
Scraping knife
Essence of turpentine

BRUSHES?
Pointed marten-hair brushes
Flat hog-hair brushes

Indifference to everything except your canvas.
The ability to work like a locomotive.
An iron will.

"You know, you paint like a locomotive, Alfredo."
"That's right, Ray. A loco with a motive."

(Conversation between Alfredo and his friend, Raymond Carver.)

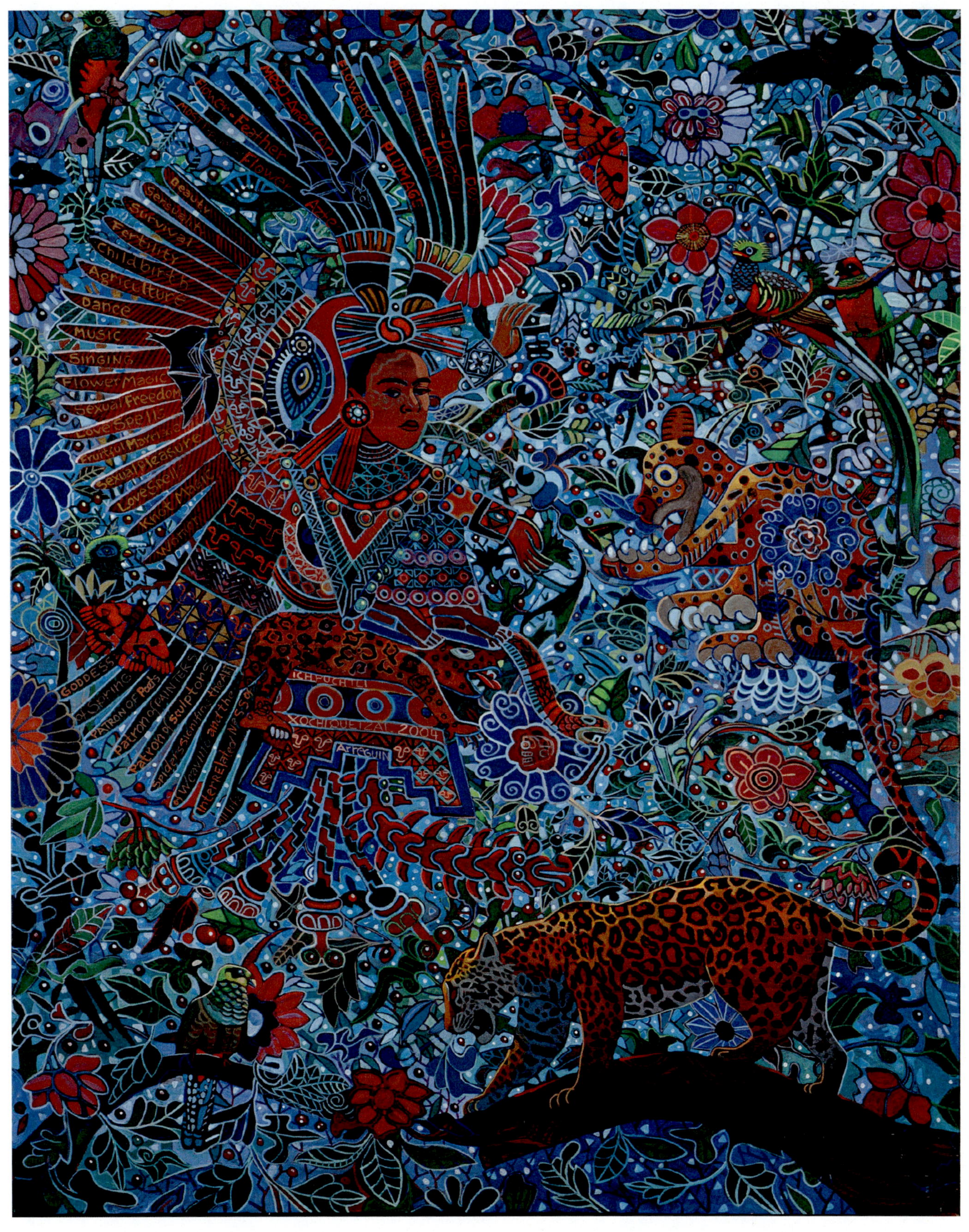

Xochiquetzal, The Birth of Flowers, 2004, 60 × 48 in., private collection

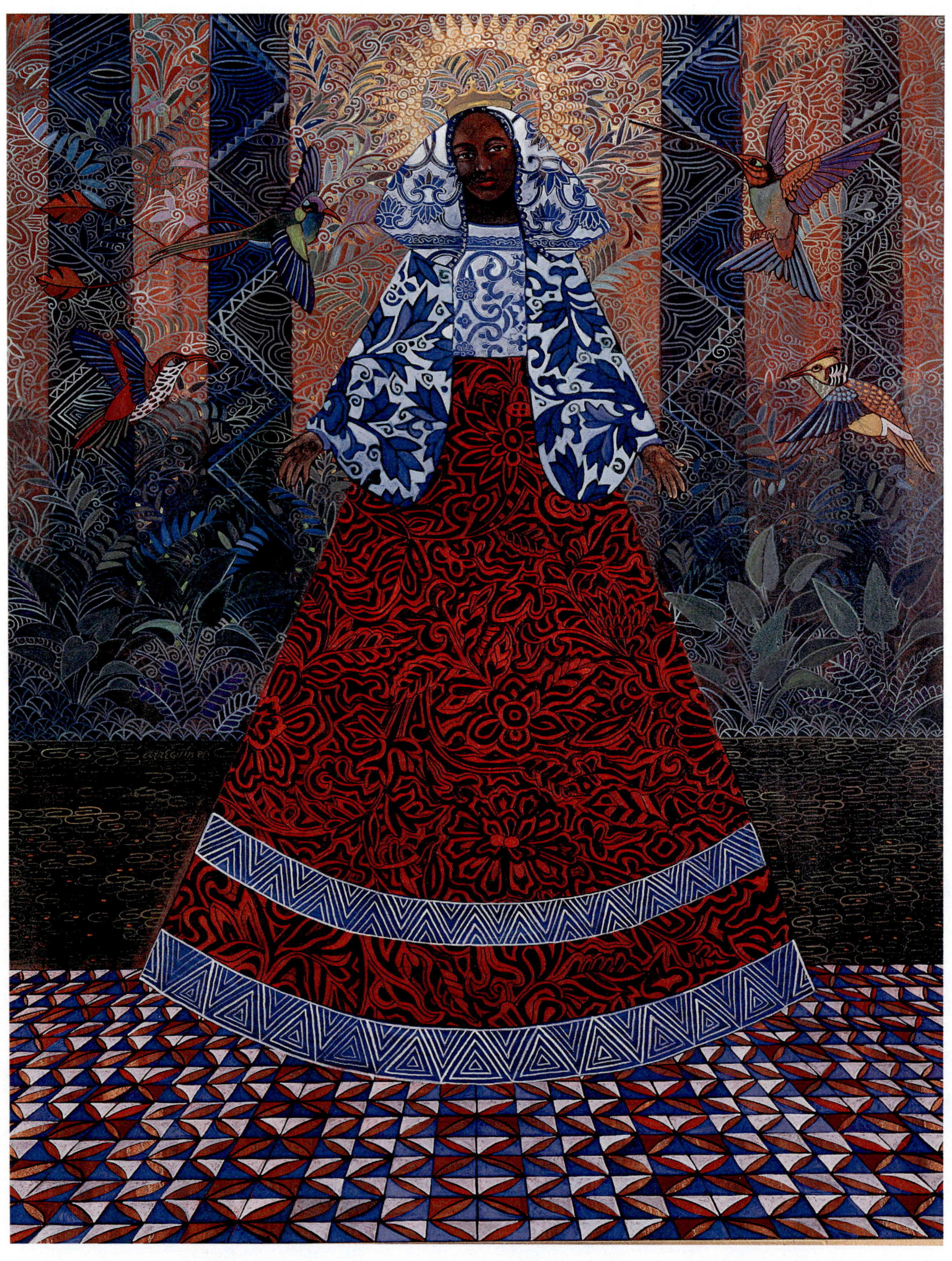

Madona Afro-Latina, 1989, 54 × 42 in., private collection

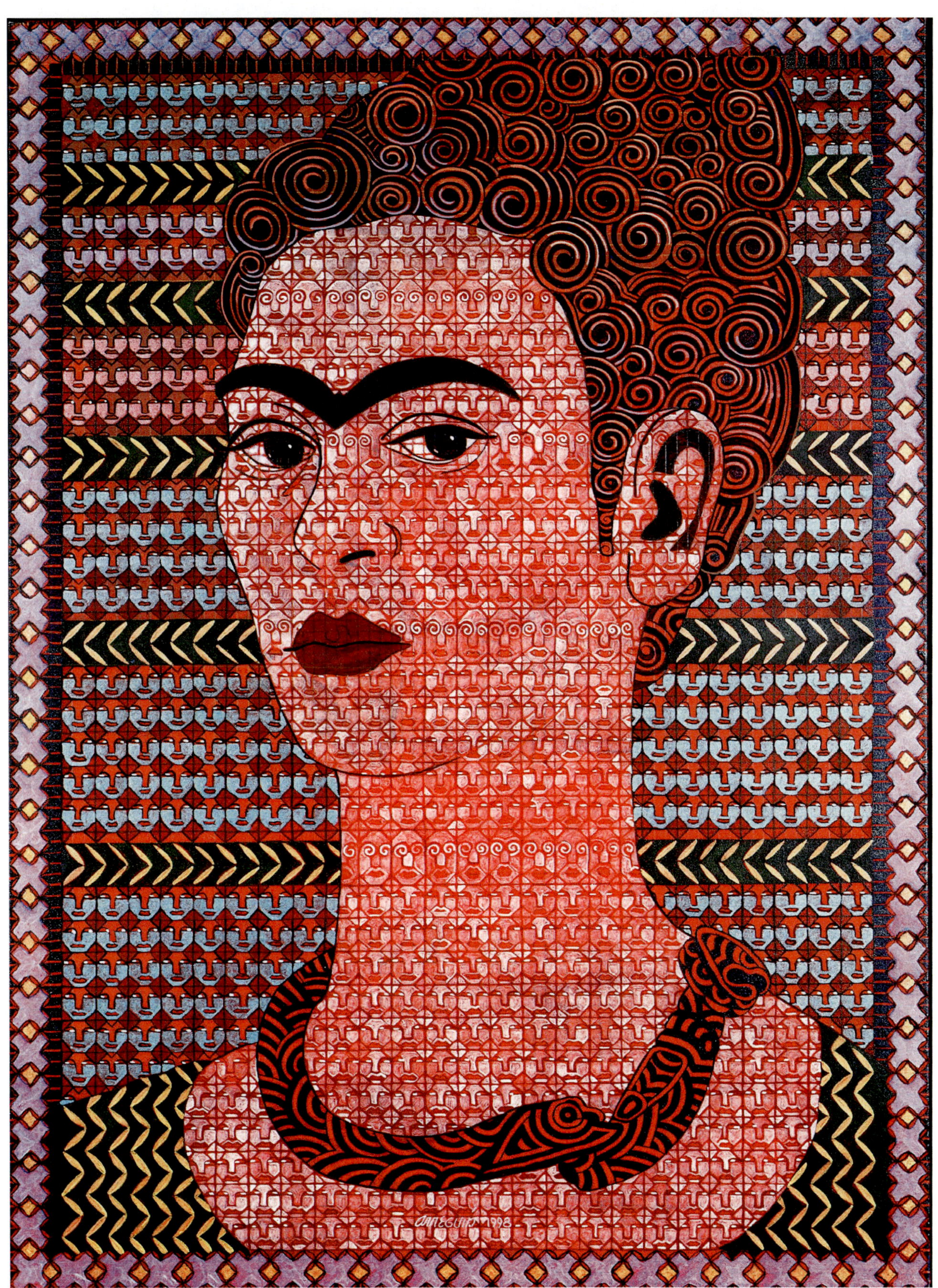

El Collar, 1998, 60 × 48 in., collection of the artist

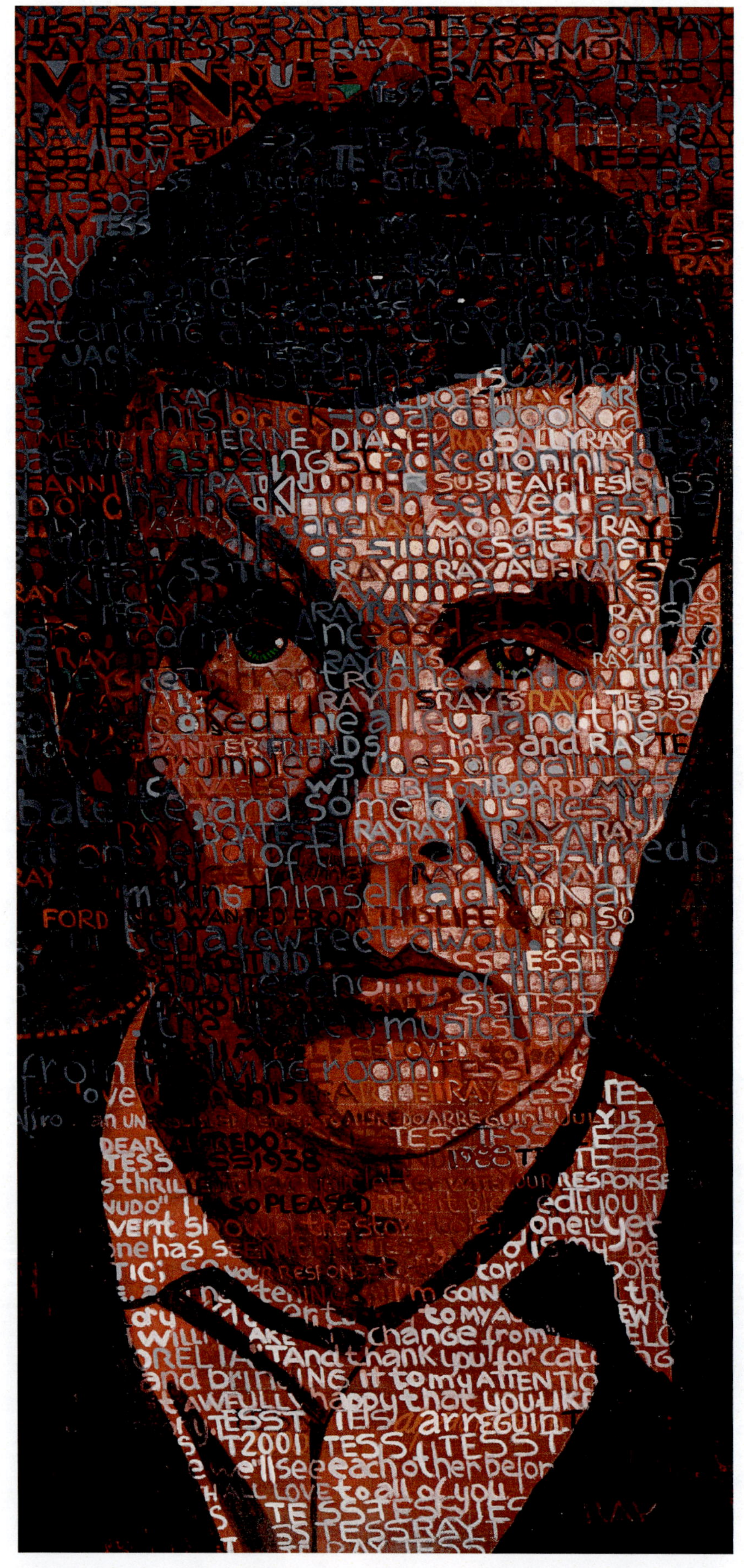

Mi Amigo, Ray, 2001, 36 × 18 in., collection of the artist

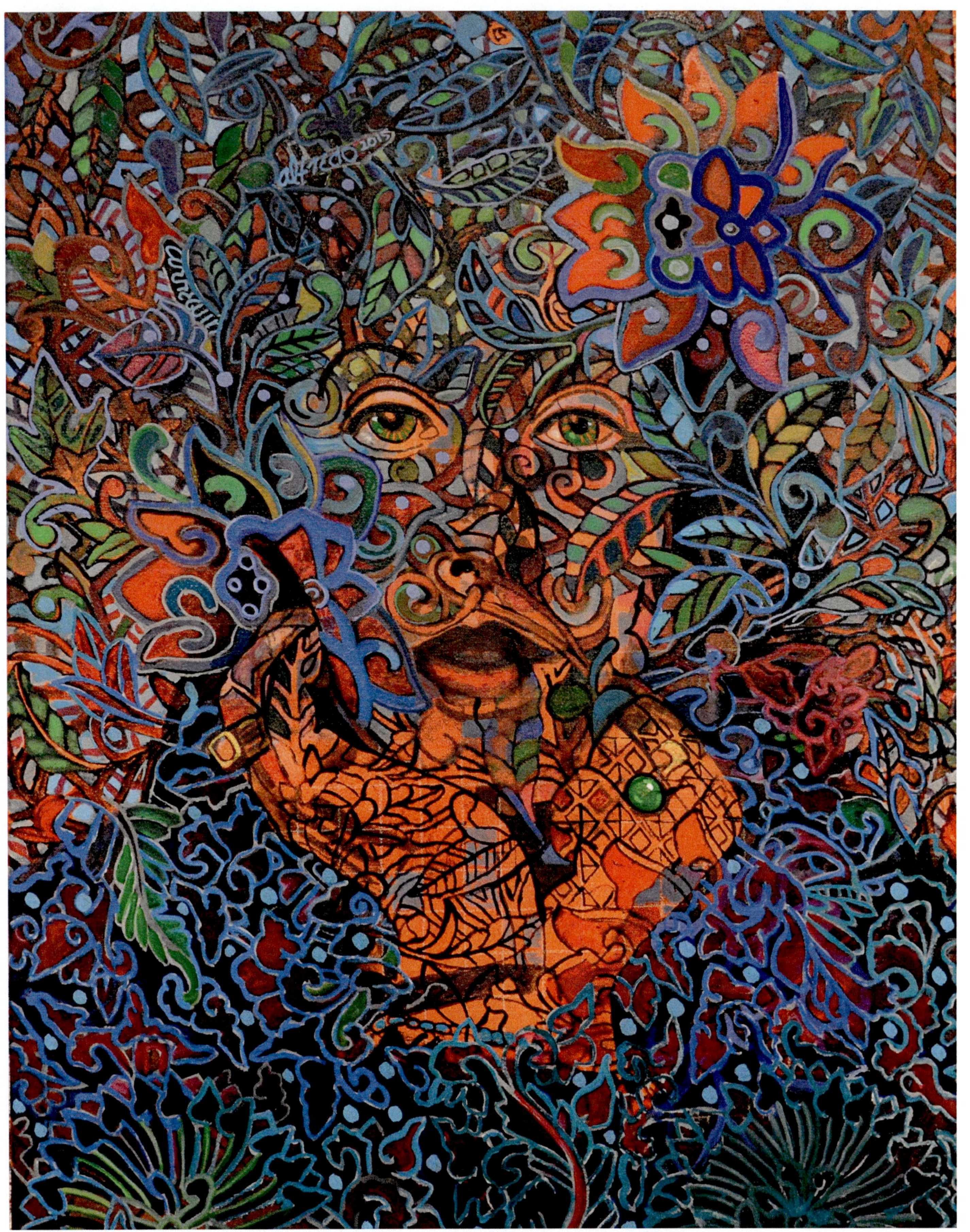

Green-eyed Poet, 2015, 30 × 24 in., private collection

Tess Gallagher

Reaching

Eyes, mouth, hands—you've left me equipped
in your portrait "Green-eyed Poet" with essentials, all
for moving outward, to touch, to open
what may be touched and opened. The eyes
open other eyes, have opened
hearts, hundreds of books, have met
the stolid searching eyes of the doe
in the orchard beside her fawn, teaching it to run
or stay. Fifty-three years we've shared

art and lives, with and without Ray,
whose ring of marriage is on my finger
yet. As is your right, you've turned the lapis
of his love-ring from blue
to green, to match my eyes, yet
exceeding them in that early spring promise-green.
The lips parted to the eternal 'would-speak' or
'about-to-speak' or 'have spoken', the past

edging out future. The hands nest the head,
cradle the chin, anchoring the flower
of the face, otherwise subsumed
by filigree of blue tendrils. My gypsy soul—out
of which I reach for words to
carry my life and the lives of those I love--
gazes like a fountain of wonder from every corner
where your brush has touched down. You know

that the soul of a poet, like blue gentian
growing alone in the forest, should never be
lifted from its incubation of shade. Providing
against this, you hide the stem, the long pedestal
of neck Modigliani might have exposed. Your life's work
forbids the soul-death of any living thing--so we are joined
in our reaching and finding, our having slept
under the same stars, wandering the fields

of our ever-emerging imaginations,
as if our vagabond natures could exact something
precious from air itself. Your poetry--of strokes,
of line and color—un-words me, stammers me
into myself like laughter in rain, so I am
lifted by your intensity out of self, by
gratitude. In every painting you bestow a democracy
of means as we gaze, re-making the world as

accessible and renewing to even the poorest of us.
What can a poet give in return--I who suffer often
the condition of word-poverty in the universe
of the ready-made?
Water-borne moonlight can lave a shore. It's
yours. Candles lit in a circle charm
and protect. I give them to you. The sky-white bay
below my window. All yours—with its ocean liners,

cruise ships, tug boats and skiffs. They are to dream
on. May a halo of hummingbirds attend you,
so when you go for your walks you'll be recognized
instantly as a deity from the Administration of
Delight for the Banishment of Misery. While I'm
at it, wouldn't you like a few golden eggs that won't
bother to hatch? And a bunch of blue grapes picked
by hands from your birthplace, Morelia? I'll also

empty my sack of about-to-be-dreams near
the basement wall that is your easel. There is
no last thing I wouldn't give you, my friend
and collaborator in the offices of Mysteries Unlimited.
This poem, like your portrait of me, can never
end or be finished, only pause, waiting to be seen
back into our precious continuing lives
made of light, of air.

for Alfredo Arreguín
on the gift of his portrait of me,
"Green-eyed Poet" —Tess Gallagher

Valentine Delivered by a Raven

—For Alfredo and Ray

Its beak is red and it has a battlefield-look
as if it's had its pickings and come away
of its own volition. Elsewhere the Emperor Frederick
sleeps on, guarded by ravens, and may yet rise
from deathly slumber and walk the earth
again. Who knows what's long enough
when death's involved. I stand on my love's grave
and say aloud in a swoop of gulls over
the bay, "I kiss your lips, babe," and it's not
grotesque, even though the mind knows what it
knows, and mostly doesn't. Language,
that great concealer, is more than generous, gives
always what it doesn't have. I stare into the dazzling
impertinent eye of the messenger. He's
been tending the dead so long his eyes are garnets,
his wings cracked open to either side, two
fissures savage with light. I bend
in recognition and take up a holly bough left
as in the old adornment of doorways. The hard, red
berries glisten and tremble in their nest of
green, so when he speaks I hear him

with the attention of a red berry before a covetous

bright eye, and what I need l take

in empires before he flaps away on my love's errands

and I am cinnabar and fog in the doorway.

With love on Valentine's Day, February 14, 1990—Tess

Raymond Carver

Menudo

I can't sleep, but when I'm sure my wife Vicky is asleep, I get up and look through our bedroom window, across the street, at Oliver and Amanda's house. Oliver has been gone for three days, but his wife Amanda is awake. She can't sleep either. It's four in the morning, and there's not a sound outside—no wind, no cars, no moon even—just Oliver and Amanda's place with the lights on, leaves heaped up under the front windows.

A couple of days ago, when I couldn't sit still, I raked our yard—Vicky's and mine. I gathered all the leaves into bags, tied off the tops, and put the bags alongside the curb. I had an urge then to cross the street and rake over there, but I didn't follow through. It's my fault things are the way they are across the street.

I've only slept a few hours since Oliver left. Vicky saw me moping around the house, looking anxious, and decided to put two and two together. She's on her side of the bed now, scrunched on to about ten inches of mattress. She got into bed and tried to position herself so she wouldn't accidently roll into me while she slept. She hasn't moved since she lay down, sobbed, and then dropped into sleep. She's exhausted. I'm exhausted too.

I've taken nearly all of Vicky's pills, but I still can't sleep. I'm keyed up. But maybe if I keep looking I'll catch a glimpse of Amanda moving around insider her house, or else find her peering from behind a curtain, trying to see what she can see over here.

What if I do see her? So what? What then?

Vicky says I'm crazy. She said worse things too last night. But who could blame her? I told her—I had to—but I didn't tell her it was Amanda. When Amanda's name came up, I insisted it wasn't her. Vicky suspects, but I wouldn't name names. I wouldn't say who, even though she kept pressing and then hit me a few times in the head.

"What's it matter *who*?" I said. "You've never met the woman," I lied. "You don't know her." That's when she started hitting me.

I feel *wired*. That's what my painter friend Alfredo used to call it when he talked about friends coming down off something. *Wired*. I'm wired.

This thing is nuts. I know it is, but I can't stop thinking about Amanda. Things are so bad just now I even find myself thinking about my first wife, Molly. I loved Molly, I thought, more than my own life.

I keep picturing Amanda in her pink nightgown, the one I like on her so much, along with her pink slippers. And I feel certain she's in the big leather chair right now, under the brass reading lamp. She's smoking cigarettes, one after the other. There are two ashtrays close at hand, and they're both full. To the left of her chair, next to the lamp, there's an end table stacked with magazines—the usual magazines that nice people read. We're nice people, all of us, to a point. Right this minute, Amanda is, I imagine, paging through a magazine, stopping every so often to look at an illustration or a cartoon.

Two days ago, in the afternoon, Amanda said to me, "I can't read books anymore. Who has the time?" It was the day after Oliver had left, and we were in this little café in the industrial part of the city. "Who can concentrate anymore?" she said, stirring her coffee. "Who reads? Do you read?" (I shook my head.) "Somebody must read, I guess. You see all these books around in store windows, and there are those clubs. Somebody's reading," she said. "Who? I don't know anybody who reads."

That what she said, apropos of nothing—that is, we weren't talking about books, we were talking about our *lives*. Books had nothing to do with it.

"What did Oliver say when you told him?"
Then it struck me that what were saying—the tense, watchful expressions we wore—belonged to the people on afternoon TV programs that I'd never done more than switch on and then off.
Amanda looked down and shook her head, as if she couldn't bear to remember.
"You didn't admit who it was you were involved with, did you?"

She shook her head again.

"You're sure of that?" I waited until she looked up from her coffee.

"I didn't mention any names, if that's what you mean."

"Did he say where he was going, or how long he'd be away?" I said, wishing I didn't have to hear myself. This was my neighbor I was talking about. Oliver Porter. A man I'd helped drive out of his home.

"He didn't say where. A hotel. He said I should make my arrangements and be gone—*be gone*, he said. It was like biblical the way he said it—out of his house, out of his *life*, in a week's time. I guess he's coming back then. So we have to decide something real important, real soon, honey. You and I have to make up our minds
pretty damn quick."

It was her turn to look at me now, and I know she was looking for a sign of lifelong commitment. "A week," I said. I looked at my coffee, which had gotten cold. A lot had happened in a little while, and we were trying to take it in. I don't know what long-term things, if any, we'd thought about those months as we moved from flirtation to love, and then afternoon assignments. In any case, we were in a serious fix now. Very serious. We'd never expected—no in a hundred years—to be hiding out in a café, in the middle of the afternoon, trying to decide matters like this.

I raised my eyes, and Amanda began stirring her coffee. She kept stirring it. I touched her hand, and the spoon dropped out of her fingers. She picked it up and began stirring again. We could have been anybody drinking coffee at a table under fluorescent lights in a run-down café. Anybody, just about. Ii took Amanda's hand and held it, and it seemed to make a difference.

Vicky's still sleeping on her side when I go downstairs. I plan to heat some milk and drink that. I used to drink whiskey when I couldn't sleep, but I gave it up. No it's strictly hot milk. In the whiskey days I'd wake up with this tremendous thirst in the middle of the night. But, back then, I was always looking ahead: I kept a bottle of water in the fridge, for instance. I'd be dehydrated, sweating from head to toe when I woke, but I'd wander out to the kitchen and could count on finding that bottle of cold water in the fridge. I'd drink it, all of it, down the hatch, an entire quart of water. Once in a while I'd use a glass, but not often. Suddenly I'd be drunk all over again and weaving around the kitchen. I can't begin to account for it—sober one minute, drunk the next.

The drinking was part of my destiny—according to Molly, anyway. She put a lot of stock in destiny.

I feel wild from lack of sleep. I'd give anything, just about, to be able to go to sleep, and sleep the sleep of an honest man.

Why do we have to sleep anyway? And why do we tend to sleep less during some crises and more during others? For instance, that time my dad had his stroke. He woke up after a coma—seven days and nights in a hospital bed—and calmly said "Hello" to the people in his room. Then his eyes picked me out. "Hello, son," he said. Five minutes later, he died. Just like that—he died. But, during that whole crisis, I never took my clothes off and didn't go to bed. I may have catnapped in a waiting-room chair from time to time, but I never went to bed and *slept.*

And then a year or so ago I found out Vicky was seeing somebody else. Instead of confronting *her*, I went to bedwhen I heard about it, and stayed there. I didn't get up for days, a week maybe—I don't know. I mean, I got go to the bathroom, or else to the kitchen to make a sandwich. I even went out to the living room in my pajamas, in the afternoon, and tried to read the papers. But I'd fall asleep sitting up. Then I'd stir, open my eyes and go back to bed and sleep some more. I couldn't get enough sleep.

It passed. We weathered it. Vicky quit her boyfriend, or he quit her, I never found out. I just know she went away for a while, and then she came back. But I have the feeling we're not going to weather this business. This thing is different. Oliver has given Amanda that ultimatum.

Still, isn't it possible that Oliver himself is awake at this moment and writing a letter to Amanda, urging reconciliation? Even now he might be scribbling away, trying to persuade her that what she's doing to him and their daughter Beth is foolish, disastrous, and finally a tragic thing for the three of them.

No, that's insane. I know Oliver. He's relentless, unforgiving. He could slam a croquet ball into the next block—and has. He isn't going to write any such letter. He gave her an ultimatum, right? —and that's that. A week. Four days now. Or is it three? Oliver may be awake, but if he is, he's sitting in a chair in his hotel room with a glass of iced vodka in his hand, his feet on the bed, TV turned on low. He's dressed, except for his shoes. He's not wearing shoes—that's the only concession he makes. That and the fact that he's loosened his tie.

Oliver is relentless.

I heat the milk, spoon the skin from the surface and pour it up. Then I turn off the kitchen light and take the cup into the living room and sit on the sofa, where I can look across the street at the lighted windows. But I can hardly sit still. I keep fidgeting, crossing one leg and then the other. I feel like I could throw off sparks, or break a window—maybe rearrange all the furniture.

The things that go through your mind when you can't sleep! Earlier, thinking about Molly, for a moment I couldn't even remember what she *looked* like, for Christ's sake, yet we were together for years, more or less continuously, since we were kids. Molly, who said she'd love me forever. The only thing left was the memory of her sitting and weeping at the kitchen table, her shoulders bent forward, and her hands covering her face. *Forever,* she said. But it hadn't worked out that way. Finally, she said, it didn't matter, it was of no real concern to her, if she and I lived together the rest of our lives or not. Our love existed on a "higher plane." That's what she said to Vicky over the phone that time, after Vicky and I had set up housekeeping together. Molly called, go hold of Vicky, and said, "You have your relationship with him, but I'll always have mine. His destiny and mine are linked."

My first wife, Molly, she talked like that. "Our destinies are linked." She didn't talk like that at the beginning. It was later, after so much had happened, that she started using words like "cosmic" and "empowerment" and so forth. But our destinies are *not* linked—not now, anyway, if they ever were. I don't even know where she is now, not for certain.

I think I could put my finger on the exact time, the real turning point, when it came undone for Molly. It was after I started seeing Vicky, and Molly found out. They called me up one day from the high school where Molly taught and said, "Please. Your wife is doing handsprings in front of the school. You'd better get down here." It was after I took her home that I began hearing about "higher power" and "going with the flow" —stuff of that sort. Our destiny had been "revised." And if I'd been hesitating before, well, I left her then as fast as I could—this woman I'd known all my life, the one who'd been my best friend for years, my intimate, my confidante. I bailed out on her. For one thing, I was scared. *Scared.*

This girl I'd started out with in life, this sweet thing, this gentle soul, she wound up going to fortune-tellers, palm readers, *crystal ball gazers*, looking for answers, trying to figure out what she should do with her life. She quit her job, drew out her teacher's retirement money, and thereafter never made a decision without consulting the *I Ching*. She began wearing strange clothes—clothes with permanent wrinkles and a lot of burgundy and orange. She even got involved with a group that sat around, I'm not kidding, trying to levitate.

When Molly and I were growing up together, she was a part of me and, sure, I was a part of her, too. We loved each other. It *was* our destiny. I believed in it then myself. But know I don't know what to believe in. I'm not complaining, simply stating a fact. I'm down to nothing. And I have to go on like this. No destiny. Just the next thing meaning whatever think it does. Compulsion and error, just like everybody else. Amanda? I'd like to believe in her, bless her heart. But she was looking for somebody when she met me. That's the way with people when they get restless: They start up something, knowing that's going to change things for good. I'd like to go out in the front year and shout something. "None of this is worth it!" That's what I'd like people to hear.

"Destiny," Molly said. For all I know she's still talking about it.

All the lights are off over there now, except for that light in the kitchen. I could try calling Amanda on the phone. I could do that and see how far it gets me! What if Vicky heard me dialing or talking on the phone can came downstairs? What if she lifted the receiver upstairs and listened? Besides, there's always the chance Beth might pick up the phone. I don't want to talk to kids this morning. I don't want to talk to anybody. Actually, I'd like to talk to Molly, if I could, but I can't any longer—she's somebody else now. She isn't *Molly* anymore. But—what can I say? —I'm somebody else too.

I wish I could be like everybody else in this neighborhood—your basic, normal, unaccomplished person—and go up to my bedroom, and lie down, and sleep. It's going to be a big day today, and I'd like to be ready for it. I wish I could sleep and wake up and find everything in my life different. Not necessarily just the big things, like thing with Amanda or the past with Molly. But things clearly within my power.

Take the situation with my mother: I used to send money every month. But then I started sending her the same amount in twice-yearly sums. I gave her money on her birthday, and I gave her money at Christmas. I thought: I won't have to worry, period. It went like clockwork for a long time.

Then last year she asked me—it was in between money times, it was in March, or maybe April—for a radio. A radio, she said, would make a difference to her.

What she wanted was a little clock radio. She could put it in her kitchen and have it out there to listen to while she was fixing something to eat in the evening. And she'd have a clock to look at too, so she'd know when something was supposed to come out of the oven, or how long it was until one of her programs started.

A little clock radio.

She hinted around at first. She said, "I'd sure like to have a radio. But I can't afford one. I guess I'll have to wait for my birthday. That little radio I had, it fell and broke. I miss a radio." *I miss a radio.* That's what she said when we talked on the phone, or else she'd bring it up when she'd write.

Finally—what'd I say? I said to her over the phone that I couldn't afford any radios. I said it in a letter too, so she'd be sure to understand. *I can't afford any radios,* is what I wrote. I can't do any more, I said, than I'm doing. Those were my very words.

But it wasn't true! I could have done more. I just said I couldn't. I could have afforded to buy a radio for her. What would it have cost me? Thirty-five dollars? Forty dollars or less, including tax. I could have sent her a radio through the mail. I could have had somebody in the store to do it, if I didn't want to go to the trouble myself. Or else I could have sent her a forty-dollar check along with a not saying, *This money is for your radio, Mother.*

I could have handled it in any case. Forty dollars—are you kidding? But I didn't. I wouldn't part with it. It seems there was a *principle* involved. That's what I told myself anyway—there's a principle involved here.

Ha.

Then what happened? She died. She *died.* She was walking home from the grocery store, back to her apartment, carrying her sack of groceries, and fell into somebody's bushes and died.

I took a flight out there to make the arrangements. She was still at the coroner's, and they had her purse and her groceries behind the desk in the office. I didn't bother to look in the purse they handed me. But what she had from the grocery store was a jar of Metamucil, two grapefruits, a carton of cottage cheese, a quart of buttermilk, some potatoes and onions, and a package of ground meat that was beginning to change color.

Boy! I cried when I saw those things. I couldn't stop. I didn't think I'd ever quit crying. The woman who worked at the desk was embarrassed and brought me a glass of water. They gave me a bag for my mother's groceries and another bag for her personal effects—her purse and her dentures. Later, I put the dentures in my coat pocket and drove them down in a rental car and gave them to somebody at the funeral home.

The light in Amanda's kitchen is still on. It's a bright light that spills out on to all those leaves. Maybe she's like I am, and she's scared. Maybe she left that light burning as a night-light. Or maybe she's still awake and is at the kitchen table, under the light writing me a letter. Amanda is writing me a letter, and somehow she'll get it into my hands later on when the read day starts.

Come to think of it, I've never had a lever from her since we've known each other. All the time we've been involved—six months, eight months—and I've never once seen a scrap of her handwriting. I don't even know if she's *literate* that way.

I think she is. Sure, she is. She talks about books, doesn't she? It doesn't matter, of course. Well, a little, I suppose. I love her in any case, right?

But I've never written anything to her, either. We always talked on the phone or else face to face.

Molly, she was the letter writer. She used to write me even after we weren't living together. Vicky would bring her letters in from the box and leave them on the kitchen table without a word. Finally the letters dwindled away, became more and more infrequent and bizarre. When she did write, the letters gave me a chill. They were full of talk about "auras" and "signs." Occasionally, she reported a voice that was telling her something she ought to do or some place she should go. And once she told me that no matter what happened, we were still "on the same frequency." She always know exactly what I felt, she said. She "beamed in on me," she said from time to time. Reading those letters of hers, the hair on the back of my neck would tingle. She also had a new word for destiny: *Karma.* "I'm following out my karma," she wrote. "Your karma has taken a bad turn." I'd like to go to sleep but what's the point? People will be getting up soon. Vicky's alarm will go off before much longer. I wish I could go upstairs and get back in bed with my wife, tell her I'm sorry, there's been a mistake, let's forget all this—then go to sleep and wake up with her in my arms. But I've forfeited that right. I'm outside all that now, and I can't get back inside! But say I didn't. Say I went upstairs and slid into bed with Vicky as I'd like to do. She might wake up and say, *You bastard. Don't you dare touch me, son of a bitch.*

What's she talking about, anyway? I wouldn't touch her. Not in that way, I wouldn't.

After I left Molly, after I'd pulled out on her, about two months after, then Molly really did it. She had her real collapse then, the one that'd been coming on. Her sister saw to it that she got the care she needed. What am I saying? *They put her away.* They had to, they said. They put my wife away. By then I was living with Vicky, and trying not to drink whiskey. I couldn't do anything for Molly. I mean, she was there, I was here, and I couldn't have gotten her out of that place if I'd wanted to. But the fact is, I didn't want to. She was in there, they said, because she *needed* to be in there. Nobody said anything about destiny. Things had gone beyond that.

And I didn't even go visit her—not once! At the time I didn't think I could stand seeing her in there. But, Christ, what was I? A fair-weather friend? We'd been through plenty. But what on earth would I have said to her? *I'm sorry about all this, honey.* I could have said that, I guess. I intended to write, but I didn't. Not a word. Anyway, when you get right down to it, what could I have said in a letter? *How are they treating you, baby? I'm sorry you're where you are, but don't give up. Remember all the good times? Remember when we were happy together? Hey, I'm sorry they've done this to you. I'm sorry it turned out this way. I'm sorry everything is just garbage now.* I'm sorry, Molly.

I didn't write. I think I was trying to forget about her, to pretend she didn't exist. Molly who?

I left my wife and took somebody else's: Vicky. No I think maybe I've lost Vicky, too. But Vicky won't be going away to any summer camp for the mentally disabled. She's a hard case. She left her former husband, Joe Kraft, and didn't bat and eye; I don't think she ever lost a night's sleep over it.

Vicky Kraft-Hughes. Amanda Porter. This is where my destiny has brought me? To this street in this neighborhood, messing up the lives of these women?

Amanda's kitchen light went off when I wasn't looking. The room that was there is gone now, like the others. Only the porch light is still burning. Amanda must have forgotten it, I guess. Hey, Amanda.

Once, when Molly was away in that place and I wasn't in my right mind—let's face it, I was crazy too— one night I was at my friend Alfredo's house, a bunch of us drinking and listening to records. I didn't any longer what happened to me. Everything, I thought, that could happen had happened. I felt unbalanced. I felt lost. Anyway, there I was at Alfredo's. His paintings of tropical birds and animals hung on every wall in his house, and there were paintings standing around the in the rooms, leaning against things—table-legs, say or his brick-and-board bookcase, as well as being stacked on his back porch. The kitchen served as his studio, and I was sitting at the kitchen table with a drink in front of me. An easel stood off to one side in front of the window that overlooked the alley, and there were crumpled tubes of paint, a palette, and some brushes lying at one end of the table. Alfredo was making himself a drink at the counter a few feet away. I loved the shabby economy of that little room. The stereo music that came from the living room was turned up, filling the house with so much sound the kitchen windows rattled in their frames. Suddenly I began to shake. First my hands began to shake, and then my arms and shoulders, too. My teeth started to chatter. I couldn't hold the glass.

"What's going on, man?" Alfredo said, when he turned and saw the state I was in. "Hey, what is it? What's going on with you?"

I couldn't tell him. What could I say? I thought I was having some kind of an attack. I managed to raise my shoulders and let them drop.

Then Alfredo came over, took a chair and sat down beside me at the kitchen table. He put his big painter's hand on my shoulder. I went on shaking. He could feel me shaking.

"What's wrong with you, man? I'm sorry about everything, man. I know it's real hard right now." Then he said he was going to fix *menudo* for me. He said it would be good for what ailed me. "Help's your nerves, man," he said. "Calm you right down." He had all the ingredients for *menudo,* he said, and he'd been wanting to make some. Anyway.

"You listen to me. Listen to what I say, man. I'm your family now," Alfredo said.

It was two in the morning, we were drunk, there were these other drunk people in the house and the stereo was going full blast. But Alfredo went to his fridge and opened it and took some stuff out. He closed the fridge door and looked in his freezer compartment. He could something in a package. Then he looked around in his cupboards. He took a big pan from the cabinet under the sink, and he was ready.

Tripe. He started with tripe and about a gallon of water. Then he chopped onions and added them to the water, which had started to boil. He put *chorizo* sausage in the pot. After that, he dropped peppercorns into the boiling water and sprinkled in some chili powder. Then came the olive oil. He opened a big can of tomato sauce and poured that in. He added cloves of garlic, some slices of white bread, salt, and lemon juice. He opened another can—it was hominy—and poured that in the pot, too. He put it all in, and then he turned the heat down and put a lid on the pot.

I watched him. I sat there shaking while Alfredo stood at the stove making *menudo.* talking—I didn't any ideas what he was saying—and, from time to time, he'd shake his head, or else start whistling to himself. Now and then people drifted into the kitchen for beer. But all the while Alfredo went on very seriously looking after his *menudo.* He could have been home, in Morelia, making *menudo* for his family or on New Year's day.

People hung around in the kitchen for a while, joking, but Alfredo didn't joke back when they kidded him about cooking *menudo* in the middle of the night. Pretty soon they left us alone. Finally, while Alfredo stood at the stove with a spoon in his hand, watching me, I got up slowly from the table. I walked out of the kitchen into the bathroom, and then opened another door off the bathroom to the spare room—where I lay down on the bed and fell asleep. When I woke it was mid-afternoon. The *menudo* was gone. The pot was in the sink, soaking. Those other people must have eaten it! They must have eaten it and grown calm. Everyone was gone, and the hour was quiet.

I never saw Alfredo more than once or twice afterward. After that night, our lives took us in separate directions. And those other people were there—who knows where they went? I'll probably die without ever tasting *menudo.* But who can say?

Is this what it all comes down to then? A middle-aged man involved with his neighbor's wife, linked to an angry ultimatum? What kind of destiny is that? A week, Oliver said. Three or four days now.

A car passes outside with its lights on. The sky is turning gray, and I hear some birds starting up. I decide I can't way any longer. I can't just sit here, doing nothing—that's all there is to it. I can't keep waiting. I've waited and waited and where's it gotten me? Vicky's alarm will go off soon, Beth with get up and dress for school, Amanda will wake up, too. The entire neighborhood.

On the back porch I find some old jeans and a sweatshirt, and I change out of my pajamas. Then I put on my white canvas shoes— "wino" shoes, Alfredo would have called them. Alfredo, where are you?

I go outside to the garage and find the rake and some lawn bags. By the time I get around to the front of the house with the rake, ready to begin, I feel I don't have a choice in the matter any longer. It's light out—light enough at any rate for what I have to do. And then, without thinking about it anymore, I start to rake. I rake our yard, every inch of it. It's important it be done right, too. I set the rake right down into the turf and pull hard. It must feel to the grass like it does whenever someone gives your hair a hard jerk. Now and then a car passes in the street and slows, but I don't' look up from my work. I know what the people in the cars must be thinking, but they're dead wrong—they don't know the half of it. How could they? I'm happy, raking.

I finish our yard and put the bag out next to the curb. Then I begin next door on the Baxter's yard. In a few minutes Mrs. Baxter comes out on her porch, wearing her bathrobe. I don't acknowledge her. I'm not embarrassed, and I don't want to appear unfriendly. I just want to keep on with what I'm doing.

She doesn't say anything for a while, and then she says, "Good morning, Mr. Hughes. How are you this morning?" I stop what I'm doing and run my arm across my forehead. "I'll be through in a little while, " I say. "I hope you don't mind."

"We don't mind," Mrs. Baxter says. "Go right ahead, I guess." I see Mr. Baxter standing in the doorway behind her. He's already dressed for work in his slacks and sports coat and tie. But he doesn't venture onto the porch. Then Mrs. Baxter turns and looks at Mr. Baxter, who shrugs.

It's okay, I've finished here anyway. There are other yards, more important yards for that matter. I kneel, and, taking a grip low down on the rake handle, I pull the last of the leaves into my bag and tie off the top. Then, I can't help it, I just stay there, kneeling on the grass with my rake in my hand. When I look up, I see the Baxters come down the porch steps together and move slowly toward me through the wet, sweet-smelling grass. They stop a few feet away and look at me closely.

"There now," I hear Mrs. Baxter say. She's still in her robe and slippers. It's nippy out; she holds her robe at the throat. "You did a real fine job for us, yes, you did."

They stand in front of me a while longer, and none of us says anything more. It's as if we've come to an agreement on something. In a minute, they turn around and go back to their house. High over my head, in the branches of the old maple—the place where these leaves come from—birds call out to each other. At least I think they're calling to each other.

Suddenly a car door slams. Mr. Baxter is in his car in the drive with the window rolled down. Mrs. Baxter says something to him from the front porch which causes Mr. Baxter to nod slowly and turn his head in my direction. He sees me kneeling there with the rake, and a look crosses his face. He frowns. In his better moments, Mr. Baxter is a decent, ordinary guy—a guy you wouldn't mistake for anyone special. But he *is* special. In my book, he is. For one thing he has a full night's sleep behind him, and he's just embraced his wife before leaving for work. But even before he goes, he's already expected home a set number of hours later. True, in the grander scheme of things, his return will be an event of small moment—but an event nonetheless.

Baxter starts his car and races the engine. Then he backs effortlessly out of the drive, brakes, and changes gears. As he passes on the street, he slows and looks briefly in my direction. He lifts his hand off the steering wheel. It could be a salute or a sign of dismissal. It's a sign, in any case. Any then he looks away toward the city. I get up and raise my hand too—not a wave, exactly, but close to it. Some other cards drive past. One of the drivers must think he knows me because he gives his horn a friendly little tap. I look both ways and then cross the street.

Peter Rodriguez

AMERICAS Magazine-1984

In a recent conversation with Alfredo Arreguín, I learned from him that he is becoming very aware of the important influence his ancestral aesthetic culture has had on his expression as an artist. It is difficult for an artist to escape this cultural marking . . . perhaps it is similar to human bonding or may be genetically inherited.

Alfredo Arreguín was born in Morelia, Michoacán, Mexico in the central region of Mexico that is known as the *Bajío*, or plateau. It is the capital city of the state and was an important region of pre-Hispanic America in the arts and has remained so after the Conquest. In pre-Hispanic times, this central area of Mexico produced many fine works of art that had very detailed patterning. This was true of everyday vessels used domestically, as well as the architecture and other artifacts we encounter or learn about from other sources. This patterning continued in the design motifs imposed upon the indigenous people after the Conquest, when the zealous conquerors who tried to alter the customs, religion, and other cultural manifestations super-imposed their own ideas and thought. If at first these ideas were closely followed, soon after the aesthetic sensibilities of the Mesoamerican people would become apparent. This change gave a new dimension to Mexican art: its vitality and own identity have prevailed to contemporary times.

The pre-Hispanic Mexican had a 360 day solar calendar. He was an adept astonomer and knew the concept of zero. His architecture was grand and his art was of a very high caliber. Albrecht Durer, the great German master, was in awe when he first observed the objects that were brought to the European courts shortly after the Conquest. "I also saw the things that were brought to the King from the new land of gold; a sun entirely of gold, a whole fathom wide, and a moon entirely of silver, of equal size, likewise two rooms of rare *accoutrements*, wonderful arms, strange garments, bed hangings and all manner of wonderful things for many uses, all much fairer to behold than any marvel. These things are all so precious that they are valued at one hundred thousand guilders. And in all the days of my life I have seen nothing that has so rejoiced my heart as these things. For I saw among them strange and exquisitely worked objects and marvelled at the subtle genius of the men in distant lands. The things I saw there I have no words to express." Brussels, 1521 *Extract from a diary kept during a journey in the Low Countries. July 1520-July 1521.*

Another important factor, Mexican folk art, must have had an impact on Arreguín. The artistic traditions of the region of his *natal* city, Morelia, go back to pre-Hispanic times where many of the objects that still remain are profusely decorated. This preference for patterned design did not diminish after the Conquest. A good example of a folk art tradition in this area is the painted lacquer ware that is still produced to this day. Some of the crafts were imposed by the Spanish conquerors; other influences can be attributed directly to the Manila Galleon, but the older influences prevailed. Arreguín's daily encounter with this rich tradition would appear to have had a definite effect on his work. Another source may be the rich and varied flora and fauna in his native Mexico.

Arreguín left Morelia at the age of thirteen to live in Mexico City, where he studied architecture after completing his early schooling. It was at this time that he was befriended by an American couple and invited to visit Seattle, Washington. He decided to remain in Seattle and continue his education, and turned to art as his main focus, much to the disappointment of his father. He attended the University of Washington, where he received his BA and MFA degrees in the late sixties. He has lived in Seattle since that time.

When you first meet Arreguín, you are perplexed if you are aware of his Mexican heritage, because he has the appearance of a 16th century, Italian noble who enjoys the plenty of life. He is fair complected, with clear blue eyes and speaks with a robust voice that is complemented with a short burst of laughter. He is very articulate and concerned with his fellow man. He has a great dedication to his art.

Arreguín's exposure to and involvement with the Chicano Movement, and its concerns, have made him aware of the collective attitude of the Chicano, which suggests that if you achieve success alone, you have only removed yourself from the battlefield. In an interview by Yvonne Yarbro-Bejarano in *Metamorfosis*, a Northwest Chicano magazine of literature, and culture, Arreguín goes to the heart of the issue, "*Al principio pensé, no estoy haciendo nada realamente para el barrio. Luego me di cuenta de que en realidad no vivo en el barrio. El barrio tiene que ser portátil porque tenemos que andar por dondequiera. El barrio lo tienes que llevar a dondequiera.*" [In English] "At first I thought, I am not really doing anything for the *barrio* (neighborhood where a large concentration of Mexican descended people live in an American city.) Then I understood that in reality I do not live in the *barrio.* The *barrio* has to be portable because we have to go wherever. You have to take the *barrio* with you wherever you go (Vol III, No 2; Vol IV, No. 1, 1980-81.)

Arreguín is a creative artist with his own vision. He is considered to be the inventor of pattern painting. He used this approach before any other American painter, and this type of painting is now recognized in the United States. His first works after finishing his studies at the University of Washington were done after a two-year hiatus. He did not agree with the mode of painting that was being expounded by his professors, abstract expressionism, and continued to seek his own form of expression. These works painted in light, over-all washes of color are super-imposed with highly patterned images. They depict the natural world with a focus on exotic animals, reptiles, fowl, lush tropical tropical imagry and are without any human representation. These evocative and translucent works that glow with brilliant color, or complex hues, have since evolved to include some human representation. Included are famous Mexican heroes or personalities,[like] Emiliano Zapata, Frida Kahlo, or persons in regional dress. Concurrently there was a move toward pattern painting without representational imagery where the pattern becomes the important element. Some references to textile weaving is suggested in his works entitled *Sarape,* and in a more abstract work, *Penumbra.* The brilliant color is less intense and is used with more restraint in which the hues rely less on the primary spectrum.

Arreguín lives in Seattle, Washington, with his wife, Susan Lytle, a fine painter in her own right, and their daughter, Lesley, who is a fledgling artist. Their home is their studio and daily life revolves around creative efforts. As a respite from his painting Arreguín creates some mysterious ceramic reptiles that reflect the *nagual* in Mexican folk art . . . a creature that is part animal-part human.

Arreguín has served on the Seattle Art Commission where his concern was to help the talented, underrepresented artist. Although he was the first artist in the United States to develop pattern painting, recognition has eluded him from mainstream sources. He is not represented in the Seattle Museum of Art's painting collection. Nonetheless, his painting continues to flourish and achieves an increasingly higher artistic level.

Jeffree Stewart

Art In Public Places: Arreguín and Ecology

My first meeting with Alfredo Arreguín was in the main lobby of Washington state's Department of Ecology's Headquarters Building. On that day in 1997, Alfredo was the Guest of Honor for an unveiling and dedication of his works, commissioned by Washington State. It was 2010, many years later, when we met again. I visited Alfredo's north Seattle home, shared with his wife and fellow painter, Susan Lytle. My 2010 studio visit was given to selecting works, from which to compose a large exhibition of his works for *Art in Ecology*.

Entering the studio where Alfredo does his paintings was both startling and surprising. By then, I was long accustomed to seeing large Arreguín works, and imagined the studio was large. Instead, I walked into close quarters. Half the basement was Susan Lytle's studio, and half, including storage of large canvases, is where Alfredo paints. Quietly amazed by this, I was...such large works, from here!

Thirty years after the fact, I'll describe a major installation of art in Ecology headquarters, north of Olympia. Arreguín's influence will be considered, relative to his intentions with that commissioned work. I'll reflect on where Alfredo's painting comes from, physically. How the work meshes with, and contributes to, a broader context of Pacific Northwest art will be explored.

Alfredo Arreguín's backstory

One of the strong currents in Alfredo's oeuvre is a visual celebration of ecological vitality and diversity. As a child, Alfredo remembers, he would spend hours in the jungle. Here, he watched and wondered about the amazing diversity of life forms all around him....snakes and spiders, droplets of water on leaves, huge trees and tiny fungal forms, mammals sneaking, crouching, and stalking in dense foliage. His painting career records a journey, deeply rooted in those early and vital experiences of Mexico.

Arreguín immigrated to the United States from Mexico in 1956, when he was 21 years old. As a young man, Arreguín served his new country as an infantryman, stationed in Japan and Korea. These postings brought the young painter into contact with Asian art traditions, which were later embraced, being integrated with imagery reflecting his own Latino culture of origin. Throughout his career, shaking off cultural stereotypes has mattered to Alfredo.

Speaking with Alexia Fernández Campbell, Arreguín said, "It is very difficult as an artist, not matter where you are from, but it's much, much, much harder to be a Latino or Mexican or Chicano artist," He added, "I don't think that we're taken very seriously because people have said Chicano artists aren't very skillful," he adds. "There's a lot of criticism of artists that don't have a formal education."

Arreguín studied art at the University of Washington, earning a BA and later an MFA. I recall having spoken with the late Sculptor Harold Balasz at his home in Spokane County. This was in 2016. Harold described the time when he was working with Alfredo at the University of Washington. He spoke fondly and with respect, describing a young man he recognized as having great potential as an artist.

Painter Boyer Gonzales, known as an abstract expressionist, was Chairman of the UW Art Department when Arreguín was there. As current UW professor Lauro Flores has noted, "Alfredo Arreguín took classes with Boyer, but turned in a different direction, based on his exposure to Japanese art and his love of the complex natural world of the jungle." Among those he studied with, Alfredo mentioned San Francisco painter Elmer Bischoff having been important.

Sharing a Studio

My own appreciation for Arreguín's work as a painter was enhanced by that 2010 visit to the artist's home. His painting plainly has deep roots in this lovely, enchanting home created by two artists. Alfredo and Susan Lytle have worked in side-by-side studios now for decades. Alfredo works long hours with many small brushes in his basement studio. Then he ascends into a realm of deep hued walls, colorful Mexican ceramics, and family photographs upstairs. These are gathered artfully among houseplants sprawling foliage, over wooden floors beside a river rock fireplace.

There are small ponds outdoors with green waters that are swimmingly alive with gold fishes. Forks and spoons on strings dangle near bells in lovingly tended gardens. Hummingbirds come and go with their vibrant and colorful feathers. Alfredo's connection with nature in Seattle is also replenished during walks at Greenlake. Here he attends the shapes of birds and trees, with the glimmers of light on silvery waters and ripples moving out, so akin to how his paintings appear to move.

Susan Lytle's paintings are akin to Alfredo's mostly in their ways of working. Both painters work up close, building up images methodically, and with great care. A table in the center holds oil paints they share. Their styles are distinct, and also related. Both have particular qualities of inwardness and exactitude in their work, as well as a lingering sense of luminosity in results.

Susan paints what she sees- elaborate and mysterious interiors, atmospheres with complex still life arrays. Through a window beyond the tableaux, appears a quiet lake. The paintings convey a sense of richness in their living spaces, filled as they are with Mexican ceramic figurines, tiny mirrors, and all manner of earthy mystery and magic. She celebrates the ephemeral beauty of orchid species and others like Night Blooming Cereus. Her botanical execution, and the sense of implicit moisture in portrayal, reminds me of the skillfulness in Martin Johnson Heade's works from South American jungles. In 2013, 15 of Susan Lytle's paintings were brought to Art In Ecology for a solo show. We have continued to appreciate one of her mystery-laden still life works since that time.

Friends and Scholars

In Lauro Flores' 2002/2007 book on Arreguín, *Patterns of Dreams and Nature*, Lauro wrote the preface, noting:

> "In a recent conversation at the University of Washington, Eduardo Galeano commented, as he has written before, 'the universe can only be seen through a small keyhole: the largest thing through the smallest one.' The brilliant Uruguyan also said he wishes that he had many eyes and could see things from many different angles at the same time....This profusion of eyes is common motif in Alfredo Arreguín's paintings, especially in his jungles, where, para phrasing one of Pablo Neruda's poems, eyes and leaves become entangled with each other. If the eyes are windows to the soul, it is precisely the soul of the jungle that Arreguín captures in his canvases."

A Mexican scholar, Agustín Jacinto Zavala, wrote some insightful words about Arreguín:

> "In the dreamlike landscape of Arreguín's canvases we find motifs belonging to the indigenous traditions of Michoacán, which he took in as a child, as well as others from the jungle, which he visited in early youth. Alongside them, however, appear elements of the contemporary North American panorama, of his adopted country's cultural and social life, and still others, of Asian origin, which mingle freely with the rest."

A Lively Presence of the Sea

Arreguín was close friends for many years with the short-story author Ray Carver, and poet Tess Gallagher, living in Port Angeles. Bobbing around in small boats on the Straits of Juan de Fuca, fishing with his good friends, sharing stories and laughter while pulling up the silvery travelers from beneath the waves in icy waters almost certainly lent some enthusiasm and vitality to many of his paintings.

Long before the 1996 Ecology Commission, Alfredo Arreguín made works which carried stories and awareness of the natural world. Many Arreguín works, for example, are inspired by the life cycles of salmonids, going from high mountain streams down rivers to long ocean journeys, then returning, cyclically, to their stream of origin. Arreguín paintings in this vein include *At Night the Salmon Move, The Fish People of the Blue Agate River*, and *The Last Salmon Run.*

Art in Ecology / 2010 Arreguín exhibition

2010 was the 40th Anniversary of the Department of Ecology. The agency was created by the Washington legislature in 1970. A strong focus on water quality testing was the impetus, with passage of the federal Clean Water Act. Legislative assignments have increased over the years, adding air quality, nuclear radiation, shoreline and floodplain land use, toxic waste reduction, social justice, and many other environmental concerns to the work done by the agency.

As a way of broadening the Ecology Department 40th Anniversary celebration, a large exhibition of Arreguín paintings was composed. The idea was to broaden appreciation for the range of Alfredo's work beyond the commissioned works. My selections focused on ways Alfredo's work relates to the agency's mission. Thirty two Arreguín paintings, done from 1985 to 2008, spanned three gallery settings.

Along with landscape works, a couple of portraits were notable, one of Frida Kahlo, whom Alfredo regards as a symbol of Mother Nature...and another, a portrait of one of Alfredo's heroines, longtime Washington environmental advocate and activist, Hazel Wolf.

The Arreguín show brought visitors to Ecology from sometimes great distances. Many individuals from various places around the state made appointments for tours in the weeks that followed. It was a popular show, and stayed in place for several months. A group of 12 docents from La Conner's Museum of Northwest Art came one afternoon. Their goal was seeing such a large sample of Arreguín's work along with his commissioned works.

Likewise, the *River of Words* brings together school children from all over Washington state. They have competed and been recognized for making poems and pictures about environmental themes. *Art in Ecology* hosted the event, several years running. The 2010 celebration happened while surrounded by 12 of Arreguín's paintings in the spacious Dining Hall, with hundreds of children, teachers, and parents in the ceremony.

Art in Ecology is an ongoing exhibition program, run by employees. Arreguín's large works serve as a cornerstone, imaginatively outstanding. Around these commissioned works, volunteer efforts have made the Department of Ecology building a notable art-in-the-workplace venue. Art in Ecology is informal, by-artist and for-artist oriented, and revenue-neutral (there is no budget for the work we do.)

Works by northwest artists-paintings, photographs, prints, and sculpture are circulated throughout the Ecology Headquarters Building. We are honoring artists' efforts, while increasing awareness of their work to new audiences. This presence of art encourages creativity and contemplation. For departmental staff, exploration of art and science intersections is encouraged. The concrete, glass, wood, and steel surroundings are colorfully enhanced.

The work being shown is on loan. Loans are from collectors and gallerists, the State Arts Commission, and often, by the artists themselves. Some are long term. The "collection" viewers are able to enjoy here is not "permanent..." This also means Washington taxpayers are not footing the bill. While not a hard and fast rule, Art in Ecology especially looks to show artists whose works have resonance with Ecology's work, protecting and enhancing the physical and social environment of Washington State.

Department of Ecology Headquarters

The Ecology Building in Lacey is a story of its own. Prior to the Arreguín commission, the Ecology Department had been growing, in size and complexity of mission. Agency staff worked from 23 separate and leased locations around Olympia. Chris Gregoire was the departmental Director in the early nineties. In 1992, her concern about inefficiency was translated to action that became a turning point for the agency. Working with the egislature, Gregoire arranged for construction of a headquarters building to consolidate the agency in one place. It was completed in 1993.

Sited on a 27 acre parcel with meadow and forest surroundings, just north of Olympia, on land leased from Saint Martin's University. The 322,000 square foot structure is a pair of long (400 plus feet) rectangles, set at right angles. It has three floors above ground, and one below. With a rock garden running the length at ground level, there is open space from the ground floor up, creating an atrium soaring upwards 54 feet. From one end of the building to the other is nearly a quarter mile walk.

It is designed and built with many sophisticated technologies for energy conservation, and recently achieved a LEED Platinum ranking. The Designing Architect was Richard Keating, with McGranahan Architects overseeing construction, and McKinstry doing upgrades and maintenance in recent years.

Although art exhibits were not envisioned nor included in specifications or criteria for design, the building lends itself wonderfully to the display of visual art. It allows for observation from various angles and distances. The scale of the spaces plays especially well to larger work. A characteristic feature of the building is how it receives and transmits natural light.

Clerestory windows bring in south light from above the third floor, which permeates to all levels above ground. Constantly changing, all the natural light gives further interest to the rotating art displays around the building.

The Rock Garden affords viewing spaces for three dimensional works. It continues outside on the west end, establishing visual links from within to outside. Several gallery spaces have been outfitted with track lighting and hanging systems, transforming ordinary hallways so they double as galleries, ideal for display of paintings and photographs.

Half percent for Art Selection Process

Construction of the Ecology Headquarters triggered an investment in the arts, through funding from the budget for new buildings, administered by the Washington State Arts Commission.

Steve Fry is an architect who began his career overseeing construction of the Washington State Department of Ecology Headquarters building in Lacey, WA. Thirty years later, Fry still manages maintenance of the 322,000 square foot building, which houses more than 1,200 employees.

Fry says there was controversy, back in the early nineties planning phase, about whether to spend art funds for specialty building materials, such as mosaic tile settings. Eventually this was settled in favor of a 0.5 percent allocation of the budget for art purchases. The Percent for Art selection process was done by a committee which included local artists, the State Arts Commission, and representatives of the agency.

From an array of almost 60 artists who were in the Artist Resource Bank, two became finalists: Alfredo Arreguín, and Dale Chihuly. Each artist came to Olympia in July of 1995 and made presentations of what was proposed to the selection committee. Dale Chihuly proposed an unspecified number of 2 ½ - 4 inch "Persians" or glass forms, mostly in blue and green hues, that would be arrayed across the front windows above the main lobby. Biannual cleaning of the works, and special lighting-both were recommended, but not included in the cost estimate.

Arreguín's proposal included mock-ups showing how the glass installation called *The Froth* would be constructed, how the glass panels would appear- and a representation of the three-panel work which became *Jungla Encantada*. In the proposal materials preceding installation of these works, Alfredo wrote:

> "The Department of Ecology has an important mission in the State of Washington, and the art work for the building needs to reflect that mission. The artwork should also reflect and record our unique time and place here in the Northwest. In the last three months, we have surveyed the building and talked to D.O.E. employees about their feelings on the potential art work in an effort to present a project that will grow from the existing conditions rather than a solution that is imposed from without."
>
> "The building itself presents both opportunities and limitations for the potential art work. The huge grey building seems to desire warmth and color in many areas. The scale of the building is quite large, and there are many potential sites for large installations, however, I feel that Human Scale art work would soften and personalize the building for the people who use it, so I have refrained from proposing a single, large installation that would reinforce the super human scale."

About *Jungla Encantada* (1994), Arreguín noted:

> "While ecological themes run through most of my work, this painting especially speaks to the complicated interrelationships of natural forces here on the home planet. You will find plants, animals and humans woven together with rhythmic forms in a tapestry of the balance of life."
>
> "A great part of the motive of my painting is to portray a positive ecological integration of the forest, jungle, animals, and the human spirit. Many faces arise from the nature of my canvasses. It could be a pre-Columbian character, or the Madonna, Chico Mendez, Frida Kalo [stet], Ray Carver, a monkey, or a fish. For me, all of these faces, forests, and jungles s serve to remind us of what Cezanne once said, that nature is on the inside." I believe that it is possible a person can discover the forest inside themselves by looking at my work."

Describing what would eventually become *The Froth* (1996), Arreguín wrote:

> "For this site we have chosen a high visibility site in the main entry lobby. This installation would be seen from both inside and outside of the building, and would help to identify the main entry. For this site, I propose a unique stained glass interpretation of my painting, *As Long as The Fish Shall Swim*, measuring 10' X 18". This interpretation in glass shall be executed by Bill Hillman of the Mansion Glass Co. in Olympia....Crossing the fields of painting and stained glass has necessitated the invention of new techniques and has lead to a whole new vision in stained glass."
>
> "The composition abstracts ecological ideas of harmony, rhythm, and the interconnectedness of the forces of nature. Its color composition is muted and pastel, so it will not overwhelm the relatively colorless surroundings, but will gently elevate and integrate with the environment. The composition has forms that eem, at one moment, to be North west Indian styles and the next moment Japanese or Latin. The larger images are made up of maller elements, much like the molecular underpinnings of nature. Many tide pool creatures spiral from the background upon close examination, and the currents and eddies reveal their ecrets to the imaginative."

Tess Gallagher explained to me (in 2018 correspondence) that *The Froth* title (which replaced the working one from the proposal) had originated with Painter Morris Graves. She said it was after he saw another example of Arreguín's work, *The Hero's Journey*. This was during a conversation with Morris Graves and Robert Yarber, at a California gathering in honor of Ray Carver. Gallagher told me, "I had carried another Alfredo painting reproduced inside the fly leaf of Raymond Carver's *A New Path to the Waterfall* book- Graves looks at the painting, and says to me: "I love how he does the froth!" She continues, "Then I came back to Alfredo in Seattle, sharing with him that remark, which then inspired Alfredo painting *The Froth*!

Ecology Employee Perspectives

There were discussions in 1995 about how art should best be fit to the existing architecture. At the time, many Ecology employees weighed in with how they saw the two proposals being considered by the selection committee.

An example was from Jordan Taylor, who noted:

> "Chihuly's presentation is, as always, beautiful and imaginative. With Arreguín's work, however, I felt immediately the intimacy, interconnectedness, and complexity of the web of life. The Arreguín/ Hillman collaboration would be visually stunning as well as connecting us to our bountiful and beautiful Northwest heritage. The paintings invite us in, drawing us deeper and deeper into the layers of interrelationship among animal/plant/human forms of life. It reminds us that we are all connected, and it all matters. My vote goes with Arreguín-reminding us why the care and stewardship of this planet is crucial. His work is inspiring, intimate, immediate!"

John Erickson reflected back (in 2018) to when proposals were being evaluated by a committee from the Arts Commission in 1996:

> "It was felt that the competing proposal from Dale Chilhuly was colorful and spectacular, yet really it had nothing in particular to do with Ecology's mission. It seemed clear, on the other hand, that Arreguín had thought a great deal about doing work which did relate to the northwest natural world and celebration of its protection."

An excerpt of another comment, from Robert Garrigues, reflects on having read the many others:

> "I notice a few comments about the Arreguín paintings not being a NW theme. It seems to me that the Pacific Northwest is only a small part of the whole, and any work that depicts the diversity of life includes the NW as well."

The Commission

When all was said and done, the 0.5 percent allocation was awarded by the Washington State Arts Commission to Alfredo Arreguín. Better for taxpayers, it had less long term maintenance and special lighting costs than what was proposed by Chihuly. It was recognized by the committee as being better aligned with Ecology's mission. Based on the comments that were collected in 1995, the committee's choice also reflected the general preference of most Ecology employees who expressed interest. Installation by Mansion Glass was completed, and the works were dedicated in October of 1997.

Collaboration and Fabrication

The Froth (1996) was fabricated by Olympia's Mansion Glass Works, using glass from Seattle's Fremont Glass Company. I spoke with Macy Jewell, an Olympia glass artisan. She and her husband have worked on many projects with Mansion Glass over the years, including works at Saint Martin's College and Saint Placid's Priory....both of which are within a mile of the Ecology Headquarters building.

"It was really exciting when our proposal was the one chosen..." she told me, as they were in competition with Dale Chihuly. Macy did sandblasting on laminated panels of specialty glass which *The Froth* (1996) is composed from. She told me that Jim Flanagan of Fremont Glass had made annealed panels that she "blasted down through..." to "reveal different layers of color."

Macy described working the sandblast in a box, lit fluorescently from behind, and using carbide abrasives in a reductive process. Bill Hillman had prepared stencils off Arreguín's painting, translating into designs to apply on glass. All the sand and vaporized glass was then recycled. Macy said she found much to see in the raw material, such as ripples and air bubbles..."These idiosyncrasies give the work a lot of depth when seen up close..." she noted.

Living with the Work

Thirty plus years ago, these works were installed. Because they are in the most public part of the building, hundreds of passersby have experienced them daily for many years. 1200 or so employees of Ecology and four other natural resource agencies work in this building. On an average day, Ecology has about 60 visitors-which adds up to roughly 1600 per year.

Arreguín's *Jungla Encantada* (1994) and *The Froth* (1996) are located in Ecology's Main Lobby, near the reception desk. There are large panels of translucent glass across the entire lobby area, a north-facing wall of light. As light levels change through the day, so does the atmosphere inside. The appearance of The Froth is always changing subtly. One can walk back and forth between the 2 large works, being given to see quite different ways his pattern designs appear-on canvas, and in glass.

Bill Yake worked for nearly 25 years at Ecology. As an environmental scientist his efforts evolved to focus on the statewide toxic contamination of water, sediments, soils, fish, and shellfish. Writing poetry and serving on the Art Committee helped balance his perspective. Bill retired from Ecology in 2002. In 2018, he offered the following reminiscence:

> "I recall little about events leading up to the selection and placement of the Arreguín works in the Ecology building. But I do remember a sense of transformation when they were in stalled. It felt as if the building-previously mostly linear and pale-had been imbued with a soul. We had joked that the tiers of interior railings and cubicles drew their inspiration from the early video of Elvis Presley performing *Jailhouse Rock.*
>
> The interior sterility and linear order was reflected symmetrically in the daily activities of its denizens: employees, 'clients', and visitors. We planned meetings, developed and reworked policies, crafted memoranda, and administrated a presumably efficient bureaucracy. It was too easy for the scientists, engineers, planners, geologists, fiscal staff and information officers to forget the larger picture. Easy to forget what inspired us to choose this line of work. And too easy for visiting functionaries to dismiss the natural world while "doing business at Ecology."
>
> For me (and many others?) Arreguín's pieces changed all that. They lit up the atrial heart of the building. Both were central to entry and departure. They brought some of the natural world into the heart of a technical, political, administrative world of human considerations. It was hard to leave or enter without considering, at least subconsciously, all the life that depended on our collective efforts.

The pieces, specifically, were:

> *The Froth* (1996)—a tribute to translucent air and water populated by the fecundity of native salmon. A clear stream overhead lit by exterior, seasonal light.

Jungla Encantada (1994)—(which I thought of as The Rainforest Triptych)—a tribute to earth and rainforest populated by entwined and half-hidden birds, primates, and jungle cats. The great damp fecundity of earth's lungs.

At the personal level, *The Froth* (1996) reminded me of aeration-the intersection of air and water. Puget Sound and salmon health were and remain central concerns of Washington's environmental law. We were concerned about toxic organic pollutants that collected at the air-water interface—whether sea surface or fine bubbles. And, when I passed it, The Rainforest Triptych drew my long attention as I searched its foliage for life forms and absorbed its greens.

This was also an era tuned to fractals-the variously scaled and derived repetitions central to natural designs. Arreguín's works were replete with them, with homages to fractals. For those of us working there, these works offered a communal reminder of the value and momentum of our work. The works buoyed us.They gave the building a soul."

Steve Fry notes:

"The two works that get the most attention, both from people who work in the building but also visitors, are *Jungla Encantada* and *The Froth*. They get attention for different reasons. The Jungle Encantada painting, with its nude figures, sparks controversy, while The Froth, reflecting the northwest with leaping salmon and flowing waters, evokes harmony with the building's architecture."

Janet Hyre is another long term Ecology employee, whose work is focused on promoting safety and well-being for Ecology workers statewide. Janet is a member of an art committee which coordinates art exhibitions and occasional receptions for northwest artists who show their work through *Art In Ecology*. About the Arreguín works, Janet notes:

"I love that every time you look, there's something different you see…and it [Jungla Encantada] is like a tapestry, which to me is the same as being like life itself…"

John Erickson works on sustainability planning at Ecology, and he analyzes fiscal implications of actions proposed at the Washington State Legislature. Erickson described his impressions about the work:

"With the *Froth*, it is easy to have the feeling that one is immersed in the river with the fish…" About *Jungla Encantada*, he notes: "The painting is vibrant, energetic-one can peacefully, serenely engage with the jaguar, parrot, monkey as well as the female figures, which bring a human dignity and vulnerability to the piece. We view them in their natural state…there is nothing salacious in these images…they are figures rendered with dignity and respect."

Sean Mellon works in Ecology as a Grant Manager supporting small communities in upgrades to their stormwater treatment systems. He became familiar with Alfredo's work when he started

working here in 2010.

> "You can tell [by his paintings] he is a man of many experiences." Sean appreciates the colorful nature of Arreguín's paintings, saying "they have an innocence and playfulness about them, and evoke something like a dream-I love the way he uses his art to educate and to inspire-it draws you in. Sean told me, "Seeing the Hazel Wolf painting got me to do some research—I looked into who was this person, wondering why Arreguín would have portrayed her...I learned a lot about Pacific Northwest history and environmental activism."

Doyle Fanning was known to her Ecology colleagues as Pat McLain, and for a number of years she was our Budget Director, and also served enthusiastically as the Executive Sponsor for Ecology's art Committee before retiring. Doyle notes:

> "Here's what I'm thinking about Arreguín's work at ECY specifically but it may apply more broadly. Encantada is the feminine form of the Spanish or bewitched, enchanted, or charmed. His work does that....enchants and charms me....with childlike visions he draws me in...the more I look the more I see and at some point...like a dream....I am transported...not to another world, bt it is as if I am being drawn in to a deeper layer of this world...he peels back the façade and reveals the true world we have forgotten how to see. It is a wild and untamed world of primary colors and childlike forms. His work always makes me think of what it must have been like 40,000 years ago to discover geometry or paint or music for the first time. Can you imagine? He can! And about the feminine form...he is a high priest glorifying the Anima Mundi which for me expresses itself in the feminine. Just look at his portraits of Frida! He gets her! He gets the soul and our connection to the wild world within and all around us."

Juxtaposing Northwest Painters

Having addressed the Ecology Building as a context for Arreguín and other northwest artists, I'll speak of my own impressions about these works using one last arc or tangent. At the heart of the matter, to my mind, are different ways of working with paint, variously expressing the Pacific Northwest. I found comparisons of these painters revelatory, though doing so may seem anything but obvious.

One day along Hood Canal, I found myself reflecting on how Guy Anderson painted the northwest, as it relates to the way Alfredo Arreguín does. I continued the juxtaposing muses with Gaylen Hansen.

Differences in style and effect are obvious between these painters. Washington residents, Arreguín, Anderson, and Hansen each have decades of landscape painting in common. Place (the Northwest) figures prominently. Each of these painters apply drawing skills to their paintings. While their works all have some abstract qualities, the work of each can be named as fundamentally figurative.

There are many ways of being creative, and each artist, poet, musician finds an environment that best serves that work. In his brightly lit studio, Gaylen Hansen stapled his canvases to the wall, tearing them down to finish with tattered edges. For many years, he lived in the high plateau grasslands of the Palouse. He taught art at Eastern Washington University for many years, and was well-liked by students.

Hansen grew up in Utah. His eccentric landscapes are less obviously specific about the northwest, except as suggested by the common presence of Palouse grasshoppers, crows and salmon. A single, bearded man always wears a wide brimmed hat, and rides around in open spaces on a skinny legged horse. Hansen's palette is bright and cheerful, blues and greens and yellows, often charged with bold red. His animal figures often are intertwined, at times in conflict or confrontation, yet almost always playfully. For music with Gaylen Hansen, I can hear the sounds of a crackling campfire, howls of coyotes in the air, and a lone harmonica drifting into the wilderness.

Guy Anderson worked among rolled up paintings, using pans and large brushes on roofing paper, upstairs in the La Conner house he built. He was fond of poetry and fossils, rusted steel and weathered wood. A voracious reader, he loved walking, and spent hours meandering the shorelines of Skagit Bay. He loved listening to opera, and he played piano. He watched his paintings unfold in outdoor settings, hung on weathered fences among rhododendrons in a rusty metal ornamented garden. A great old cedar and a rock formation towered over the slate patio where his friends came to converse.

A painting of Guy Anderson's brings to mind a solo cello, echoing and reverberating, his deeply fluid shadows coalescing in dark puddles of Brahms and Ravel. The brushstrokes are sweeping, like strong north winds blowing in off the Pacific. They coalesce the swirls and eddies of a deep green river, showing an endless flow as it crosses a vast coastal plain. His sweeping strokes were made in motion from above—fluidly lavished onto paper on the floor. Anderson's limited-palette suffusions of muddled umber are bold; they come with small red accents. They are brooding and also grounded to earth. In paintings, horizontal figures are afloat, suspended in a paper brown sky. There are wispy accents of white gouache. His paintings feel profoundly northwestern by nature, and always evoke the seeming endless winters of the northern forests and headlands where Guy grew up near Puget Sound.

The Imagination Carries On....

Where Anderson expresses the northwest land, air and seas expansively, from a northern viewpoint, and Hansen does so more with bemused allusion, Arreguín shows vistas of the natural world more inwardly, and from the south.

At a cellular level, almost...his countless brushstrokes evoke tapestries of neuronal bursts, flickering fields, colorful atmospheres.

Although Arreguín was for a time a soldier, his paintings do not dwell on the darkness of war. Volcanoes loom over bright blue waters, seen with orcas breaching up close, or else quietly in the distance. Honoring portraits of heroines and heroes are commingled in liminal atmospheres where grand fireworks displays are seen but not heard.

Arreguín, whose boyhood was in Mexico, shows us the dancing, sparkling droplets of the water of life. Suspended in air is the lively spray, of a cresting wave, or dancing above an elaborate fountain. The water is always sparkling, and it is seen in the eerie sunlight of a strangely familiar environment, one suffused with mystical enchantment, encouraging our imagination easily to wonder.

In my mind, the sounds of an Arreguín painting are lively trumpets, playing a mariachi rhythm in the near distance. Marching is suggested, possibly toward the Fountain of Youth. A bustling cantina is festive and celebratory. As if in a dream, these drifting, lively notes are intermittent with silence. Sometimes there is a high-pitched tinkling of wind chimes. This nearby music is heard from a quiet cave, where the phosphorescing cavern walls are alive with subterranean color. The air is cool and moist.

The structures in Arreguín's paintings are intricate, delicate, and percussively staccato. Architectural in their function, hosting ideas of many kinds, cultural, political, ecological. Among the crystalline lattice-works of light, leopards and lions stalk in the jungle, and curious humans peer from the foliage.

Art In Public Places

Not all commissions for public art end up being well-received. Some of them become subjects of ridicule or disdain. They don't always get sturdily built or competently installed. Sometimes their initial interest fades over time, or the works physically deteriorate, and have to be revised or removed.

Ecology is blessed with hosting other large works which, like Arreguín's, were commissioned by a selection committee. Unlike what happened here, these works were later refused by the institutions who paid for their creation. to the State Art Commission, they were later loaned on long term to Ecology. In this context, works by Mo Bach and Roy DeForest are treasured presences.

I think Alfredo Arreguín's 1995 intentions, well-expressed at the time, have also been wellrealized. He had a vision, and found competent collaborators to help realize the work. He was able to convince others of its worth, and the work has held up well over time. In the Washington State Art Collection, these Arreguín installations continue affording a source of contemplation for many.

The ripples of imagination carry on, in a context well related to Alfredo's vital concerns—as a human who cares deeply about the earth and its creatures. For many, work days at Ecology are enlivened by his art. Walking past
Arreguín's beautifully hand-crafted works, North and South America are reunited, with a celebrant Mexico given lively expression. Singular visions of the diversity of life have been crafted into durable and exuberantly symbolic images. Withthem, as we strive to protect and preserve, we can celebrate the majesty and mystery and complexity of the natural world.

Andrew Connors

Interview with Andrew Connors Senior Curator at the National Hispanic Cultural Center in Albuquerque, New Mexico (2003)

Yvette: We'll just gather some information about the development of the cultural center, how that came to be and the role you played in it. I think Alfredo was here earlier in the Lalu Show and then he's come back again, so he's a repeat visitor, so those are the two things. You ready, Mike?

Andrew: Do you want me to talk to you or the camera?

Mike: Look at her.

Yvette: So the first question I had was about how you came to meet Alfredo and what happened with him being collected in the Smithsonian?

Andrew: Well, I first saw his work at the opening of the Chicano Art Resistance and Affirmation exposition that opened in L.A. at the White Art Gallery of UCLA. That opened, I think, in September of 1990 and there were several artist in that show that just sang. They really popped out as artists of significance and artists of heft that were doing something worthwhile that communicated across cultural boarders. They weren't artists that rejected acts of doing heritage and background. Rather, they created acts that celebrated that and also made it accessible to a larger public. As that exhibition traveled around the country it came to the Smithsonian Institute and I realized at that point that the others, many of my colleagues, the art world folks, also responded very warmly to Alfredo's work. So it wasn't just a cultural communication but an esthetic communication and at that point, we were working on to build a collection, filling in the hundreds of years of absence of Latinos artists in the Smithsonian collection. I was able to go out to Seattle and visit with Susie and Alfredo and spoke with them, looking at a lot of his work and talking with him about how he would best see himself represented at the Smithsonian.

So I brought back a sheet of slides and we talked it over with the collections committee and we were able to acquire *Sueño, (Dream: Eve Before Adam)*, for the Smithsonian American Art Museum and that was a very important acquisition for us because it was sort of the breakthrough acquisition that made people realize that not all Chicano artists working today are angry or express themselves through political actions. Rather, there are others that express themselves through visual complexity, strength, and power. They make a presentation, or make a statement, that's very strong, but the piece doesn't come across as a pure political enterprise. Furthermore, Alfredo is one of those artists that make strong statements about the world, about what he feels is important, and they are all statements that we all get swept up in right away. His paintings speak to all of us. They become eternal. They become visceral statements about our lives, who we are, and what is important to us. There are not many artists that can do that without banging you over the head and Alfredo bangs you over the head with lushness, beauty, and a representation of unseen forces.

That's the thing that makes Alfredo's work so powerful because he visualizes, or makes visible, the things that we sense we cannot see. Alfredo sees things that most of us don't see, but we have a sense that they might be there. Alfredo shows us how they are there and because he was telling us this morning, when he was in the jungle, he saw eyes everywhere and those eyes are everywhere in his work. I think in today's society we think of people watching us all the time and Alfredo makes it very straight forward. It's the sort of work that crosses many different boundaries. There's the boundary of political art vs. beautiful art—of contemporary art vs. patterned art— ethnic art vs. mainstream art. Alfredo's works in all of those different fields and he is inclusive as an artist, as opposed to exclusive. I think that's what makes all the difference with Alfredo. The, the work is serious, significant, full of content and full of meaning.

However, it's also the sort of thing that a two-year old can appreciate and love just as much as a Ph.D. in Environmental Studies. All of that works very well. I'm thinking of the American Academy of Science exhibition when Alfredo was shown in the world of science. I think that made it very clear that the scientist loved his work as much as the art world loved his work. He just has an ability to speak to people that don't think they want to hear anything and I think that's what made him such an easy sell at the Smithsonian. I think everybody, everybody agrees that he is an artist that deserves a much greater representation and I think he is getting it bit by bit. But he is certainly a favorite and a household name to everyone who works at the Smithsonian. Unfortunately, he is just not at other art museums, so we still got work to do.

Yvette: You said something this morning about how when the painting, when it was first acquired, it went into the board room, I think. That was an interesting little sequence there that you talked about how it was a unanimous vote.

Andrew: Well, I guess he meant to back up and talk a more about the process and acquiring his work at the Smithsonian. We had a group of slides to show and I was striving to be reasonable and present something that was not the most expensive, that was the most grand, but was really solid so we went through a number of pieces and our director said, "Well, let's see all of the slides," because they kept responding to all of them. I showed one of the slides of one of the panels of *Sueño* and the director said, "This one is just incredible." I said "That was just one third of the whole painting here are the other images." She said, "Well let's get the biggest, the best, and the most important if we are going to build an important collection." The rest of the committee agreed. When the painting was brought in for the final review it was unanimous. The people in the shipping and packing office, when they unpacked this thing, they could not believe the extent of the painting the depth of the painting and the complexity of the painting. Then it was installed for the board meeting, when and it installed— do you want me to wait for that? When it came time for the commission meeting, which came twice a year, the director would usually pick some of the most significant acquisitions that had occurred in the six months previous and she choose *Sueño*. So, *Sueño* was on the big wall of the board room of at the Smithsonian American Art Museum. Everyone on the board of commissioners were just enthralled by it and they voted unanimously to accept the piece into the collection. A major abstract contemporary painting was taken down in the contemporary art gallery of the museum the next day and this was put up in its place.

So, it was on view basically all time and always with a bench in front of it so people can sit down and just and constantly watch the painting and it's not a question of just looking at the painting, but watching because its constantly changing and shifting just as soon as you know a work art by Alfredo Arreguín it shows you 15 other faces that you never saw before. Just the other day, just yesterday, there was a group that I was taking on a preview tour of the exhibition. In the family portrait, a painting I've seen dozens of times, I saw yet another face just when it was down on the floor because I was at a different perspective, a different angle. There aren't many artists who can do that, who can make work of art that never stop surprising you. Alfredo's work has that sense of surprise, and that sense of enthusiasm for life. I think it is very important in this day and age that we have an artist who has something to say and that something is optimistic and I very much appreciate him for that and I think most of us in the art world feel the same way.

Yvette: *Sueño*. I was interested in *Sueño*, in particular, that theme of *Sueño*—

Andrew: Well, the wonderful thing about *Sueño* is that Alfredo is willing to poke fun at himself and everyone else. The fact that Alfredo's self-portraits often are on the bodies of monkeys, shows that he doesn't take himself all that seriously, but the whole notion that Sueño is what Alfredo sees the world being like if God had make Eve first, or never got around to making Adam. It is a great celebration in, of the strength in the feminine ability to negotiate through problems and I think it's very much a strong statement that Alfredo feels that it's the man that have really messed up the world and if women were left to run it, it would be a much better place, much more idyllic place. That painting is an idol, it is a jungle paradise that is populated by thousands of different creatures, presumably all, which are female—and it looks like a pretty great place to be and I love that Alfred put his face on the monkey. So he could view the world that he idealized through that dream and that statement I think is very relevant for many people even if it's not just a sexist question as to who are making the biggest mistakes in the world today. It's a question of what would happen if things are better. If we didn't make some of the decisions that we did and that's another level of interpretation of Alfredo's work. It just appears to be pattern. It appears to be lush jungle life, and yet is a very strong political statement.

Yvette: And the idea of the mother factor, the birth factor, Mother Nature, mother Earth. Earth goddess, that kinda of thing. You had contact with Alfredo from the beginning days or beginning months, I guess of the opening of the National Hispanic Cultural Center I think he was in that earlier show. Can you talk about Lelu and how all that worked for him?

Andrew: Well, when Helen Lucero became the director of the art museum here she asked me if I would apply for the senior curator position. I applied and got the position and she said "The first thing you have to do is do a national exhibition, highlighting artists from across the United States." So, basically what I had to do was Rolodex curation, you know, I had to curate from my Rolodex those people that I knew, those people that I felt would be willing to lend to a center that didn't exist. We had no track record. We had no staff than anybody necessarily recognized and so I pulled together those artists that I felt were some of the best artists working in the United States today. Alfredo, very graciously, from the beginning agreed to participate and he said "These are the paintings that are available, which one would you like to borrow?"

So, we requested the *Tree of Life*, and it became the poster image and the image used on our press package and all the different materials we generated for that exhibition. It was very popular and people loved it and realized on this center, The National Hispanic Cultural Center, is going to be different than we expected. It's going to show different sorts of things than what we had originally proposed. What I had originally proposed titling the exhibition was, La Luz, contemporary art in the United States because there had been so many exhibitions in the United State that are called American art. The problem was that they have no Latinos or Asians. They have no women. In fact, they have no minorities of any kind, and I felt it would be fun to counter that by simply saying these are all contemporary artists in the United States. Ultimately, it was decided that was not helpful enough because it didn't really explain that they are all part of some Latin American heritage.

So, we added Latino to the title, but I really felt that it would be important to show all of the artists in the exhibition as simple American artists, not artists with a hyphenated ethnicity or some shared background, but artists from our country. I also think that's one of the great things about Alfredo. He is also a Mexican artist as much as he is a United States artist. He is a Mexican-American artist with whichever naming system people choose to apply to him. He gets all of them and he doesn't reject any naming system. He doesn't say, "I'm not this. I'm not that." He just doesn't need outsiders to tell him who he is. He knows very strongly who he is and what's doing, so these categories, don't apply. The fact that his work doesn't look like the work of a lot of Chicano artists doesn't make him any less of a Chicano artist. It simply means he has his own vision and he's creating his own painting style. Nobody paints like Alfredo. I don't know of anybody who does the sort of thing that he does—and I can't imagine anybody doing it better. For instance, for him to take a Mexican revolutionary and turn that into a pattern painting in the most dense of jungles, or to paint salmon swimming upstream against the current. Who would ever think of doing paintings on all those different subjects? Yet, even with the variety of subjects, he makes them his own. His subject matter is incredibly broad, incredibly diverse, and yet you would never mistake his work for the work of any other artist.

Yvette: Kinda developing that idea a little bit. Dr. Wilson from the University of Washington. Did you meet him when you were in Seattle at one point? Robert Wilson? He's an art history professor at the University of Washington? Do you agree with his assessment of Alfredo's work as monumental?

Andrew: Well, I think there is something to that in terms of physical scale, but what I think Alfredo is continuing is something that is not really celebrated in contemporary society. That's the folk arts, the tile patterns—the incredible complexity of geometric designs from pre-conquest art that continues to this day. Generally those art forms are continued and carried on and innovative by people with very little training, very little education, in many cases illiterate artist. So, Alfredo is taking the hallmark, the community based arts, the arts based in hundreds of years of tradition and bringing those up to date by translating that complexity of pattering and that sophistication of geometry into painting styles, rather than decorating on gourds or weaving and brocading, or any of the traditional Mexican folk art forms. I think Alfredo is much more based in that tradition, but because he has very, sophisticated art training people tend to lump him more with the trained artists. However, I see what he is doing as ever more Mexican than what Los Tres Grandes [Rivera, Orozco and

Siquieros] among other of the 20th century contemporary artists have done. That is because he is simply taking that exuberance of patterning, that exuberance of color, and transmitting it into an entirely different medium so I don't know if that contradicts what—

Yvette: No, no I totally agree and I was just wondering about your perspective on that in terms of heritage and tradition. I agree completely, a more close up label coming into the heart of the patterns. In closing, any other comments?

Andrew: Well, one of the things I always would love to see Alfredo while he painting. I don't know if he lets many people watch him while he's painting, but the times I've been up there I've never been able to see him painting because this gregarious, this, this all giving personality of his, to me doesn't seem to be selfish enough to spend the time painting a painting. So, I just find that very contradictory. In order to achieve what he does in his studio,

I would think there are times when he simply has to be an absolute private person and shut down all the influences from the outside and just lock himself away to make art work. But, his personality doesn't seem to be that sort of person at all, so that again, that's another semi-conflict. Who he is as a person and how he presents himself as an artist seem to be different because he is so giving and so generous and he gives in the paintings. I sort of wonder when he takes the time to even make those paintings.

Yvette: Well, I'll send you some footage. I'm working on a sequence and I've been going up there and staying overnight at their place on the weekends. He finally got to, you know, that point where I got to come in the studio and do some shooting in the studio. So, I got some images I really love of him painting and then he set up, at our request, a time lapse image series of one of the Frida paintings, so it just is all its coming together, the patterns are getting filled in. So, like a coloring book really being colored in a sense, you know, being filled in, so that's a very fun sequence and you probably enjoy that. But, he is very strict, you know, the social business is finished in the evening that fine and then in the morning he go for his walk then it is down in the studio. The routine is there and so the hours and the lifetime standing before the easel and painting. But he has a, he has a commitment that very few artists do. Very few people do and that commitment is so rich and complex. There are thousands of pages in writing in each one of his paintings and as I said he takes the larger picture of the world around us and encapsulates it so thoroughly that, that you can't help but, but recognize what a keen observer he is. You can't help but recognize that he knows the world, that he know situations, he knows how human beings work and all though human beings in many of his paintings seem to be absolutely non-existent they are all ultimately highly humanist work of art that they are about our perceptions of the natural world. They are about our perceptions of hero, of our perception life and space and ultimately our perception of time because the longer that we spend with the works the more we realize they don't just exist in a static two dimensional form. They really exist in three dimensions and four dimensions because the longer that we look at them the more they change and each time you see one of his painting you see it differently and depending on the light, the time of day, depending on your attitude, depending on the mood you're in Alfredo's paintings can reflect and talk back to you in this dialogue and it's pretty wonderful that art can still move people in such a dynamically way because most art is currently about ideas. Alfredo's art is about ideas, but ultimately is is about the human soul and the heart and he has a heart and soul that is bigger than anybody I know.

Antonio Sánchez

Decoding the Arreguín Codices:
Mexican, Mestizo, Chicano/a and Náhuatl Patterns, Phantasmagoria & Symbols

I sing the pictures in the book
and see them spread out
I am an elegant bird
for I make the codices speak
within the house of pictures.
Náhuatl Poet[23]

Memorizing Mexican jungles with foliage gently embracing stoic and ageless dark-skinned Mestizo Madonnas; radiant butterflies and moths that drift effortlessly in search of the jungle's sweet nectar; a rainbow of parrots, macaws, raptors and sacred hummingbirds firmly clutching the exposed tree branch or taking flight into the rare fissure created among the relentless bursts of colored flora, reflecting portraits of persuasive social and artistic protagonists; felines striding arrogantly across their familiar terrain; monkeys that expertly seek your gaze with their peering deliberate intent of mischief, or maybe protection; and the ever-present plethora of guarding Naguals, transfixed and motionless in a sublime state of spiritual readiness. These are just hints of the kaleidoscope of Mexican, Mestizo Chicano and Nagl imagery that have become elements of Alfredo Arreguín's signature and hypnotizing coded masterpieces.

Although Alfredo's mastery of patterned paintings quickly captivates the viewer's eye with a dizzying array of shapes, patterns, protagonists and themes, can we really be sure that our mind's eye is seeing what we think it is, or has this masterful shaman artist cleverly deceived us into believing that each canvas only speaks to the viewer in a colorful and alluring one-dimensional aesthetic plane, like seeing just the saccharine icing on the surface of a layered cake? This is the polemic that needs to be discussed, and to do so we must dig deeply into the conscious and subconscious visual elements and the profound cultural meaning ascribed to them to decode his complex layered pattern paintings.

Studies using voxel-based morphometry of human brains have found that the template for an artist's imaginative expression is etched deep within, as part of their being, long before they were ever old enough to pick up an artist's brush and during their formative years. Alfredo explains the process he uses during the construction of his paintings as a deliberate but subconscious event that begins from the first moment he rhythmically applies each stroke of a wet brush to an empty canvas. In this process he delves deeply into the culturally implanted layers of subconscious references. In the case of Alfredo, these references are taken from his formative Mexican, Mestizo and Chicano roots. His most dominant guiding place of reference is Mexico, where his imaginative expression was profoundly embedded during the formative years of his youth. It is here where he was first immersed in the patterns associated with the tangled breathing jungles of Guerrero Mexico, awash with mystery and

23 Miguel Leon Portillo, *Pre-Columbian Literatures of Mexico* (Norman University of Oklahoma Press 1986)

pulsating rays of color; the dazzling and chaotic public markets filled with fragrances and mounds of fresh sweet fruits and nurturing vegetables; the redundant structured patterns of Spanish colonial tiled floors and walls; the playful expressions of the regional folk art that are so much a part of the uniqueness, tradition and talent found among Mestizo Mexican village artists and the rich nature-based wisdom and lore of the autochthonous and Mestizo Mexicans. Alfredo literally absorbed and assimilated the colors, shapes, shadows, light and patterns of this Mexico and filtered these elements through a process of creative osmosis. Like a life-giving capillary action, he took in the visual context of the culture-rich Mexico that surrounded him and etched it into his creative subconscious. Even the sounds of these experiences were transformed and transplanted into colors and patterns. However, it is important to also highlight that shortly after these formative years spent in Mexico, he came to live and study art in the Pacific Northwest in the very early 1960s. This inspiring artist arrived just in time to witness the birth and zenith of one of the most radical social, sexual and cultural upheavals in the history of the United States. Whether he adopted the mantel of a Chicano artist at that time or the activist movement adopted him, is not entirely clear. We may be sure, however, that the formative experience also left an indelible mark on his creative conscious, and his combined experience of Mexico and bearing witness to the 1960s Chicano social and civil rights revolution has now become his unconscious creative springboard.

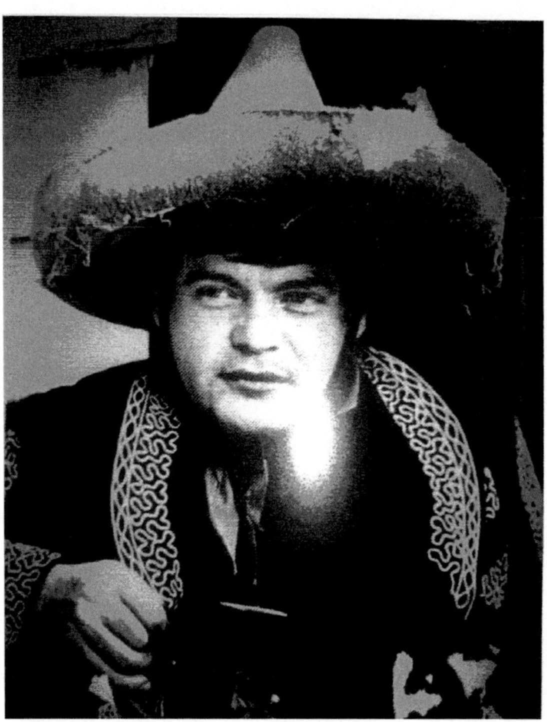

A tantalizing insight into the visual alchemy of Alfredo's creative immersion into Mexico's profound cultural and aesthetic palette, was partially revealed during one special occasion while I was visiting with him in his studio. I gently, but imprudently, attempted to pry out of him the meaning of the tabby cat on the painting that he had done for the official Washington State Centennial commemoration. "Why the cat?" I said to him. His quick and bemused but playful glance and the spontaneous response, broken only by his characteristic and endearing laughter, lanced my innermost soul and yanked at every cell of curiosity in my being. Alfredo quipped, "Maybe that cat is me."
That brief sentence precipitated an epiphany of thought and meaning which opened my prism of

visual awareness and unfurled a valuable and extraordinary roadmap that I now use to accompany me during every optical sojourn into his paintings. Alfredo had armed me with a new insight into both the context and meaning found in the rubric of his masterfully layered paintings. This valuable new awareness allowed me to assign a cultural algorithm to the remarkably concealed layers of proscribed complexity of Mexican, Mestizo and Chicano patterned symbols, the animals and fish, the ostensibly Catholic Madonnas, and the iconic protagonists that adorn his paintings.

The key that unlocks both his patterns and themes was not that every animal was an anthropomorphic rendition of the artist himself or even of others. That would be an oversimplification and much too uninteresting for this complex artist. Rather, it was insight into the belief held by indigenous Indians about Naguals, the belief of transformation of animal forms. It is also a window into the veiled or coded dichotomy of the real world and corresponding spirits, a belief held by Mexican mestizo and native Indians. It is an understanding that the world exists in a constant state of duality. This understanding is best epitomized in their belief of the existence of animal spirits called Naguals which can be seen depicted in many of his paintings and grounded in a very profound belief system strongly held by native Mexican Indians and Mestizos, even to this very day.

The term Nagual, also spelled Nahual, refers to a personal guardian spirit that is understood by some Mexican Indians and mestizos (mixed-race Mexican Indians) to belong to an animal or insect, such as a deer, jaguar, butterfly or parrot. It is often used by anthropologists to describe a healer or shaman who claims to have the power to transform into an animal form – to figuratively "shift" into another form. The term Nagual was made very popular in the 1960s by the charismatic anthropologist Carlos Castaneda. He popularized the term Nagual in his books and used it to describe those who have the skills to transform themselves physically and spiritually in order to guide others to new areas of awareness and alternate realities.[24]

The earliest European description of a Nagual or Nagualism was by Antonio de Herrera's 1530 book titled *Historia de las Indias Occidentales.* The Mayan Indians provided him with a trove of insight and information about Naguals. Translated from the Spanish, the author writes: "The Devil was accustomed to deceive these natives by appearing to them in the form of a lion, tiger, coyote, lizard, snake, bird, or other animal. To these appearances they apply the name Naguales, which is as much as to say, guardians or companions; and when such an animal dies, so does the Indian to whom it was assigned. Either in his dreams or half awake, he would see some one of those animals or birds above mentioned, who would say to him, 'On such a day go hunting and the first animal or bird you see will be my form, and I shall remain your companion and Nagual for all time.' Thus their friendship became so close that when one died so did the other; and without such a Nagual the natives believe no one can become rich or powerful."

The clear presence of animal spirits, or Naguals, can be found throughout many of Alfredo's paintings. To the unaware, these animals appear at times to be secondary aesthetic components of his art. However, in many cases, the animal, bird, or insect Nagual is essential to understanding the thematic meaning of his paintings. They are richly coded symbols that speak to the duality, metamorphosis, transposition and even marginalization he is distinctly capturing.

24 *Teachings of Don Juan: A Yaqui Way of Knowledge*, University of California Press 1968

By looking at his painting through this culturally based Mexican lens, you can see that he has consciously or subconsciously chosen to simultaneously depict an existence of two symbiotic and parallel universes: the spiritual and mundane; the human form and the animal spirit guide Nagual; the good and the bad; the beast and exquisite stark beauty; the powerful and the fragile; the past and the present; the protector and the protected; and remarkable stillness amid turmoil and chaos. He is, unquestionably, the master of creating a visual portal into this Mexican realm of duality and transforming Naguals through the use of layers of culturally coded symbols.

When the Spanish arrived in Mexico in 1519, only an extremely small fraction of the entire Mexican Indian population was literate in the written pictographic and ideographic Aztec Nagualtl writing, a written system that used a complicated set of logograms and syllabic signs. As a result, just the most basic written Aztec language could be understood by the common Aztec, if any at all. Alfredo clearly follows this Mexican Aztec tradition by creating symbolic codes to be understood by those willing to look deep into their intended meaning. Through the depiction of Mexican coded symbolism, he invites us to be Mexican and to understand the use and expression of Mexican duality and transformation. Through his use of animal and insect guides, Naguals, he constructs a remarkably complex and deeply meaningful and transcendent cultural bridge into the realm of the Aztec religious, cultural worldview and aesthetic.

It is astounding to witness how this master artist skirted the line between Mexican tradition and creative innovation as he carefully constructed the multiple layers of culturally-coded meaning in the symbols and duality he employed to depict La Virgin of Tonantzin, found in his 1993 painting Tonantzin. The word Tonantzin is the native Mexican Nagualtl Indian name which has been given by the Mexican Indians to the Catholic Madonna, most commonly referred to as the Virgin of Guadalupe. The name "Virgin of Guadalupe" is the most recognized and most common name used in reference to this rendition of the Madonna by the majority of Mexicans, Mestizos and Chicanos. However, by referring to this Madonna in his 1993 painting as Tonantzin, Alfredo has invited—if not teased—the viewer into accepting the importance, legitimacy and duality of the native Mexican Indians' spiritual universe. It is also an expression of the depth of expressed and real duality found in Mexican culture and profound religious history.

The story of Guadalupe/Tonantzin, according to both native Mexican oral tradition and official Catholic tradition, was a Mexica Indian woman who appeared to Juan Diego in 1531 on the hill of Tepeyac near *present-day* Mexico City.

The apparition of this Madonna goddess appeared to a Mexican man named Cuauhtlatoatzi (Talking Eagle). He later became known as Juan Diego, after his conversion to Catholicism. It is believed that this woman, the living Madonna Guadalupe / Tonantzin, appeared to him and spoke directly to him in the Náhuatl language. She asked him to convey a message to the Catholic Spanish bishop, saying that her name was La Virgen de Guadalupe and that she asks that a church be built on the hill of Tepeyac. When Juan Diego delivered this story to the bishop, as instructed by the apparition, Juan Diego was not believed. As proof of his story, Juan Diego returns to the hill of Tepeyac, where the Madonna goddess then instructed him to fill his tilma (a cactus-fiber mantle) with roses, take them to the Catholic bishop and instruct him, yet again, to build a church on that same site.

However, when Juan Diego returned to the Catholic Bishop and opened his tilma to show the skeptical bishop the roses he had requested, instead of just roses he also saw that the image we know today as Our Lady of Guadalupe/ Tonantzin was miraculously embossed upon the cactus fabric. That original tilma, is now enshrined at the Catholic Basilica in Mexico City and serves as the template for all of Alfredo's depictions of this Madonna.

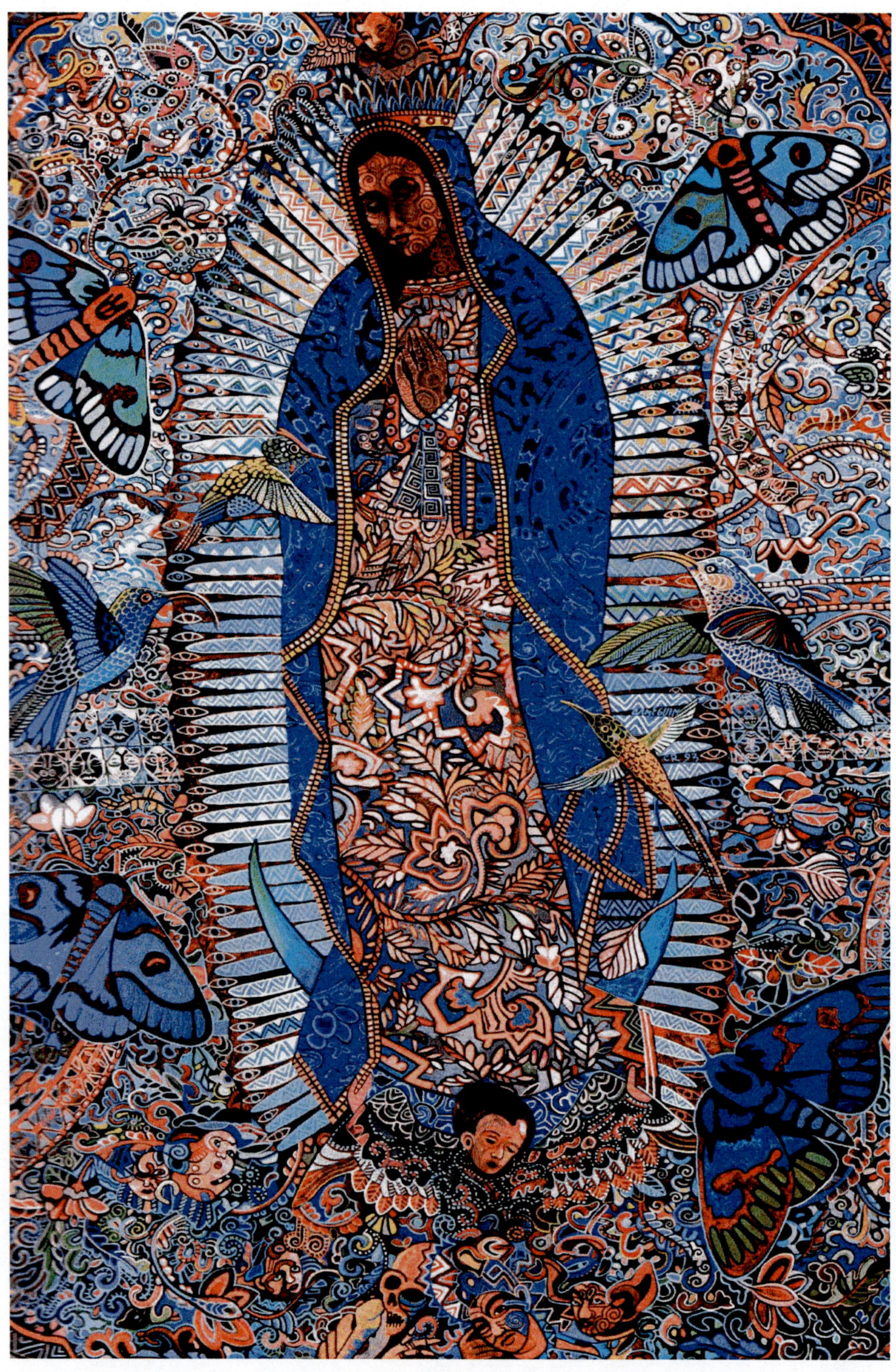

La Virgen de Tonantzin, 1993 72x48 in., Sea Mar Community Health Center, Seattle Washington

The devout Mexican Catholic will often explain that the Madonna is Our Lady of Guadalupe who appeared in Mexico to this Indian peasant to prove her devotion to the Mexican Indian people in a true demonstration of Catholic faith, and in honor of the conquering Catholic Spaniards. However, the story of the Madonna as Our Lady of Guadalupe / Tonantzin told by a Mexican Mestizo or indigenous person might be quite different. What might be said is that Our Lady of Guadalupe is really Coatlaxopeuh, which is another name for Earth Mother Tonantzin, to whom sacred offerings were made by Aztec Mexicans on that same hill of Tepeyac many hundreds of years prior to the cataclysmic arrival of the Spaniards. The widely shared Mexican Indian story explains that Tonantzin/Coatlaxopeuh appeared to Juan Diego /Cuauhtlatoatzi as a divine gesture to provide inspiration, protection and hope to the Mexican Mestizo and Indian people who were being oppressed by the Spanish.

It was only later when the Catholic Church officially acknowledged Our Lady of Guadalupe as the Patroness and mother of Mexico and all the Americas that the Mexican people were allowed to honor her in safety and under this cloak of hidden symbolic religious duality (Aztec/Catholic).
The miraculous and well-timed appearance of this dark-skinned Madonna, on the hill of Tepeyac Mexico in 1531, is considered the most important element responsible for the mass conversion to Christianity of literally hundreds of thousands of Mexican Indians and mestizos. To these converts, she is not either/or, but rather a mirror or sacred duality: Tonantzin/Guadalupe. Her blend of indigenous and European physical features represents the beauty of Mestizo racial duality and the sacredness of both Indian and Spanish cultures. Her brown face is the face of today's Mexican, Chicano, Mestizo people, and an unquestionable depiction of the spiritually based cultural and racial duality.

True to the original miraculous image of the Virgin of Guadalupe Madonna, Alfredo's Tonantzin is a testament to the cultural complexity and profound Mexican mestizo duality. She is surrounded by a spectacular aureole, or luminous light, that shines behind her. In the Catholic tradition, this is in keeping with her Christian description as the "woman clothed with the sun" of Revelations 12:1. From the Aztec tradition, the light is a sign of the power of God, who has sanctified and blessed the one who appears. However, in the Aztec tradition, the rays of the sun would also be recognized by the native people as a symbol of their highest God, Huitzilopochtli. Thus, the Aztec story that has been handed down for centuries is that the Madonna comes forth hiding and controlling – but not extinguishing – the power of the Aztec sun. This symbol depicts to the Mexican Indians that she possesses the power to block the all-powerful Aztec Sun God and God of War, Huitzilopochtli, and her mission and appearance is to announce the coming of the Christian God, Jesus Christ, who the Spanish now say is greater than their Aztec Sun God. For the Spanish Catholic evangelistic zealots, the Virgin of Guadalupe provided the divinely inspired symbolism and coded messaging that bridged the two cultures and two religions, proving to be the only real method for converting the native people to the Christian religion. The extent to which this conversion was realized is best determined by witnessing how strongly Mexicans today still hold the Virgin of Guadalupe / Tonantzin in the highest reverence. The image of the Virgin of Guadalupe is ubiquitous in Mexico and also throughout every Hispanic community in the United States.

Another duel-coded Aztec/Catholic symbol of the Madonna's power, depicted in Alfredo's painting and common to the original 1531 miraculous rendition, can be found in the way that the Madonna is shown standing upon the crescent moon. The Christian symbolism of this is explained in the Bible, Revelations 12:1, she who has the "moon under her feet". However, for the Aztecs, the symbolism for the moon under her feet was understood as the God of the Night and God of War, Tezcatlipoca. By standing directly on the moon, the Aztecs' Madonna shows that She is more powerful than the Aztec God of Night. However, in Christian iconography, the crescent moon under the Madonna's feet is also commonly understood to be the symbol of the Madonna's perpetual virginity, and sometimes it can refer to her Immaculate Conception or Assumption. For the Mexican Indians, the flowered bow around her waist is a sign of her virginity, but it also has several other meanings. The bow appears as a four-petaled flower. To the native Indians this was the nahui ollin, the flower of the sun, a symbol of fertility and new life. This symbol of the bow and the slight swelling of the abdomen show that the Lady is with child.

It is also important to note that, in Alfredo's original complex rendition, you will find that directly below the feet of the Madonna he has skillfully placed a small skull, or *calavera*. By placing this skull in this context he has created another clever and culturally understood symbolic duality: one of life and death, so essential to the ultimate meaning of both the Aztec and Christian religions. Tonantzin/Guadalupe is creating life and the skull is a reminder that death is part of life. In the Christian religion it is Jesus Christ who is crucified and dies in order to provide eternal life to his believers. In a remarkable religious parallel, for the Aztecs death through actual human sacrifice was believed to be an essential final act that provided sustenance for the Gods to give life on earth and heavens. Aztec sacrifices provided the human blood that was considered the crucial nourishment for many of their Gods who, with this sustenance, would in turn keep nature and the cosmos in balance, preserve the sun for yet another day, and allow life on earth to continue. It is very difficult to escape the symbolic duality so boldly found in Alfredo's exquisite rendering of this rendition of Tonantzin, the Mexican Madonna. The more familiar iconography of Christianity is in clear juxtaposition with that of Native Aztec religion, cosmology and Mexican culture that Tonantzin symbolizes. It is in this icon Alfredo reveals that the titans of both religions and both continents are clearly locked together in a powerful, dueling, and composite yet complementary religious messaging in two languages, using two symbolic reference points that are constructed for and aimed directly toward the hearts and souls of the Mexican Indian and mixed-race Mestizo people of the Americas.

This important messaging would be symbolically inert and almost meaningless to the Indian and Mestizo people without adding the symbolic imagery found in the accompanying Naguals that Alfredo has incorporated in this painting. The Naguals in this context are present to symbolically carry the complex coded message of religious duality, transition and transformation. In Alfredo's rendition of Tonantzin (Virgin of Guadalupe), She is depicted surrounded by her subtle but powerful array of sentinel spiritual guides, her Naguals. One of the most prominent Nagual attending her is a platoon of Lucifer (Calothorax or Trochilus lucifer), Long-tailed Hermit (Phaethornis superciliosus), and Rufous-crested Coquettes (Lophornis delattrei delattrei) swift and vibrant hummingbirds common to Mexico. The hummingbird, in the Aztec religion, is arguably one of the most powerful Nagual animal symbols. The Aztec believed that the highly prized, tiny and commanding hummingbird never died, and was the embodied symbol of the most powerful Aztec God, Huitzilopochtli, the God of war. Huitzilopochtl is usually translated literally as the left-handed hummingbird.[25]

In the Mayan cosmology, it is believed that the Gods created all living things on earth; that every

25 *In the Book of Chilam Balam of Chumayel "it is called the hummingbird as a referral from a*

animal, every tree and every stone was a commissioned work. However, when the Gods finished, they realized that they lacked a way to communicate their wishes and thoughts from one place to another. According to Mayan lore, having run out of mud or corn to create another animal, they took a stone carved jade and with it a small arrow and gave it their breath, and the little arrow flew. At that instance it was no longer a simple jade arrow. Now it had life. The gods had created the *x ts'unu'um* (hummingbird).[26]

The Mayan Gods noticed that it was so fragile and so nimble that the hummingbird could approach even the most delicate flowers without damaging a single petal. It was also admired because its feathers reflected in the sun, like the refracted rainbow light created by raindrops, reflecting all colors. It was said that because of the beauty of their feathers, men tried to capture the hummingbird to use its feathers to adorn their finest garments. The Mayan legend has it that the Gods saw this, became angry and said: "If someone dares to catch a hummingbird, it will die." For this reason, no one has ever witnessed a hummingbird in a cage, or in the hand of a man. In this way, this mysterious and delicate bird has been able to carry out the task of the Gods: "Hummingbird leads from here to there the thoughts of men. From now on, the hummingbird will take all your wishes and thoughts from one place to another.[27]

Alfredo's selection of the hummingbird as one of the principal Naguals to accompany the brown-skinned Madonna was a deliberate effort to build into the painting the precise Nagual that symbolically enhances and promotes her sacred duality as both a significant and revered Native Mexican religious deity and a Christian saint. The hummingbird, for the Mexican Indian, was the Nagual messenger who is recognized for its qualities necessary to transport Tonantzin sacred Christian and Mayan messages, prayers, and hopes to the believers. The hummingbird could translate the native languages and Spanish, and her messages were not only understood but also had value and legitimacy because Tonantzin was culturally and religiously syntonic with the Aztec people and had the same skin hue as the Native Mexicans.

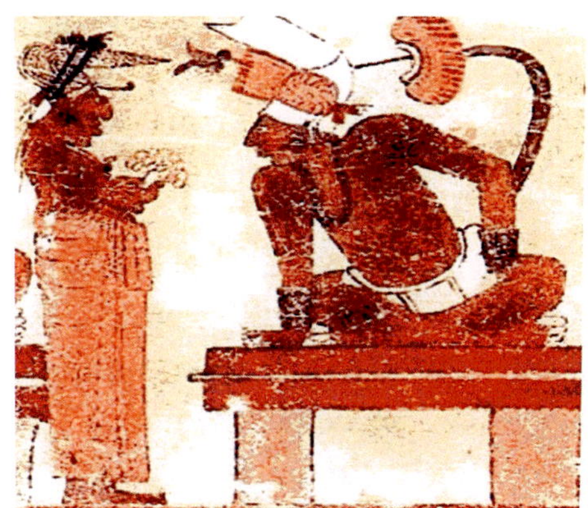

Scene from a Tikal vase with an anthropomorphic hummingbird facing an enthroned ruler.

Nahuatl name, Pizlimtec, also Xochipilli, Aztec goddess of music, song, flowers and hallucinogenic plants.

26 *The Maya names for birds, generally relate to the sounds they make, their songs or sounds are produced by feathers, for example x ts'unu'um for hummingbirds. There are over 50 difference types of Hummingbird found in Mexico and are refered to differently depending on the region. These names include quindes, tucusitos, picaflores, chupamirtos, chuparrosas, huichichiquis, or by name in indigenous languages: huitzilli Nahuatl, Mayan x ts'unu'um, Tzunún in huasteco or Jun in Totonac, among others.*

27 *Mercedes de la Garza Aves sagradas de los Mayas UNAM, 1995.*

Another spiritual Nagual messenger depicted in this painting is the moth. The moth, just as the butterfly, goes through an intense metamorphosis from caterpillar to adult. The native Mexicans believe that this ability possessed by moths indicated that they were sent to the world because of this transformational quality of duality and could serve to mitigate between the earthly and spiritual worlds. The moth Nagual spirit guide in this painting symbolically shows that the Native Indians believed that Tonantzin was the transformation of the Virgin of Guadalupe. She was the living essence of religious power contained in the duality of the Aztec Goddess Tonantzin and the Catholic Madonna Virgin of Guadalupe. The moth Nagual uses this transformational power to serve as the Nagual guide who was believed could translate religious meaning from one culture to the other, from the Aztec spiritual world to a transformed Catholic one. Ultimately, with these qualities, the transforming moth could serve as a greatly revered guide needed to provide the necessary path and help transition humans into the other world after death.

In addition, the sorcerers of the Yaqui Indians of Mexico refer to moths as Naguals and symbols that possesses great knowledge and skills as Nagual translators. Although considered to be an academically incomplete anthropological work by Carlos Castaneda, he describes, in the book *Tales of Power*, that the moth is a key spiritual figure. It was so central to his polemic that it was depicted on the cover of the book. In that book, it is explained that Castaneda was told by Yaqui sorcerer don Juan that "knowledge is a moth." He expresses metaphorically that: "the moths are the heralds, or better yet, the guardians of eternity," don Juan said after the sound had stopped. "For some reason, or for no reason at all, they are the depositories of the gold dust of eternity." (p. 28) He goes on to say, that "The moths have been the intimate friends and helpers of sorcerers from time immemorial." He adds, "Moths are the givers of knowledge and the friends and helpers".[28]

Naguals appear throughout most of Alfredo's paintings in a multitude of culturally recognized forms. However, the Nagual in his painting, entitled *Family Portrait*, (1992) is not at all camouflaged. The Nagual in this painting, is caught frozen in its state of transformation, exposing the symbolic process of transformation and duality. In this brilliantly playful painting, the Nagual is clearly revealed as the artist himself. Alfredo has taken the undisguised form of a monkey, confidently glaring at the observer from his rather stern portrait. As the monkey Nagual, Alfredo is shown as the protector of his family, located above the members of his intimate troupe. His wife Susan and his daughter Lesley are the most recognizable faces. The others faces depicted in the painting most likely include additional family members who accompany them in the jungle of life.

One of the most compelling examples of Mexican duality and transformation is found in Alfredo's 1993 portrait of La Malinche. Although Alfredo's depiction of La Malinche appears to the untrained eye to represent one of Mexico's ubiquitous pious Madonnas, this figure is definitely not religious in nature, neither in the Catholic religious tradition or that of the Aztecs. Alfredo's artistic genius captures in this painting the epic true story of one of the most reviled and controversialfigures in Mexican history. This story begins in 1519, shortly after the Spanish conqueror, Hernan Cortés, arrived on the Gulf Coast of Mexico. This is when Malinche, the woman depicted in the painting, was gifted by a Maya lord to Cortés as a slave in an act of appeasement. Written documentation from that time states that she distinguished herself by her keen intellect, ability to translate

28 *Tales of Power by Carlos Castaneda*, Published January 1, 1992, by Simon & Schuster. First published 1974.

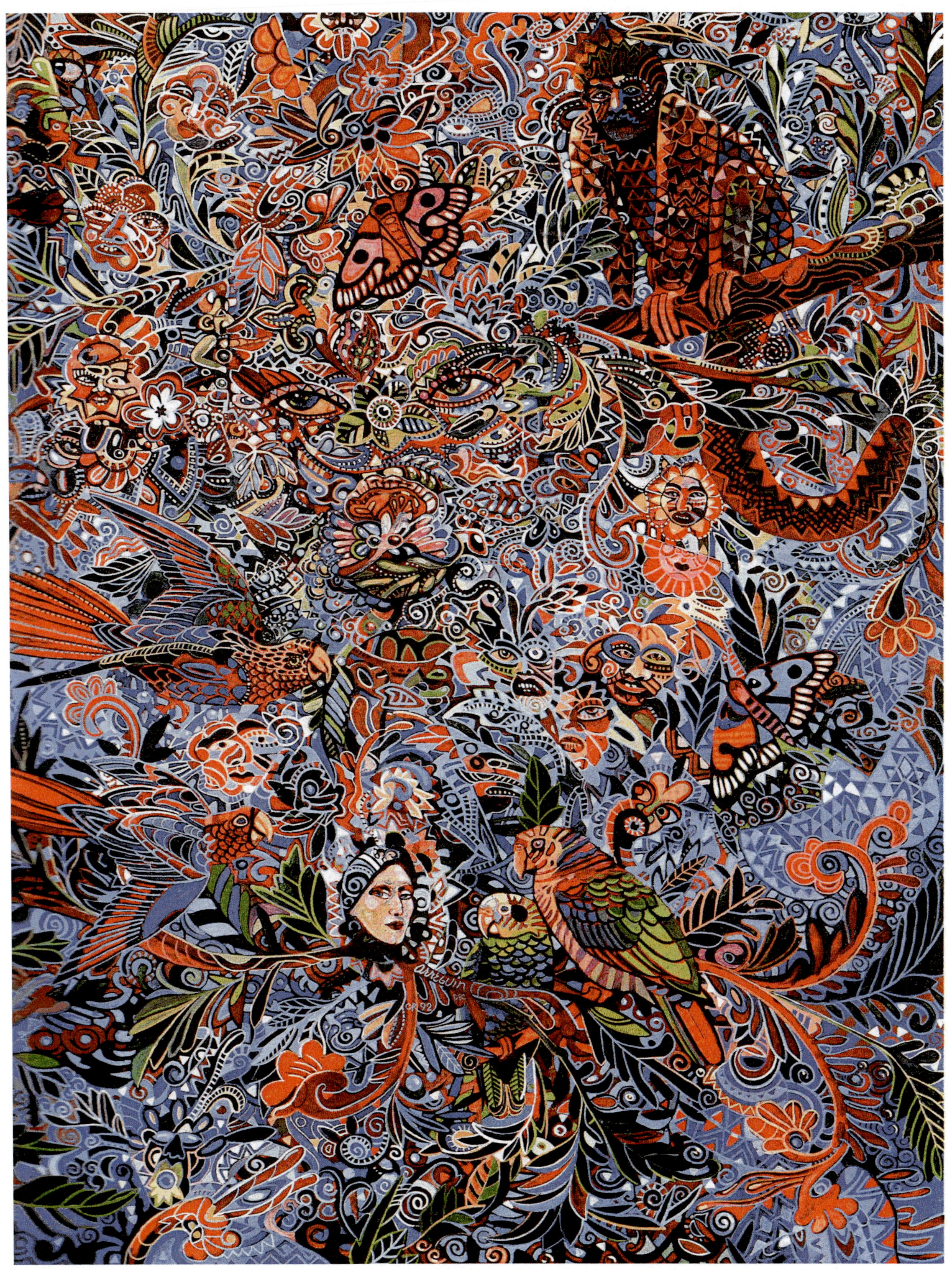

Family Portrait, 1992, 60x 48 in., collection of the artist.

languages, and amazing aptitude for quickly assessing military and political strategies. Her talents became extraordinarily useful, if not essential, for the Spaniards' success in achieving their seemingly impossible military ambitions and political endeavors in Mexico. She served as the primary translator, negotiator and cultural mediator for the Spanish army. She was also a concubine of Cortés and gave birth to their son, Martín. She is considered by Mexican folklore to be the mother of Mexico's first Mestizo child and her union with Cortés—literally and metaphorically—inextricably binds her to Mexico's Mestizaje legacy.

Alfredo's rendition of Malinche depicts her almost as a Madonna, but clearly show us in this rendition that her reputation as the most notorious treasonous Mexican Indian to the Mexican people and twofaced reputation, continues to remain in a state of indeterminate flux of duality—whore and traitor and savior of the new dual culture, Mexican Mestizo race. For most of history since 1519, the name Malinche has been used negatively and synonymously with traitor and whore because she provided willing aid to the conquering Spaniards, facilitating the wholesale demise of an entire nation of indigenous Mexico and promoting the domination of European rule. As you see, he has painted her face in a hue of red, like a charlatan or whore. You also see that two masks have been placed on opposite sides of her head: one mask is white, the other brown. The dichotomy is continued as she is represented in this painting as the transitional Mestizo mother, wearing atop her Indian head the European trapping of true feminine power—the queen's royal crown. She is exalted as the bilingual bicultural mother, a stoic culture broker flanked by omnipotent Aztec Gods and her powerful but weary Jaguar Nagual. Yet, despite the duality of transformation and positive and negative symbolic messaging in Alfredo's Malinche, she is ultimately portrayed as an exalted feminist icon. Alfredo paints into Malinche's persona her intellect, fortitude and survival skills. He shows her standing erect and adorned as one of the most revered nonreligious Mexican Madonnas and the most respected and consummate strategists Mexico has ever known; a woman of undeniable strength who did not waiver in the face of true adversity and who is unquestionably responsible for both the death of the indigenous Mexican and the birth of the Mexico and Mestisaje as we know it today.

There are also many of Alfredo Arreguín's images and patterns of layered artistic creation on canvas that draw deeply from his Mexican worldview and experiences along with his Chicano past. It is easy to see that some of his expressions are a likeness of the motifs and colors commonly associated with traditional Mexican village folk crafts.

The elaborately patterned costumes and garments of Mexican Indians and Mestizos that incorporate regionally inspired traditional geometrically patterned birds, animals, and stylized motifs appear repeatedly in almost all his works. These expressive and colorful indigenous designs are centuries old and can also be found in current decorative Mexican basketry, pottery, broom straw and feather pictorial creations, ceramics, and carvings of stone, wood, wax and especially in the colorful and expressive regional cotton weavings. Take, for example, one of the key components of his paintings: the underlying patterned tiled symmetry. His detailed pattern of painted quadrangles is comparable in colorful, ordered and graphic expression to patterns found in the labyrinth of ceramic Mexican architectural tiles adorning the walls and floors of the colonial Michoacán homes and cathedrals reminiscent of the ones he must have frequently encountered during his childhood.

These Mexican ceramic tiles first find their adoption in the city of Puebla, Mexico. The Indian and Mestizo people living in Puebla and its surrounding villages were taught to make and decorate ceramics using the Spanish Talavera technique during the 1571 construction of the Church of Santo Domingo. The Spanish priests and artisans instructed the native Indians in these Iberian ceramic techniques so that their new Catholic temples could be decorated in the way they were accustomed—with elaborate hand-painted tiles and religious figures. Now, these decorated ceramic tiles are an iatrical and ubiquitous part of the artistic tradition of Mexico.

The animal, bird, and insect Naguals that are often thematically central to Alfredo's paintings are not only drawn from the rich Mesoamerican historic tradition but also have their stylistic origin in the arts and crafts developed as a result of the cataclysmic cultural, religious and artistic transition that occurred shortly after the arrival of the Spanish. This artistic transition was initiated as early as 1535. The conquering Spanish, borrowing from the already known practice of using highly skilled and specialized Aztec artistic guilds to create utilitarian and decorative art, enlisted entire villages to adapt their skills, techniques, and natural resources to the production of items that were a reflection of European ascetics and utilitarian needs. Their motives were ostensibly to develop rural infrastructure in the hope of repairing and rebuilding local economies decimated by the Spanish invasion. First to implement this model was the Bishop of Michoacán, Vasco de Quiroga. In addition to rebuilding towns and replanting fields, he assembled the surviving indigenous people into working guild-like population centers and instructed them in the production of specialized crafts. The Aztec traditions and techniques that had survived the early colonization, enriched with the new techniques brought from Spain, have now become very much an integral part of Mexico's highly creative contemporary folk art tradition.

One of the centerpieces of Mexico's contemporary folk art tradition are the colorful carved wooden and paper maché Nagual figures consisting of fantasy-based renderings of fauna, birds, fish, insects and unimaginable creatures. These Nagual-like figures are now sometimes referred to as alebrijas, a term that was coined in the late 1930s. The popularized usage of this term owes its origin to Master Mexico City papier maché artist, Pedro Linares, and later to master Oaxacan wood carver Manuel Jimenez. These contemporary artists created alebrijas figures that can only be described as a conflation of the artistic stylizations found somewhere between Disney and Dali and are complete with innovative patterns of stripes, dots, geometric shapes, flowers and flames.

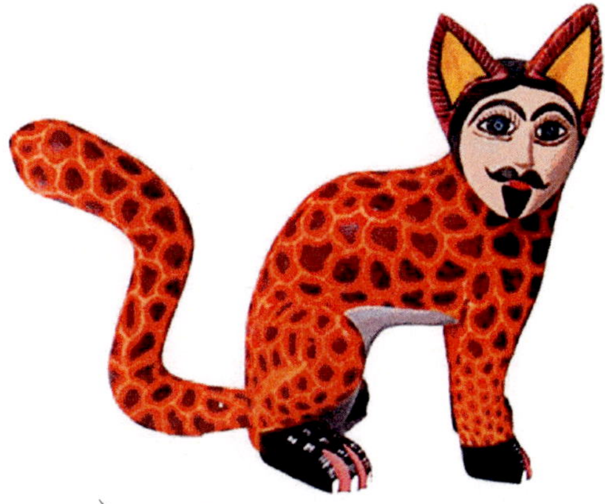

Nahual alebrije wood carving handcrafted in Oaxaca, Mexico by Jesús & Roxana Hernández.
Length/Height/Width: 6.5" x 6" x 3" - Features: Hand-crafted Copal wood

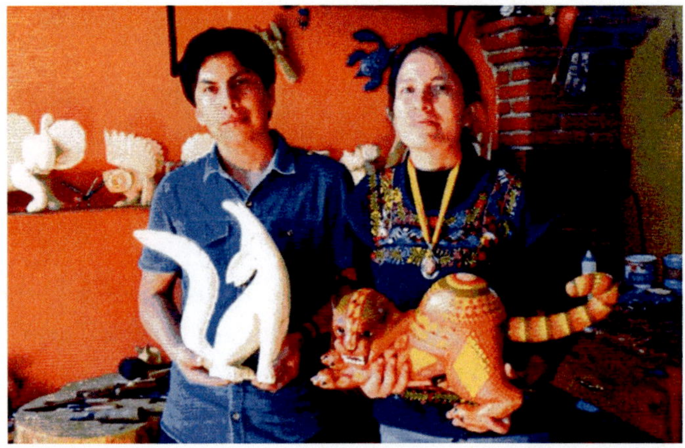

Wood Carving by Oaxacan artists Efraín Fuentes and Silvia Gómez.

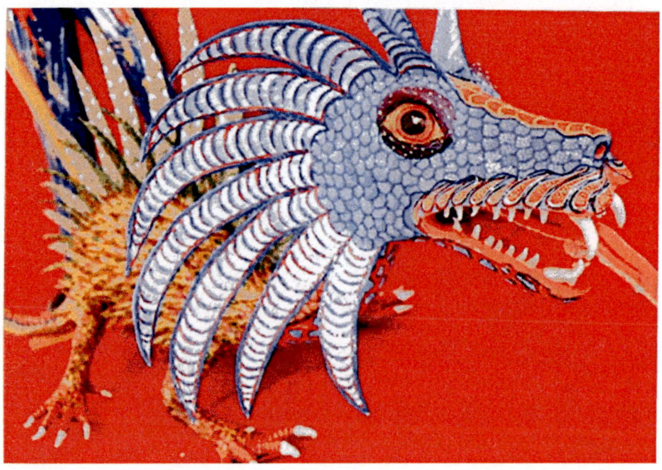

Papier maché alebrije dragon made by Pedro Linares

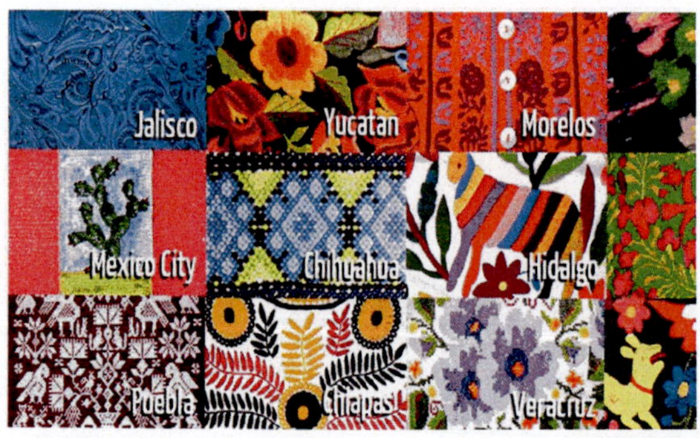

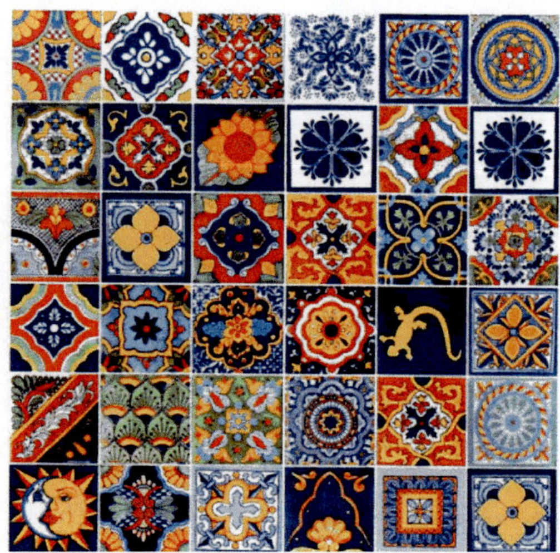

Patterns found in Mexican fabrics and tiles

As you experience, close up, the exquisite detail found in Alfredo's work and assemble his culturally complex and deliberately playful patterned graphic arrangements, a focused and serious element always emerges that is central to his thematic creations.

His paintings not only have profound meaning, based on his Mexican culture and history, but also contain a more profound socially defining purpose. He is above all, an activist artist. His paintings use beauty, color, shapes and themes that, on the surface, appear to be silent fragments of Mexican jungle topography and phantasmagoria. However, in reality, he provides us with compelling and deafening insight into the duality and inequities inherent in social power structures. Rather than representing them or simply describing them he places the social inequities in context of time and place. For example, his painting *Sal Si Puedes II* depicts Juan Diego (canonized July 31, 2002, as a saint by the Catholic Church), standing underneath the Farmworker union logo and a memorialized portrait of César Chavez. In this painting, Juan Diego is painted as an adolescent brown-faced Mexican Mestizo, complete with a field worker's hat to protect him from the beating sun. His message of martyrdom and self-sacrifice is clear and vociferously echoes the plea caught in the crystal tear in Juan Diego's eye and is. Furthermore he captures this message, not just in symbols but clearly expressed in the title, *Sal Si Puedes—Escape if you can.*

This powerful message speaks to the irony of protecting the head of a young farmworker from the relentless sun while he works in a suffocating hot field. Yet the real and more profound message tells us that, as a society, we are silent to the far more ominous treat to Mexican immigrant youth caused by child farmworker exploitation and the endemic trap of allowing migrant youth to be caught at a young age in the jaws of human trafficking and the menial labor market, almost as a life sentence. It speaks to the need for labor organization and advocacy for equal access to education as a way out of the repressive capitalistic morass. It is also a direct message to all immigrant youth who, through no fault of their own, are brought to the United States and are treated as marginal. They live in a dual system of bipolar cultural, social, economic and educational inequities. However, the painting also depicts hope. The guiding Nagual moths are there to guide Mexican youth out of an impending trap and to carry a compelling message of hope through self-determination, education and action. It is a statement that there culture and history has meaning. In the painting, you will find this message written twice. It says, Sal Si Puedes—but is it really saying, "Escape if you can, while you are young, and do so with strength, pride and courage." It is an activist's imploration.

His arrival in Seattle during the height of the civil rights movement, the student movement, the anti-Vietnam War movement, the women's movement, the gay rights movement, the environmental movement and—most importantly—the Chicano rights movement (el movimiento), became an important conceptual springboard for his talent, creativity, social conscious and his cultural voice. It was the solace for his ideals of homeland, history, the environment, civil rights, community justice and social equality. For Alfredo, this period became the critical alignment between timing and talent, when his genius was exposed to an awaiting Chicano/a community who needed heroes and heroines and loudhailers whose talent could be used to project them to a wider audience. His artistic virtuosity allowed him to create visual works that various activist communities understood, and the Chicano/a in particular used his art as a form of political or social currency.

The terms "Chicano and Chicana" were born of a proactive need for activist Mexican Americans to embrace their own personal, community, ethnic and political self-identification. They were community-crafted activist labels that were collectively adopted and embraced as our own, and as central pivot for the movimiento. The use of the term Chicana and Chicano further set us apart because it was not a mandated label manufactured by the U.S. Census Bureau or crafted by Madison Avenue capitalists.

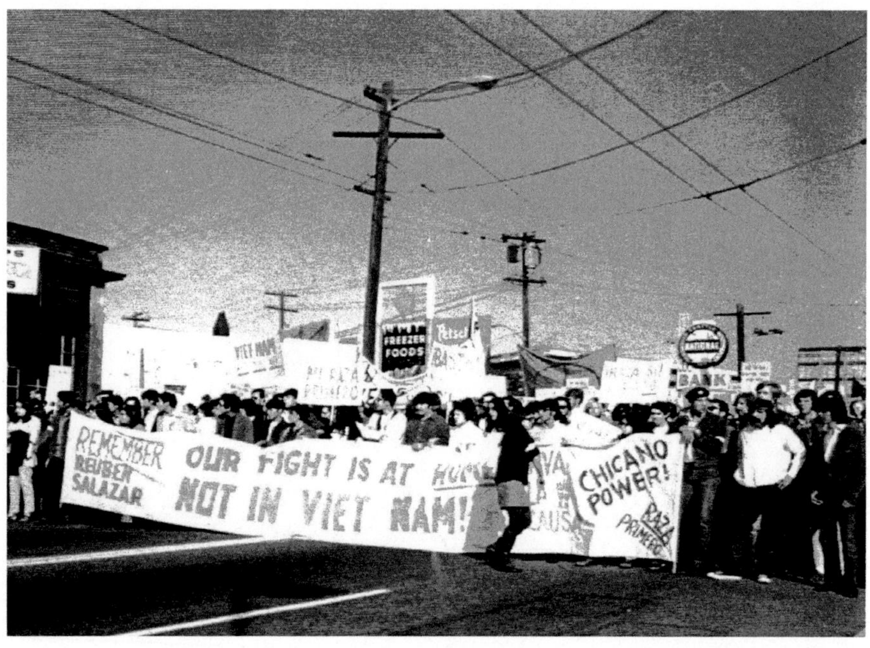

(Photo) Chicanos and Chicanas MEChA and the Brown Berets contingent in this anti-Vietnam war demonstration in the early 1970s in the streets of Seattle (UW Civil Rights and Labor History Project)

With heartfelt pride we shouted, "Somos Chicanos!" in the streets of Seattle during rallies and protests, knowing what it meant and exactly who we were and are. We wrote it boldly on protest placards and huelga (boycott) signs, and it was embedded into activist-created art as a means for branding and broadcasting our unique and deliberate message of Chicano and Chicana self-identification. During that time the Chicano/Chicana movimiento enlisted and army of talented Chicano and Chicana poets, singers and artists. Each of them, including Alfredo Arreguín, who helped the Chicano/a community and the moviemento to understand and express an array of Mexican and Chicano elements and ideas that were fundamental to the cause, la causa. During this period, Alfredo's art incorporated a deliberate set of bold and carefully re-purposed Mexican and Mexican-American heroic personalities such as Dolores Huerta, Cesar Chávez, Zapata, Pancho Villa Morelos, Frida Kahlo, and other key social or environmental activists. Arreguín drew from this historical resource to create a unique body of work that set him apart from other artists and helped define and provide meaning to his Mexican patterned style.

In keeping with the social vision of his socially and politically artistic predecessors, mentors and founders of the Taller de Gráfica Popular of last century Mexico, Alfredo uses his painting like an expertly honed blunt force weapon to give these heroes and heroines yet another stage to protect both the common people and a compromised planet. The Chicana and Chicano activist community quickly galvanized with the recognizable cultural and historical elements found in his paintings. The collective conscious of the Chicana and Chicano community resonated to the harmonic cacophony of voices coming from the heartbeat of pre-Columbian colonial revolutionary Mexico and the vanguard of the Chicana Chicano social movement. Perhaps Chicana and Chicano activists also detected in his paintings the echoed heartbeats found deep within the very soul of Mexico's Indian and its marginalized dual culture Mestizo and Chicano and Chicana people.

Alfredo Arreguín's Mexican heritage, life experience, and masterful artistic talent were skillfully suited to the times. He understood how to graphically capture the palpable emerging aesthetic and political needs of this prevailing new civic, social, cultural and pro-environmental paradigm shift in the United States. His canvas spoke clearly about and to community inequity, justice and social worth. He graphically portrayed a community-based activist paradigm that became part of the effort to build into and celebrate the awareness and creation of the movimiento. It called for the reevaluation and reexamination of the history of the Americas and United States. Alfredo drew directly from the Chicano and Chicana mantra for self-identification, and he did so by creatively and deliberately incorporating into his paintings the role and image of the indigenous and Mestizo people as active—not passive—participants in their own historical destiny.

His message became one of affirmation with the activist community, which sought out and continues to celebrate Alfredo's paintings. Alfredo Arreguín's Mexican and Chicano activist palette provided Chicanas and Chicanos a rainbow of ideas to help them to construct an even bolder message of self-identification and self-determination, especially for women.

The Chicano Movement broadly encompassed several key subjects, many of which were magnificently incorporated in Alfredo's Chicana/Chicano-centered works. These subjects were very central to the moviemento and their ideas are also coded onto the canvas by Alfredo. The messages he expressed included the cry of civil disobedience from activist Reies López Tejerina, who called for the restoration of land grants that had been stolen in New Mexico, in much the same fashion that Mexican revolutionary hero Emiliano Zapata lived and died in Mexico. Delores Huerta and Cesar Chávez were the persistent beacons for farm workers' rights. Corky Gonzales rallied Chicana and Chicano youth in an effort to enhance educational perspectives and opportunities and was tireless in his plea for civic engagement. José Angel Gutierrez and Luz Gutiérrez created the RAZA UNIDA party in an effort to create political self-determination through voting campaigns and by activating dormant political rights. In addition, the constant message captured by Alfredo was that all of these civil rights protagonist activists also created a profound awareness of the pride felt towards the collective Chicana and Chicano history.

I would be remiss, however, if I did not also highlight that, as part of this historical reassessment and recapture, many of Alfredos's activist paintings directly or indirectly spoke to the meaning, role and the broader concept that Aztlán played in the development of the moviemento. Aztlán, is the term used to denote the general geographical location where the birth of the Aztec nation occurred. It was adopted as a political and historical term during the moviemento to refer to the geographical locations of Northern Mexico that were forcefully and deliberately annexed by the United States as a result of the Mexican-American War. Aztlán, in this sense, was used as an important "symbol" for Chicana and Chicano activists who lay claim to a legal and prehistoric right to the area of land believed to be somewhere in the desert southwest, straddling a vague swath of geographical space that crosses the current Mexico / United States border.

This concept not only ignited a profound introspective look into the origin of Mexico and its subsequent history, but also became an important reference point for moviemento civil rights platform. Chicana and Chicano activists called for the use of the re-forged tools of propaganda at hand such as theater, art and literature to inform the public and to boldly construct a polemic for historical revision and political reference. Activist artists, such as Alfredo, were actively enlisted to use their talents in an effort to insure that the concept of Aztlán was seized, at the very least symbolically. In his painting, *Return to Aztlan* (2006), his goal appears to be to ensure that the Mexico/United States ersatz border was rendered irrelevant by lacing it with meaningful conduits of a Chicana and Chicano construct and purpose. It is his effort to span the chasm called the Mexican border as effortlessly as the seeds, birds, animals, insects and indigenous people had done for millennia. Mexican Indian, Mestizo and Chicana and Chicano-infused art, symbols, music, film and poetry became the chosen pabulum to continually nurture and transmit living ideas, feelings, and insights through this conceptually recaptured corridor called Aztln. Alfredo's artistic genius was harnessed as one of the mediums that fostered the transmission and resulting porousness of the physical border. His fame in both Mexico and the United States is legendary. He is recognized as one of the artists most recognized for his ability to speak to the creative and open minds on both side of the Mexico / United States border, freely and with the confidence of earned legitimacy. It is fair to say that Alfredo's artistic genius was a key element that helped foster the transmission of shared ideas across often-sealed corridors and facilitated the creation of an artistically porous physical border between Mexico and the United States.

As a testament to this important effort, Alfredo Arreguín was ceremoniously awarded Mexico's highest presidential award, the Ohtli, for the promotion of culture abroad. His paintings have also been featured at major national museums in the United States. It is clear that Alfredo's paintings have left an indelible and important mark on the Mexican and Chicana and Chicano worldview, and continue to be relevant and vital components of contemporary discussions of Mexican immigration and the historically determined geographical scar called the Mexico / United States border.

The concept of Aztlán and the protagonists and icons Alfredo depicted in graphically astonishing beauty and with complex symbolic meaning were chosen because each was soiled with Mexican sweat, blood and tears. These Chicano- and Chicana-based themes in his art became the Chicano Movement's artistic anthem, and the jungles of Aztlán and Mexico were transformed into our cultural gardens of serenity, strength and repose. Today, his works are even more relevant and speak more loudly than ever.

My association with Alfredo's art is both academic and deeply cultural. As a Chicano, his art touches the very nadir of my soul. Attempting to sort out the myriad of non-random patterns, each sodden with Mexican, Chicano, Chicana, and Mestizo-laced meaning, patterns, colors, and symbols, I am transported into his surreal world of Mexican duality, powerful Naguals and cultural transformation. From an academic prospective, I have dedicated many hours attempting to dissect the composite of patterns into their thousands of different anthropomorphic and geometric elements. Through this, I was able to discover that each patterned quadrant spoke to the next, as if they were aligned and tied together with living Mexican sinew. However, his paintings are clearly more than the sum of each of the patterned tiles and connected highly coded symbols. Each composition reveals the exquisitely complex graphic DNA that forms the origin, transition, mysticism and meaning of Mestizaje, Chicana, Chicano, and Aztlán. Their complexity, once dissected, exposes the raw elements of life itself.

In his work we see the amazing resilience of cultural elements and how cultural transmission of these elements are passed forward from century to century by one generation to the next. It speaks to ecological survival, and the marginalization created by duality and cultural adaptation. Most importantly, his paintings are lessons on how to assign meaning and proscribe action to social, political, and cultural inequities. It is as if you are looking through an electron microscope and seeing the ordered microbial patterned elements floating in a vibrant rainbow of primordial life-giving soup. By trying to understand Alfredo's graphic constructs through a cultural prism, his Mexican jungle can be seen teeming with hidden life and mystery that gives way to profound meaning and unique and valuable insight. Alfredo's paintings, upon final view, ultimately speak to the messages transported through Mestizo, indigenous, Chicano and Chicana symbols, Naguals and protagonist. They are tantalizing visual banquets bursting with color, patterns, symbolic meaning, illusions of ghostly portraitures and the allure of a powerful familiar hero, heroine, or Nagual jungle creature. For Chicano and Chicana activists, the hundreds of curious eyes in his paintings reach out, as if in an effort to solicit decoding. They recruit you to become a member of his activist army poised to save humanity, ecosystems, human dignity, and shattered self-identities created by artificial borders, both real and conceptual. His powerful codices ask you to identify, understand and appreciate the coded symbols that contain a wisdom brought to you by the Naguals who transport an important autochthonous Mesoamerican world view.

Alfredo Arreguín has painted onto each canvas the coded meaning that caused social activists to struggle, bridge hope with action, and spark an uprising of consciousness among environmentalist and Chicano and Chicana philosophies. This has become part of the new Chicano/Chicana paradigm. It is Alfredo's gift, an exquisite and meaningful visual cornucopia that radiates from Aztlán to Zapata, without borders, timeless and wherever the Mexican dysphoria transports Mexico's indigenous, Mestizo and Chicano/a people, patterns, timeless codes, styles, art and ideas. Arreguín's Mexican, Mestizo, Chicana and Chicana-centered paintings are our century's rich trove of Codices, a collective guide for community self-determination and our dual identity.

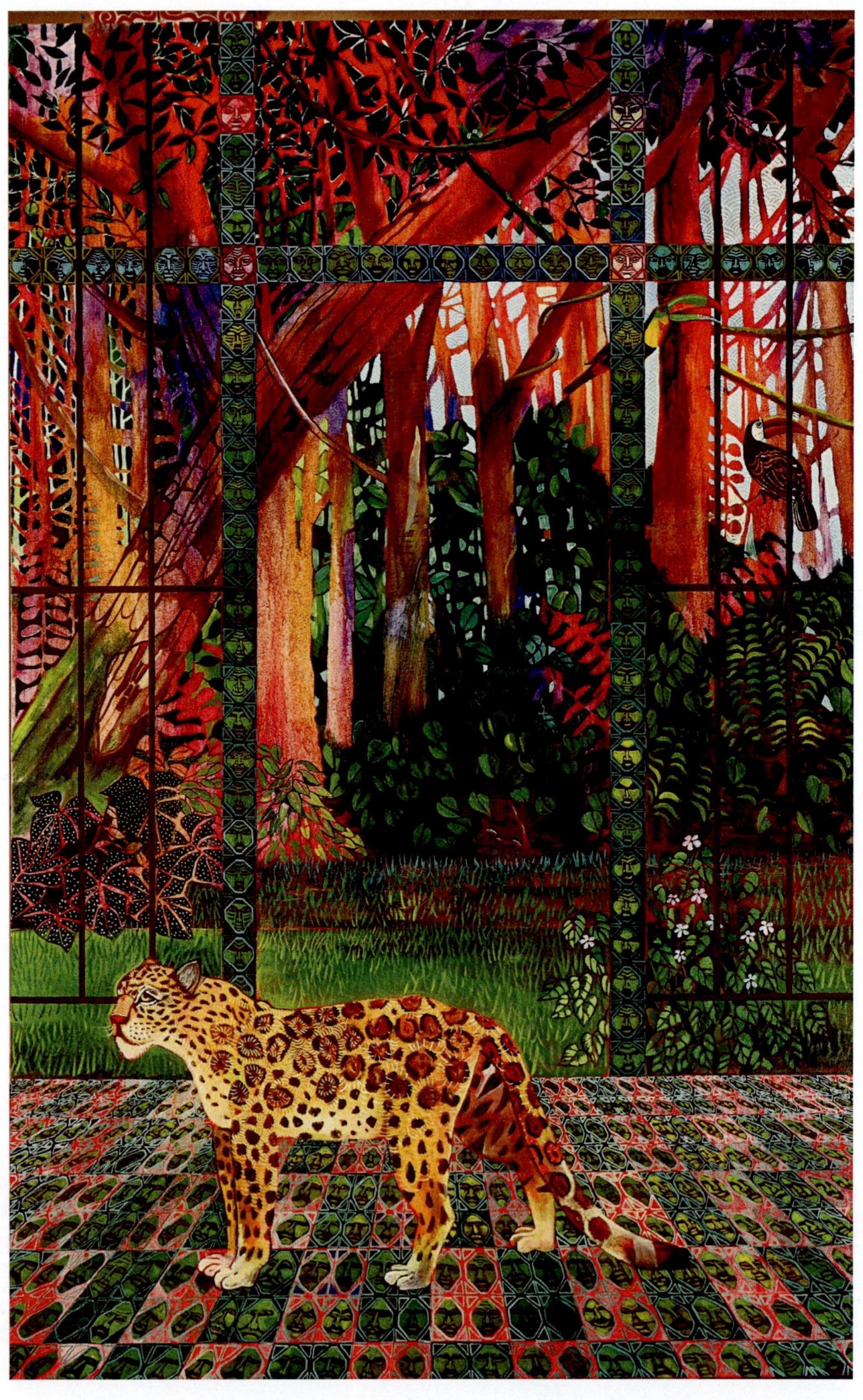

Sal Si Puedes, 1972, 72 × 48 in., Pacific Northwest Bell Telephone Company, Seattle.

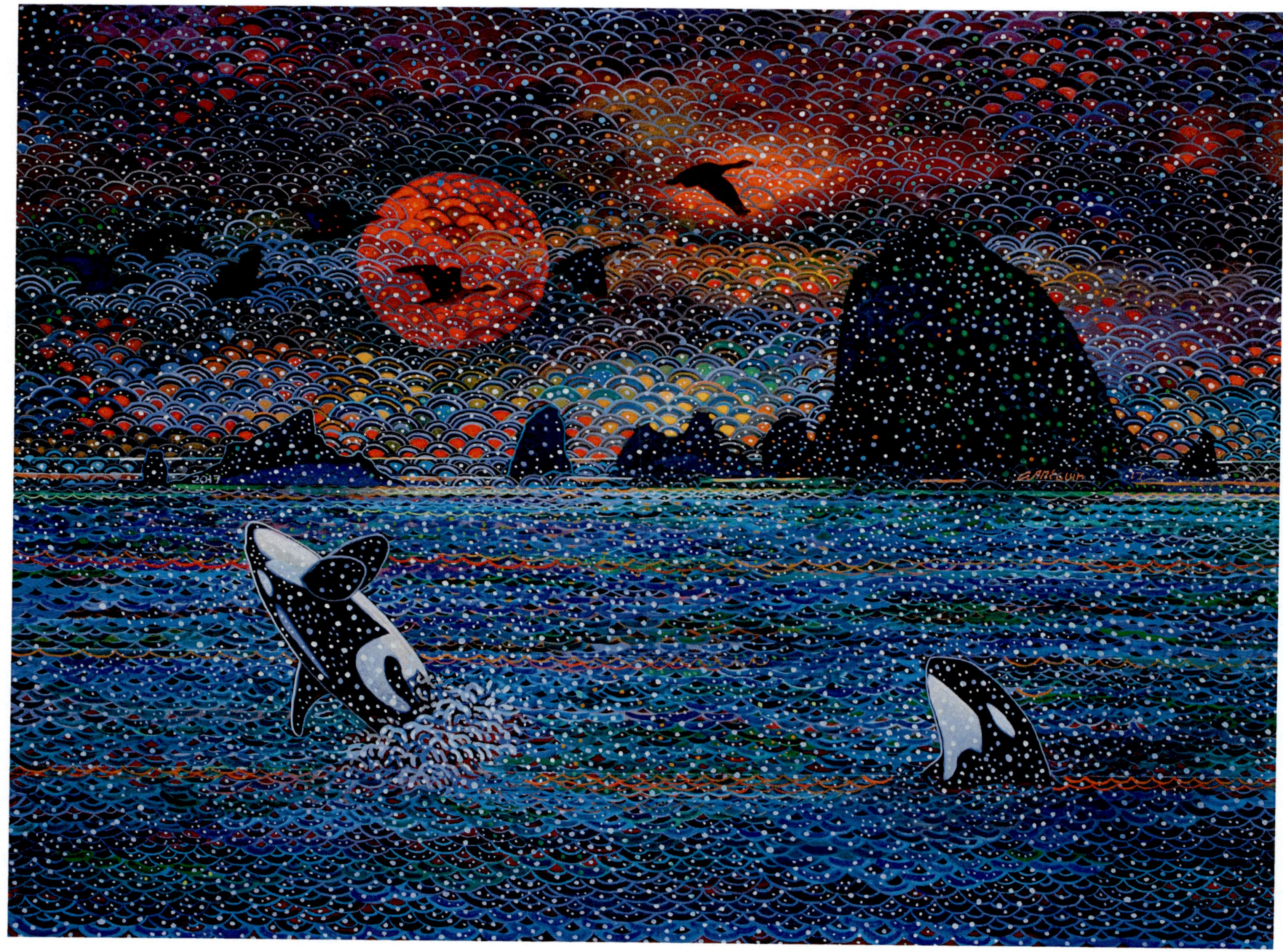

Salish Sea, 2016, 48 × 60 in., private collection

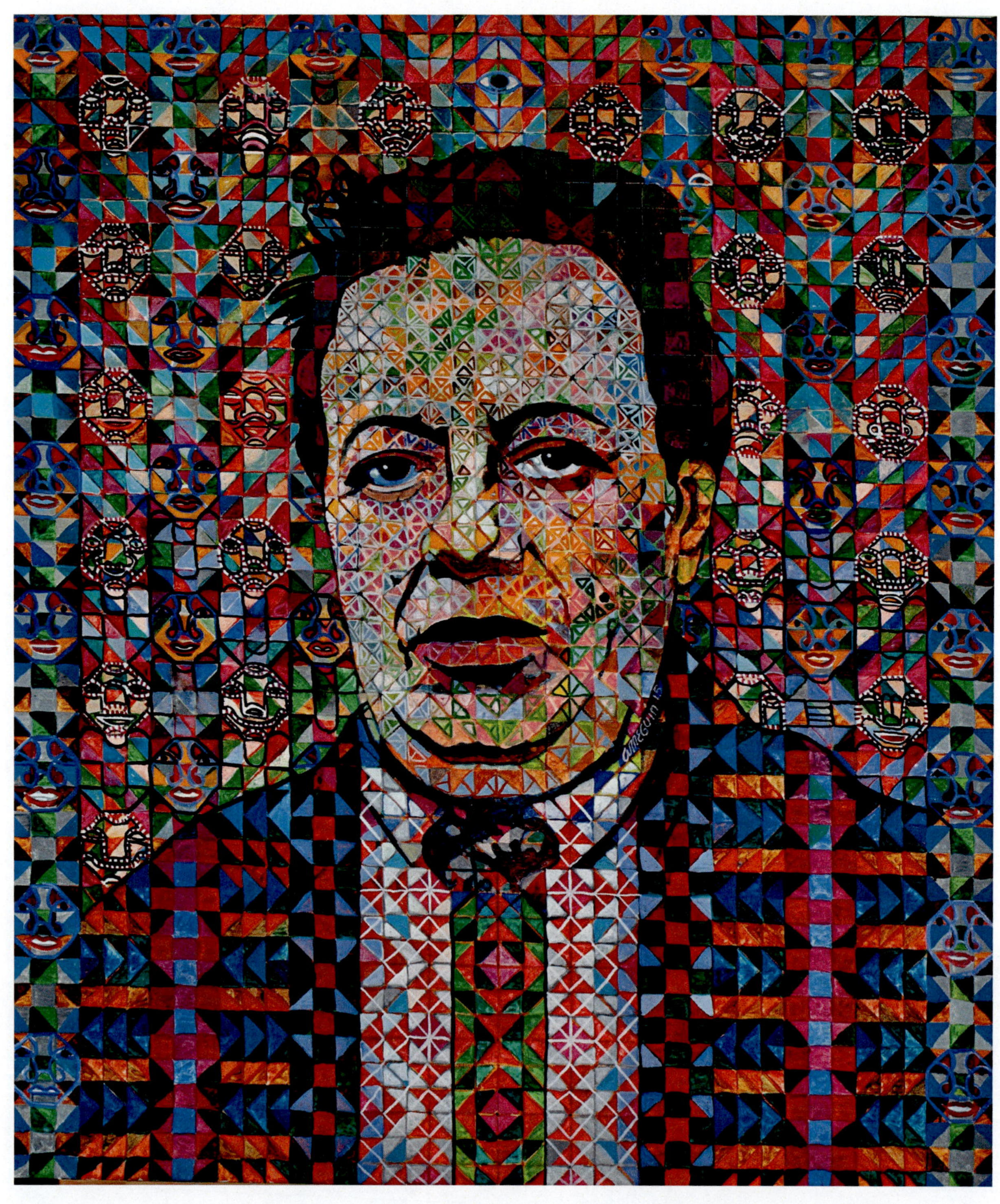

The Muralist, 2013, 48 × 42 in., collection of the artist

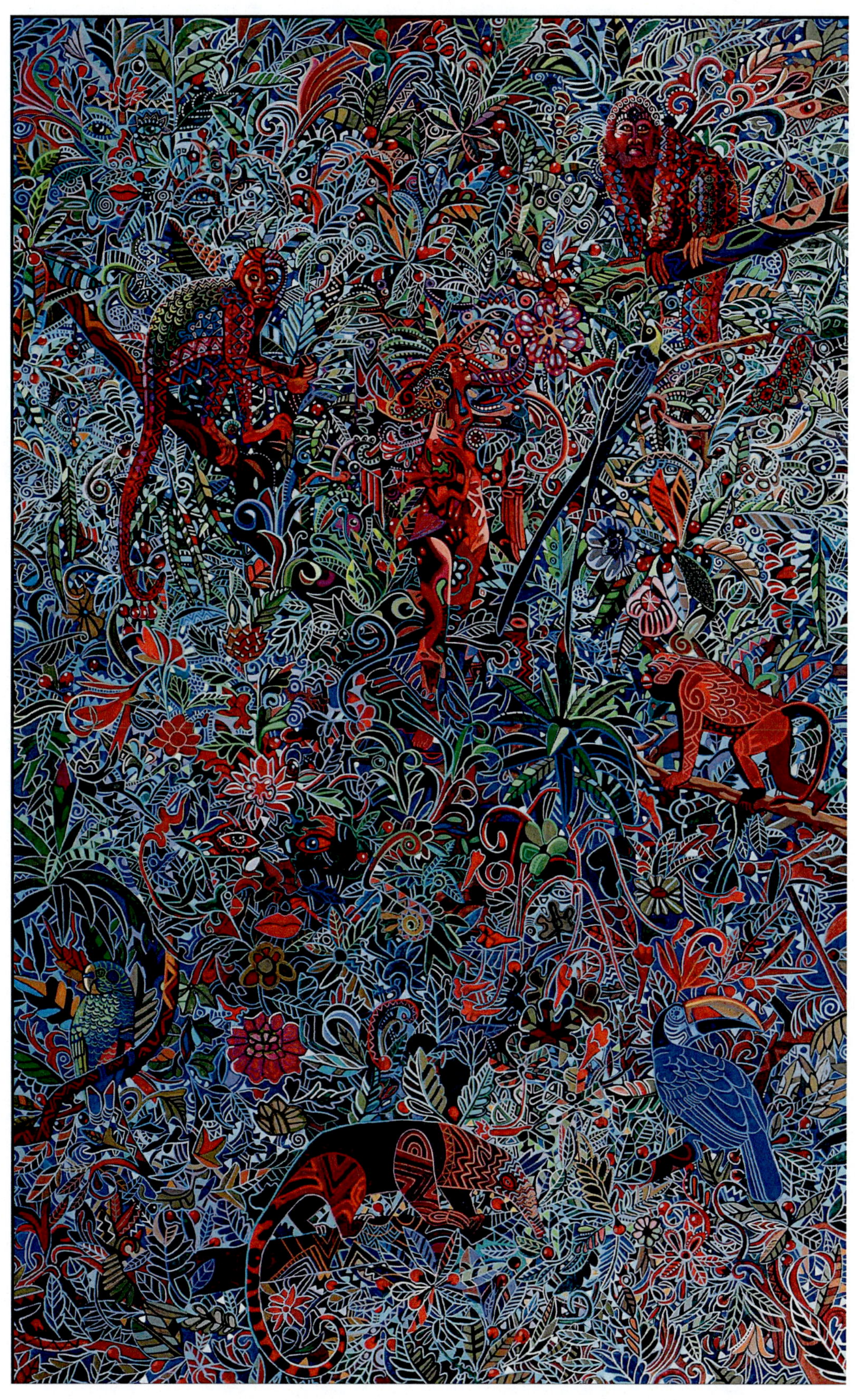

Sueño,(Dream: Eve Before Adam) (Left panel ofTriptych) 1992, 72 ¼ × 144 ¼ in., Smithsonian American Art Museum, museum purchase through the Luisita L. and Franz H. Denghausen Endowment and the Smithsonian Institution Acquistion Program

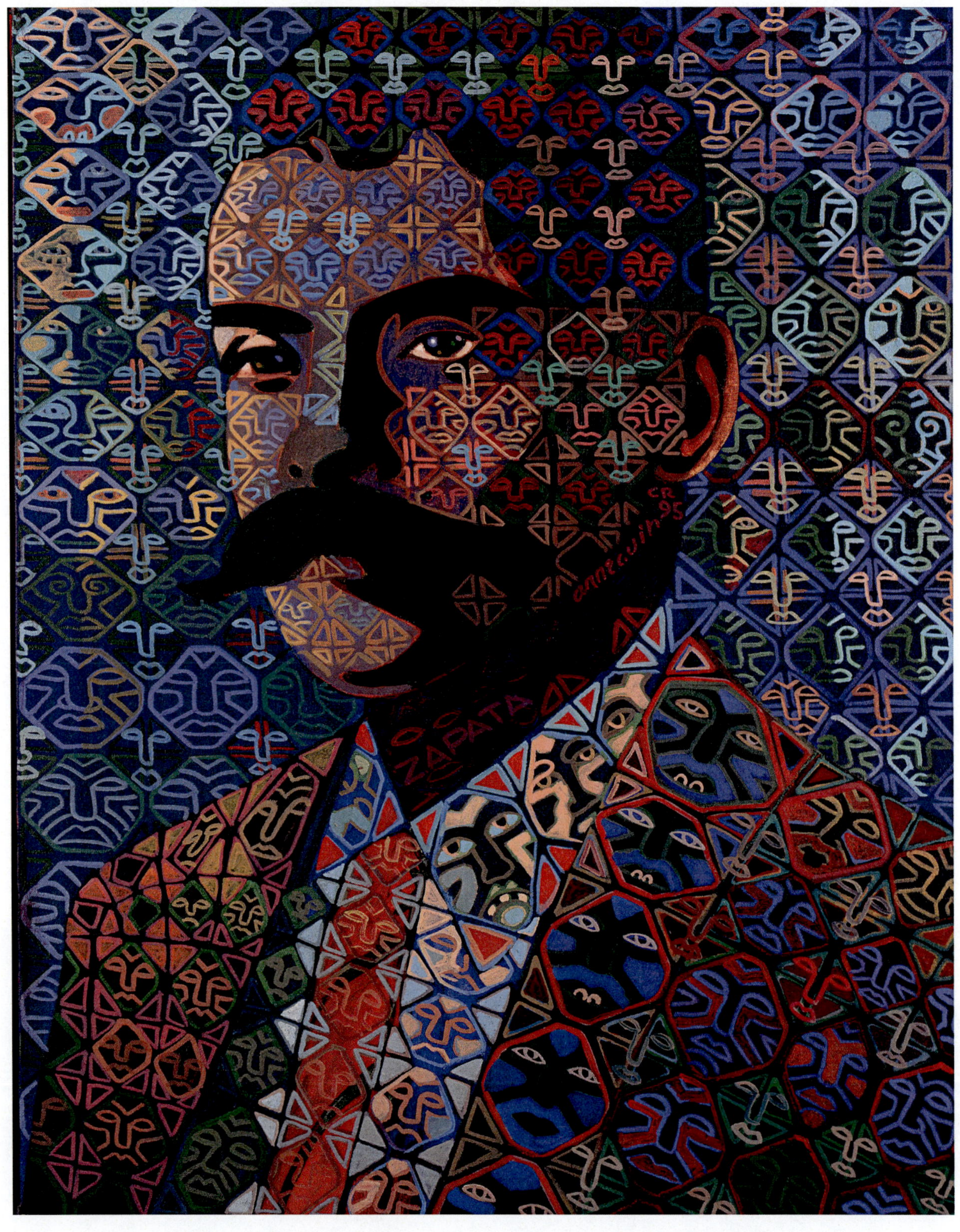

El Joven Zapata, 1995, 28 × 22 in., collectionof the artist

Rigoberto González

The Flight South of the Monarch Butterfly

They always return to make us warm here in Michoacán
because they remind us of fire: they sputter like candles,
expanding and shrinking their singed browns and reds
as they consume the air in November, finally tapering down

into the shadows like burnt paper. What message
do they carry in their wings from the North--
the place that gave them a brush of black opal
for weight and touches of white to attract the clean

clouds and fool the sun into sending its brightest rays
through the mimic of holes? The butterflies settle their lit
bodies on the naked tree, bringing back its autumn leaves,
those breaths of orange that gasp before falling off again,

this time into the hands of winter. But here, winters
are warm like manzanilla tea. Haven't we always known that,
those of us who chose to stay within arm's length
of our mothers? But for some women, sitting like wooden saints

at their doors, these butterflies are calls for blessings
from their sons, the men whose names trickled down to thirst
inside their mothers' mouths. To them, the monarch's eggs
complete their prayers like rosary beads, they are the flammable

heads of matches. But we value the chrysalis of bone,
the blue shell that brings down the sky within our reach.
By March, when the monarch leaves, a second fever
strikes: the butterflies cluster into wreaths. The trees

the women's sons once owned are set ablaze again: young boys
raise their sticks to cut them down in flames.
We watch together as butterflies drop--explosions bright
as fireworks without sound, yet loud enough to call us out.

El vuelo hacia el sur de la mariposa monarca

Siempre regresan para darnos calor aquí en Michoacán
porque nos recuerdan al fuego: parpadean como velas,
expandiendo y encogiendo sus rojos y marrones chamuscados
a medida que consumen el aire de noviembre, hasta disminuirse

en las sombras como papel quemado. ¿Qué mensaje
llevan sobre sus alas desde el Norte--
ese lugar que les dio una pincelada de ópalo negro
por peso y unos toques de blanco que atraen a las pulcras

nubes y engañan al sol haciéndolo enviar sus más claros rayos
por la imitación de agujeros? Las mariposas posan sus cuerpos
encendidos sobre el árbol desnudo, haciendo retornar su follaje de otoño,
esos suspiros anaranjados que boquean antes de caer nuevamente,

esta vez en manos del invierno. Pero aquí los inviernos
son tibios cual té de manzanilla. ¿Acaso no lo hemos sabido siempre
aquellos de nosotros que elegimos permanecer a una distancia prudente
de nuestras madres? Pero, para algunas mujeres, sentadas como santos de palo

en sus puertas, estas mariposas son llamadas de bendiciones
de sus hijos, aquellos hombres cuyos nombres gotearon en sed
dentro de las bocas de sus madres. Para ellos, los huevos de la monarca
completan sus plegarias cual cuentas de rosario, son las cabezas

combustibles de los cerillos. Mas valoramos las crisálidas de hueso,
la cáscara azul que pone el cielo a nuestro alcance.
Allá por marzo, cuando se marcha la monarca, una segunda fiebre
ataca: las mariposas se agrupan en guirnaldas. Los árboles

que los hijos de la mujeres una vez poseyeron son prendidos en fuego: los muchachos
levantan un palo para reducirlas a llamas.
Miramos juntos como caen las mariposas--explosiones radiantes
como fuegos artificiales sin sonido, mas suficientemente ruidosas para llamarnos.

—Spansh translation, Lauro Flores

Rigoberto González

Papalotzin and the Monarchs: A Bilingual Tale of Breaking Down Walls

The day finally arrived when the Great North built a Great Wall to separate itself from the Great South. Nothing and no one was allowed to pass anymore, not even the clouds, or the wind that once flowed from one side of the sky to the other.

At first, the people of the Great South didn't mind so much. Besides, they thought, they were the fortunate ones: The monarch butterflies had remained on their side of the wall, fluttering around like flakes of orange and gold every day of the year.

But Papalotzin, Royal Butterfly among the Aztecs, was very upset by this. Since time began the butterflies had moved freely back and forth. Their migration was like the circulation of life on Earth! Papalotzin was right to be concerned. When the butterflies tired of flying in circles before the imposing wall, they began to drop to the ground. Once the monarchs were gone, there was no more color in the sky and everything began to fade to gray. The sunflowers lost their yellows. The browns of the tree trunks, the reds of the apples, the pinks of people's hands—all of it began to disappear! Even the proud grasshopper became depressed when he was left invisible without his green coat.

The people of the Great South cried for help: "Oh, great Papalotzin, soon we will all be colorless ... as death!" Papalotzin peeked over the Great Wall and discovered that the people of the Great North also were suffering. Everything on the other side also was fading into gray. The strawberries were no longer red. The oranges were no longer orange. And the conversational blue jay stopped talking because he had nothing to say without the brilliant blue of his feathers. "Whatever shall we do?" the people of the Great North cried out.

Papalotzin knew he had to save the people on both sides, but also the animals, the flowers, the fruits, and even the sun, which was losing its shine, and even the moon, which was losing its sheen, and even the skies, which were becoming dull as sand.

With his Royal Butterfly foot, Papalotzin kicked and crumbled the Great Wall that divided the Great North from the Great South. He then breathed deeply and blew a gust of wind from his Royal Butterfly lungs to launch the monarchs into the air.

In flight once more, the monarchs spread across the skies; immediately the colors started coming back. Everyone celebrated, North and South: ¡Urraaa! Hooraaay! The grasshopper jumped in happiness now that he was visible again, and the blue jay sang, joyful in his brilliant blue.

The Great North and the Great South decided it was best to leave things this way, to let the monarchs, and everything and everyone, migrate back and forth for the rest of time. And Papalotzin thought so too as he flapped his great wings and pushed the beautiful rainbows high into the sky.

The Great North and the Great South decided it was best to leave things this way, to let the monarchs, and everything and everyone, migrate back and forth for the rest of time. And Papalotzin thought so too as he flapped his great wings and pushed the beautiful rainbows high into the sky.

Papalotzin y las monarcas: un relato bilingüe acerca de derribar murallas

El día finalmente llegó cuando el Gran Norte construyó un Gran Muro para separarse del Gran Sur. Ya a nada ni a nadie se le permitía pasar, ni siquiera a las nubes, o al viento que antes fluía de un lado a otro del cielo.

Al principio, a la gente del Gran Sur no le importaba mucho. Además, pensaban, ellos eran los afortunados: las mariposas monarcas se habían quedado de su lado del muro, revoloteando como copos naranja y oro todos los días del año.

Pero Papalotzin, la Mariposa Real entre los aztecas, estaba muy consternada ante el hecho. Desde el principio del tiempo las mariposas se habían desplazado libremente de un lado a otro. ¡Su migración era como la circulación de la vida en la Tierra!

Papalotzin tenía razón en estar preocupada. Cuando las mariposas se cansaron de volar en círculos frente al soberbio muro, empezaron a caer por tierra. Una vez que las monarca desaparecieron, no hubo más color en el cielo, y todo empezó a desvanecerse en gris. Los girasoles perdieron sus amarillos. Los marrones de los troncos del árbol, el rojo de las manzanas, el rosado de las manos de la gente— ¡todo aquello empezó a desaparecer! Incluso el vano saltamontes se deprimió cuando se hizo invisible sin su capa verde.

La gente del Gran Sur gritó pidiendo auxilio: "¡Oh, gran Papalotzin, pronto seremos todos incoloros ... como la muerte!"

Papalotzin se asomó por encima del Gran Muro y descubrió que la gente del Gran Norte también estaba sufriendo. Todo del otro lado también se desvanecía en gris. Las fresas ya no eran rojas. Las naranjas no eran naranja. Y la conversadora urraca azul dejó de hablar porque no tenía nada qué decir sin el radiante azul de su plumaje. "¿Qué haremos?" gritaba la gente del Gran Norte.

Papalotzin sabía que tenía que salvar a la gente de ambos lados, pero también a los animales, las flores y los frutos; e incluso al sol, que estaba perdiendo su fulgor, y aun a la luna, que perdía su lustre, y hasta a los cielos, que se hacían opacos como la arena.

Con su pie de Mariposa Real, Papalotzin pateó y desmoronó la Gran Muralla que dividía al Gran Norte del Gran Sur. Después respiró hondo y exhaló una ráfaga de viento desde sus pulmones de Real Mariposa para lanzar a las monarcas al aire.

En vuelo una vez más, las monarcas se esparcieron por los cielos; de inmediato, los colores empezaron a retornar. Y todos celebraron, Norte y Sur: ¡Hurra! ¡Viva! El saltamontes saltó feliz ahora que era nuevamente visible, y la urraca cantó, alegre en su radiante azul.

El Gran Norte y el Gran Sur decidieron que era mejor dejar las cosas tal cual, permitir que las monarcas, y todo y todos, migraran de ida y vuelta el resto del tiempo. Y Papalotzin pensaba también lo mismo a medida que batía sus grandes alas y empujaba los bellos arcoíris hacia lo alto del cielo.

—Spanish translation, Lauro Flores

José Luis Alcubilla

Alfredo Arreguín: el esplendor de la selva

¡Cantemos el bosque!
Bajo las alas verticales, oh serpientes,
de las águilas
¡cantemos el bosque!
Desde sus raíces y sus troncos gigantescos
a sus follajes liberados
por la gloria y por el viento.
Aquí se festejaron desbordados
los monarcas paternos.
Aquí Cuauhtemotzin
aprendió a llenarse los labios de silencio.
Cantemos el bosque
de cuyas entrañas sale el tiempo...

Carlos Pellicer

I

En la indefinible totalidad de la selva crece el árbol de la vida; su tronco se ancla en el centro de la tierra, sus ramas y follajes todo lo cubren. Ellas son techo y cuna, el mundo de Eva antes de Adán, la energía esencial que glorifica el crecimiento: colores a perpetuidad, la magia de la clorofila, fenomenología de lo cerrado y lo abierto. Florecimientos, geometrías, recobecos esculpidos, bordados en la piedra, laberinto de raíces y sonidos, el inusitado acontecimiento de la lluvia en el más barroco monumento de la naturaleza: la selva-entraña verde con todos sus lenguajes.

Porque en el principio fue la selva y el agua, aún antes del aire y del fuego. Eso lo sabe muy bien Alfredo Arreguín, un artista que ante todo es un paisajista que de manera magistral ha hecho de la selva, la floresta, la algaida, la frondosidad, la espesura, la catinga, el sobral, la manigua, el bosque, tanto su tema principal como la fuente esencial de sus metáforas y símbolos. Sea pues que pinte selvas o paisajes de agua o de tierra, vírgenes, terrazas con inquietantes vistas a las montañas, estructuras geométricas a la manera de alfombras o tapetes, retratos o autorretratos, siempre evoca en sus creaciones la fuerza orgánica de lo vegetal.

Es interesante por ello bordar un poco en la simbología de la selva o el bosque. Podemos decir que "entre los celtas constituían un verdadero santuario en estado natural... En la India los *sannayasa* se retiran al bosque, lo mismo que los ascetas búdicos: los bosques son benignos—se lee en el *Dhammapada*—cuando el mundo no entra allí, el santo halla su reposo. En el Japón, el *torii* designa, más que la entrada al dominio de un templo, la de un verdadero santuario natural que por lo general es un bosque de coníferas. En la China la montaña coronada por un bosque es casi siempre el paraje de un templo." [1]

1 Jean Chevalier y Alain Gheerbrant, *Diccionario de los símbolos,* Barcelona, Editorial Herder, 1999, p.194.

Entre los grandes logros del universo estético de Arreguín encontramos la reminiscencia de los mencionados santuarios naturales, tan fecundos como espléndidos en su superabundancia. En este sentido, verdaderos manifiestos pictóricos son sus cuadros: *Sueño, Eva antes de Adán* (1992) [2] y *El árbol de la vida* (1995). Obras como *Campeche* (1977), *Michoacán* (1982), *Xapuri* (1988), *Los búhos* (1992), *Acámbaro* (1993) o *Jungla encantada* (1994) son dignas de mencionarse también pues de manera contundente nos invitan a vivir la magnificencia de la selva.

Y así, desde un verdadero culto por la naturaleza adentrémonos en las significaciones de ésta y del bosque, pues no deja de ser curiosa la categoría mística que adquieren tanto por sí mismos como por los personajes que los habitan. Con dicha carga espiritual, se entiende muy bien por qué este maestro ha incluido *Vírgenes* dentro del corpus de su obra. Para explicar su presencia recordemos que para los "antiguos, griegos y latinos, como para otros pueblos, los bosques estaban consagrados a las divinidades: simbolizaban la morada misteriosa de Dios. Séneca les dedica una bella evocación: esos bosques sagrados poblados de árboles antiguos de altura inusitada, donde las ramas espesas superpuestas hasta el infinito roban la vista del cielo, el poder de la floresta y su misterio… ¿todo eso no da el sentimiento de que un Dios reside en ese lugar?" [3] Véase *Nuestra Señora de la Selva* (1989), *Nuestra Señora de Cuzco* (1990), *La Virgen de los Milagros* (1994) y, entre otras, *La Virgen de la Luz* (1996). ¿Acaso no son ellas mismas las responsables de la abundancia, el colorido y la frondosidad? ¿toda virgen o madonna en su inmaculada gloria es símbolo del más grande misterio creador? ¿son por ello el perfecto vehículo para llamarnos a la veneración del espacio donde reinan? Es un hecho, entonces, que los lienzos de este artista plástico son un himno apasionado a la naturaleza, a sus habitantes, visibles e invisibles. A través de su producción vamos comprendiendo muy bien porqué éstos son además un alegato a favor de la ecología, en el que se incluye a sus defensores. Tal es el caso de *Sacrificio na Amazonia* (Homage to Chico Mendes) (1989) y el retrato de *Hazel Wolf* (2000).

Con base en todo lo anterior, podemos identificar en este artista plástico una vocación claramente biofílica. Y es que si "la materia viva tiene la tendencia a integrar y unir, aquella tiende a fundirse con entidades diferentes y opuestas y a crecer de un modo estructural; unificación y crecimiento integrado son características pues de todos los procesos vitales, no sólo por lo que concierne a las células, sino también respecto del sentimiento y el pensamiento… El ciclo de la vida es unión, nacimiento y crecimiento…" [4] No otra cosa se nos propone una y otra vez en las obras Arreguinianas, que la sublimación de este proceso. Es definitivo que en su calidad de santuario, "la selva o el bosque sagrado es un centro de vida, una reserva de frescor, de agua y calor asociados, como una especie de matriz. También es un símbolo maternal. Es la fuente de una regeneración e interviene en este sentido en los sueños, descubriendo un deseo de seguridad y de renovación. Es una expresión fortísima de lo inconsciente." [5]

Por tanto, la selva puede verse como la depositaria de una de las aspiraciones humanas más profundas: la del crecimiento que en su proyección más pura invade todos los ámbitos de lo humano… De ahí el carácter de la selva o el bosque como sinfonía vivificante.

---

2 Cuadro de gran formato que fue elegido entre más de 600 obras y comprado en 1994 por el Smithsonian American Art Museum confirmando y ampliando con ello el reconocimiento a la obra y trayectoria de este artista.

3 Chevalier y Gheerbrant, op.cit., p. 195.

4 Erich Fromm, *El corazón del hombre*, México, Fondo de Cultura Económica, 1985, p. 46.

5 Chevalier y Gheerbrant, op. cit. p. 195-6.

II

Al recuperar la mencionada fuerza orgánica de lo vegetal desde la cual este autor concibe sus temas, digamos que el vehículo para estructurarlos es el manejo de patrones ornamentales mismos con los que, a partir de estructuras geométricas o mediante un juego de follajes y arborescencias—a modo de una segunda piel dentro de la realidad de lo que pinta-, consigue en sus composiciones una inusual efectividad plástica. Se impone por lo tanto una pregunta:
¿cuáles son las coordenadas que confluyen en su estilo personalísimo? Es interesante saber que como artista plástico se educa en la Universidad de Washington de donde egresa con una licenciatura en 1967, obteniendo tambien, dos años más tarde, el grado de Maestro en Bellas Artes. Esta es una época en la que en el contexto de la pintura norteamericana tienen importancia mayor las prácticas creativas emanadas del Expresionismo Abstracto y del Arte Pop. Lo extraordinario es que no se haya visto influído por dichas vanguardias, proponiéndose, en cambio, escuchar atentamente sus voces interiores relacionadas, por una parte, con la cultura mexicana, y por otra, con la cultura universal. Como se sabe, Alfredo Arreguín nace en Morelia, Michoacán, en 1935. Siendo niño, su abuela Pepita lo lleva a mercados donde toma contacto con el arte popular mexicano. A través de ésta, y otras experiencias, asimila el colorido, el sentido mágico, la riqueza imaginativa y, sobre todo, las estructuras ornamentales del mismo que integrará posteriormente de forma magistral en su trabajo, enmedio de un curioso horror al vacío. Esta tendencia, tal y como nos dice Rubín de la Borbolla, es de origen muy antiguo y consiste en "llenar los espacios vacíos en una composición, o de rodear el tema principal con elementos simbólicos o decorativos, lo que en el arte moderno se llama fondo o ambiente. Esta es una de las características más sobresalientes en el arte de muchos pueblos… Existen varias explicaciones de este fenómeno tan común en el arte popular universal. En muchos casos se trata de mensajes dibujados o grabados (fórmulas religiosas o mágicas), razón por la que el artesano aprovecha todo el espacio disponible. En otros se ve la intención de un enriquecimiento exagerado en la composición y la decoración." [6]

Al intentar, por lo demás, definir sus abrevaderos puede decirse, con Tess Gallagher que "los diseños (patterns) de Arreguín provienen del arte colonial mexicano, de las fachadas de las iglesias barrocas, del arte decorativo precolombino, de los motivos animales y florales de la cerámica de Tlaquepaque, pero quizás más directamente de las artesanías de Michoacán y Guerrero. Más aun, uno puede ver allí huellas de la arquitectura islámica, de la pintura tántrica de la India y de fuentes del lejano y del medio oriente..." [7]

Por tanto, en la obra de este productor plástico hay varios puntos de partida y diversas asimilaciones: lo mexicano, desde imaginerías plásticas y temas o personajes muy concretos, y lo universal, cuando dialoga con diversas tradiciones artísticas. Si todo artista verdadero parte de lo que es y de lo que aprende, éste ha de crear desde su ser más profundo, es decir, desde lo que vive y lo que siente. La auténtica originalidad surge cuando todo ello confluye proyectándose en un estilo tan inigualable como personal. Es el caso de Alfredo Arreguín, cuyo trabajo se ve condicionado por el gran espectro de la cultura mexicana, logrando a la vez dialogar creadoramente con tradiciones artísticas universales que se avienen muy bien con su iconografía y con el perfeccionismo y laboriosidad de su oficio.

---

6 Daniel Rubín de la Borbolla, *Arte Popular Mexicano*, México, Fondo de Cultura Económica (Archivo del Fondo No. 19-20), 1974, p. 22.

7 Tess Gallagher, prefacio a: Lauro Flores, Alfredo Arreguín, *Patterns of Dreams and Nature*, Seattle and London, University of Washington Press, 2007, p. xxiv.

III

Dijimos ya que este pintor es esencialmente un paisajista. Desde esta práctica sus obras conllevan un doble nivel: el que sostiene los diferentes planos y/o figuras en las composiciones y otro más donde aquéllos son transformados mediante la aplicación de patrones. Esta interesante propuesta adquiere incuestionablemente el rango de opulencia visual tal y como la caracteriza Diane Douglas. Y más, "cada uno de sus lienzos es un exuberante ecosistema de narrativa, paisaje, mito e historia… Primero está la historia subyacente, un terraplén de máscaras y otros motivos provenientes de la flora nativa y de los textiles mexicanos. Este intenso entramado de patrones y color provee una estructura… Encima de ella encontramos un toldo de gente, animales y anécdotas –los protagonistas del arte narrativo de Arreguín…" [8]

Sea pues que miremos estas obras del fondo hacia afuera o al revés, el caso es que tienen múltiples estratos: el plano, la figura, el ornamento, el símbolo. En la historia del arte unos y otros elementos han recibido diversos tratamientos y tenido las más variadas proyecciones. Puede decirse que la arquitectura siempre mantuvo una estrecha relación con el ornamento, no así la pintura o la escultura. Este último más bien se vio ligado siempre a las artes aplicadas. Por ello, si miramos hacia atrás, en decoraciones de techos o paredes, en pilares, mobiliarios y utensilios, en tejidos y bordados egipcios pueden encontrarse ya una serie de interesantes propuestas de patrones ornamentales geométricos y/o vegetales, que como se ve surgen en la antiguedad y aparecen en la historia del arte prácticamente en todas las épocas –Grecia, Roma, la Era cristiana, la Edad Media, el Renacimiento, el Barroco, el Rococó, etcétera.

Ahora bien, si nos referimos a la historia de Oriente, el arte de ornamentar, por ejemplo en el mundo islámico, adquiere especial significación. Y es que "la religión del Oriente Medio que barrió cuanto la había precedido en los siglos VII y VIII, la religión de los conquistadores mahometanos de Persia, Mesopotamia, Egipto, el Norte de Africa y España fue más rigurosa aún que el Cristianismo en este aspecto, y prohibió absolutamente las imágenes. Pero al arte como tal no se le suprime fácilmente, y los artistas de Oriente, a los que no se permitía representar seres humanos dejaron correr su imaginación en formas decorativas y lineales, creando la más sutil ornamentación de tracería: el arabesco. Si hoy admiramos la capacidad de creación, el equilibrio y la armonía en los esquemas de color de los tapices orientales, lo debemos, a fin de cuentas, a Mahoma, quien alejó el espíritu del artista de los objetos del mundo real para impulsarlo hacia el maravilloso de las líneas y los colores." [9]

Para saber muy bien a qué nos referimos conviene aclarar la significación del término arabesco: "Del italiano arabesco íd., derivado de 'arabo' árabe, por ser este adorno característico del arte musulmán, que no admite representación de imágenes. Ornamentos propios del arte árabe, hechos a base de líneas, lo más a menudo rectas, entrelazadas y que forman figuras geométricas, estrellas, etc. en dos dimensiones. Por extensión, los adornos de hojas festonadas, naturales o fantásticas, con florones o de figuras geométricas aunque correspondan a otros estilos arquitectónicos." [10]

---

8 Diane Douglas, Nota final. En: Lauro Flores, op. cit. p. 166.

9 Ernst H. Gombrich, *Historia del arte*, Madrid, Alianza Editorial, 1981, (3a. ed.) p.115.

10 Vicente Medel Martínez, *Vocabulario arquitectónico ilustrado*, México, Secretaría del Patrimonio Nacional, 1975, p. 36.

Así, los diseños basados en formas de la naturaleza, la geometría en sí misma y también la caligrafía (no estrictamente como un medio de comunicación humana sino como vehículo sagrado de relación entre Dios y el ser humano) manejada desde diferentes estilos, se proyectan ampliamente dentro de la arquitectura y las artes aplicadas del Islam. Especial mención merecen en este universo artístico las alfombras o tapetes que son un verdadero alarde de composición, simetría, armonías y contrastes de color.

Si "las grecas, líneas quebradas de diversos cánones y figuras poseen, aparte de su valor expresivo un significado tradicional: formas cuadradas asociadas a la tierra, triangulares al fuego, onduladas al agua y el aire," [11] lo significativo aquí es la reivindicación del ornamento como principal vehículo de expresión plástica. Esa es, precisamente, la afirmación de Alfredo Arreguín, un cultivador de la línea, cuyos arabescos evocan en algunos de sus cuadros la plasticidad árabe. Si uno contempla obras como: *Las iguanas II* (1983), *Totem* (1990), *Metepec* (1995), *Mariposas de Lacandonia* (1997) o *Sarape II* (1998) hay algo en la profusión decorativa –en nivel de efecto general- que nos remite al Oriente Medio, pero en este caso lo sorprendente es el trastocamiento que este autor concreta al construir cuadros donde la multiplicación de máscaras y una profusión de motivos geométricos, dan a las composiciones un marcado carácter tribal. Esta operación lo conecta, desde luego, con la tradición artística mexicana que se encuentra en textiles, sarapes y rebozos.

IV

Si al ya referido valor plástico de lo vegetal le aunamos el ornamento como símbolo estructural y el culto por la línea, tenemos entonces tres coordenadas que nos permiten explicar el estilo Arreguíniano. Y aquí una interesante coincidencia pues éstas son características del Art Nouveau, movimiento artístico de finales del siglo XIX que se proyectó primordialmente en la arquitectura y las artes utilitarias. Lo importante, sin embargo, es subrayar que como parte de este Modernismo, la pintura y la escultura se vieron, ahora sí, influídas por la línea y el ornamento. De esta manera, los Prerrafaelistas, los creadores de la Escuela de Pont-Aven y los Nabis, los Simbolistas Fernand Khnopff, Jan Toorop y otros, comenzaron a echar mano de soluciones plásticas que sólo se habían manejado en el arte aplicado o industrial.

Quizá el ejemplo prototípico de esta asimilación lo tenemos en Gustav Klimt (1862-1918), pintor simbolista que dentro de la Secesión vienesa aporta a la pintura de los inicios del siglo XX la reivindicación de los valores del ornamento. Es notable la forma en que este autor lo incorpora en los retratos de: Emile Floge (1902), Margaretha Stonborough-Wittgenstein (1905), o Fritzia Riedler (1906) en los que planos geométricos enmarcan los rostros. En el último hay además un sillón que se ha construído a base de ojos de pluma de pavo real y sin perspectiva.

Ahora, la ambición geométrica y la promoción de valores bidimensionales, con la influencia sintetizante y decorativa del arte bizantino y del oriental, halla su culminación en otro retrato de Klimt, el de Adele Bloch-Bauer I (1907) donde—entre dorados—el vestido se integra totalmente al fondo. Uno y otro dejan de presentar volúmenes o formas para ofrecernos directamente una serie de

11 Juan Eduardo Cirlot, *Diccionario de símbolos*, Madrid, Ediciones Siruela, 1998, p.222-3.

patrones decorativos. Esta voluntad de transformar la superficie pictórica es llevada a sus últimas consecuencias en la serie de mosaicos realizados por él para el comedor del Palacio Stoclet de Bruselas. En estos, las figuras se ven envueltas en tan nutrido conjunto de geometrías y líneas ondulantes que casi las hace desaparecer. En uno de los paneles vemos una imagen que es antecedente directo del famoso cuadro El beso (1907-8). En otra, la sección Árbol de la vida o de la Ciencia del Bien y del Mal, tiene en su tronco toda una serie de aplicaciones y las ramas son simplemente ondulaciones de las que cuelgan frutos de dos ojos; en una de ellas se ha posado un ave. Nada es aquí representación imitativa, sino pura estilización.

Algo más, la osadía mayor dentro del proyecto de la residencia Stoclet se encuentra en los paneles donde las formas geométricas se han manejado independientemente de cualquier motivo, es decir, con un rango abstracto. He aquí la validación total del ornamento como entidad autónoma susceptible de utilizarse dentro del todo pictórico. (Compárese éste con las propuestas de Kandinsky, Mondrian o Malevich para así comprobar su originalidad). En resumen, con este legendario artista plástico,—y también con obras, como *La Bailarina* (1916-18) donde la geometría ha sido sustituída por un ensueño floral lleno de vivacidad—asistimos a la "sorprendente aparición de una pintura decorativa," [12] o para mejor decir, al nacimiento de un tipo de pintura que conquista sus rangos plásticos a partir del uso de patrones decorativos u ornamentales.

En conclusión, no cabe duda de que la lección dejada por Gustav Klimt en cuanto al uso del ornamento ha sido llevada a sus últimas consecuencias por Alfredo Arreguín, quien ha sabido integrarlos dentro de su lenguaje y estilo muy propios. Klimt, por otra parte, no será el único artista del Art Nouveau con el que podemos relacionar a nuestro pintor, pues cuando buscamos explicar algunas de sus asimilaciones y/o paralelismos artísticos no debemos olvidar al más prominente maestro norteamericano de las artes decorativas: Louis Comfort Tiffany (1848-1933), quien, proyectándose en muchos ámbitos, es conocido sobre todo por su trabajo en vidrio: lámparas, floreros y desde luego vitrales, en los que siempre encontramos vistas de la naturaleza: árboles y arbustos en un primer plano, y más allá, un lago circundado por montañas, el horizonte y el cielo. Véanse las obras: *Vista de la Bahía* de *Oyster y Magnolias* y lirios (ambos ca. 1905). Más complejo en el primer plano pero con la misma estructura es el tríptico *Paisaje de otoño* (1923-4) (que además ha sido enmarcado por una arquería de madera al estilo gótico). Entre los cuadros de Arreguín que nos sugieren un claro efecto de vitrales –a la Tiffany- se encuentran: *Caleta* (1974), *Pátzcuaro* (1975) —que también podría ser visto como un biombo—, *Laguna azul* (1976) y de manera muy destacada: *Shilshole* (1986) y *Tukwila* (1990). Que estas pinturas podrían convertirse en vitrales generando así una nueva manera de verlas, vía la luz, lo demuestra la obra *The Froth* (la espuma que resulta del choque de las olas) que basándose en *The Last Salmon Run* (1990) se convirtió en vitral en 1997, comisionado por el Washington State Department of Ecology. Por su parte, telas como *Río Lobo Tasmano* (1981), *La maleza* (1982), *Camécuaro* (1983), y *Río Tamazula* (1992) junto a otras, incluyen lagos o lagunas en medio de la selva. En esta clasificación han de tomarse en cuenta también los que podríamos llamar paisajes acuáticos, tales como *Dentro del mar* (1975), *Cenote* (1980), la mencionada *The Last Salmon Run* (1990) y dos piezas –entre muchas más– que son un homenaje al grabador del ukiyo-e japonés, Katsushica Hokusai (1760-1849) cuya estampa *La gran ola* (1830-31) fue pretexto para llevar a cabo los trípticos: *The Nisqually* (1998) y *Chiwana (The big river)* (1999).

12 Ernesto B. Rodríguez, "Enfoque de actualidad", en: Werner Hofmann, *Gustav Klimt*, Buenos Aires, Pinacoteca de los genios, No. 149, 1964, sin página.

Por último, hablemos de otro espacio en las obras de este creador, el que llamaremos de los cuadros-terrazas. *The Window of Make Believe* (1975), *Sal si puedes* (1975), *Barandal-azulejos* (1980) o *La casa de la paz* (1994) son ejemplos de composiciones donde barandales y columnas, encuadran desde un plano medio la mirada de un interior hacia un exterior. Por supuesto se propone aquí la arquitectura como espacio habitable en la que se enmarca la experiencia del paisaje. En el destacado cuadro *Washingtonia* (1988) (que fue elegido entre 200 propuestas para servir de base al diseño de un cartel conmemorativo del Centenario del Estado de Washington) una arquería pródigamente decorada con motivos geométricos nos recuerda tanto al Medio Oriente como al propio Tiffany. Es aquí incuestionable el afán de integrar o de hacer dialogar un vitral o una pintura con la arquitectura.

V

Apartado especial, en la obra de nuestro creador, es el del retrato. A propósito del mismo puede decirse que aunque a través de mil esferas de intolerable fulgor quisiéramos cercarlo, el ser humano es indescriptible y su rostro es siempre único, amén de que éste simboliza el tránsito de los seres vivos de las tinieblas a la luz. No hay dos seres humanos completamente iguales, por tanto su semblante y sus gestos son la demostración del irrepetible y fugaz misterio de la vida. En la historia del arte, y desde tiempos inmemoriales, se ha tratado de dar permanencia a esa extraordinaria realidad humana expresada en las faccciones de alguien. Con ella, podemos remontarnos por un lado, a los retratos del Fayúm y trazar un vaso comunicante enntre éstos y las efigies sintético-cubistas de Pablo Picasso; en todos éstos la belleza de las representaciones esquematizadas que a lo largo de los siglos han definido estilos desde la simplificación o síntesis de formas.

Por otro lado, nos encontramos con las representaciones imitativas que surgen con la escultura romana y que son recuperadas en el Renacimiento y más,—de la mano de las Academias- por retratistas profesionales como: Hans Holbein, el jóven (siglo XVI), Anton van Dyck (siglo XVII), Joshua Reynolds y Thomas Gainsborough (siglo XVIII), Joaquín Sorolla, John Singer Sargent y Giovanni Boldini, entre otros (siglo XIX a XX). En este rubro el artista desarrolla una capacidad para reproducir fotográficamente lo que ve y nos sorprende con el realismo de carnaciones, drapeados, transparencias, volúmenes y todo género de detalles.

Alfredo Arreguín emplea en su retratística, ingredientes de estos dos universos, es decir, de inicio estructura las formas de acuerdo con una ubicación espacial –perspéctica- y un manejo de línea que tienen un origen académico. De suyo en ocasiones utiliza la fotografía como recurso de composición de un rostro; a la base resultante de ellole sobrepone, la sorprendente red de patrones ornamentales típica en él y que siempre evoca la fuerza y barroquismo de la naturaleza y/o un universo de geometrías. Por cierto, cuando se trata de escritores, la palabra se convierte en el vehículo para esa capa o velo que amplifica la realidad de las composiciones. Es el caso, por ejemplo de *Mi amigo Ray* (2001) dedicado a su entrañable amigo Raymond Carver y *Sirenas* (2003), cuadro que es un homenaje a Pablo Neruda.

Ahora bien, tratándose de retratos, este artista los trabaja recuperando a héroes, personajes o artistas, relacionados, muchos de ellos, justo con su patria de origen; es por ello que Emiliano Zapata, Frida Kahlo, César Chávez, Diego Rivera, José María Morelos, Miguel Hidalgo y Dolores Huerta han sido convocados para habitar los cuadros de nuestro pintor. Estas presencias implican la reivindicación de una cultura, -tanto en sus luchas sociales, como en sus artes- y lo son desde una irremediable inserción en el trópico, con toda la exuberancia y colorido que suele caracterizar a éste. Ahí es donde Arreguín recupera para nosotros el esplendor de bosques y selvas, el misterio de ríos y lagos, la distancia de las montañas y claro, a sus habitantes, las vírgenes nacientes de la tierra, el agua y la luz. Siendo plenamente consecuente con su estilo, en ese mismo escenario coloca a todos sus retratados haciéndolos partícipes de lo que en su pintura podemos llamar reinvención de la naturaleza, misma que quizá no sería posible sin el poder plástico y simbólico del *trompe-l'oeil* que nos propone. Ese engaño a nuestra vista es especialmente curioso cuando se trata de autorretratos.

Hace varios siglos Guiseppe Arcimboldo (1527-1593) concibió rostros a partir de flores, frutos, animales o incluso figuras humanas y libros (véanse: *El jurista*, 1566; *El bibliotecario*, ca. 1566; *Vertumno*—retrato de Rodolfo II- ca. 1590; *Flora*, ca. 1591); guardando las proporciones de época y contexto, parecida operación lleva a cabo Alfredo Arreguín al crear una doble realidad: la que vemos todos los días y la que turbadoramente nos ofrece a manera de una profunda y vitalísima fiesta de la tierra que en sus crecimientos todo lo toca. En sus retratos pues, recrea una memoria con la que nos demuestra que la vida es un rostro floreciente. Resuena el aire...

VI

Ya dijimos que Alfredo Arreguín nace en 1935, en México, y más específicamente en la ciudad de Morelia, Michoacán. Como antecedente en su profesión un hecho es curioso: su abuelo Carlos lo inscribe en la "Escuela Popular de Bellas Artes, institución vinculada a la Universidad Michoacana de San Nicolás de Hidalgo. Esa fue su introducción formal al arte. Así, a los doce años y durante 1947 y 1948 siguió múltiples cursos en los que aprendió, entre otras cosas, los principios básicos de dibujo y pintura." [13]

Veintiún años después –como hemos comentado- egresará de la Universidad de Washington con el título de Maestro en Bellas Artes, mas, paradójicamente, terminar sus estudios no le proporciona sino confusión, ello a pesar de que había pintado—como tesis de posgrado- nueve cuadros que podríamos caracterizar de diálogo con una figuración expresionista. Por ello abandona la pintura y se dedica al dibujo. Sin embargo—tal y como comenta Tomás Ybarra Fraustro- un nuevo encuentro con el pintor figurativo Elmer Bishoff, que había sido su maestro y mostrado interés en su obra y quien le urge a desarrollar una visión original, propicia que Arreguín regrese a la pintura. Significativo fue el hecho de que ello implicara dejar atrás las enseñanzas escolares... Es entre 1973 y 1974 que las búsquedas fructifican, pues los cuadros: *Slythe* (1973), *Stalemate* (1974), *Floating* (1974) y *Remolino* (1974)—éste último una especie de mandala- ya nos muestran a un artista que empieza a manejar patrones geométricos y coloridos que con el paso de los años refinará a grados máximos. Con los cuadros mencionados asistimos al descubrimiento de un estilo dentro del cual un importante antecedente lo es la obra *Emerald Island* (1970) que desde su estructura de mosaicos parecería el fondo de una fuente en un palacete morisco. He aquí, insistimos, el reconocimiento del ornamento como vehículo para la expresión plástica.

13
Lauro Flores, op. cit. p. 10. Para cuestiones biográficas confróntese la obra anterior y también: Tomás Ybarra-Fraustro, *El universo de Alfredo Arreguín*, en: *Alfredo Arreguín, el universo vegetal, animal y humano de un pintor moreliano*, Morelia, Mich, México, Universidad Michoacana de San Nicolás de Hidalgo, 1989.

Así las cosas, a partir de la segunda mitad de los años 70 y hasta la actualidad simplemente confirmamos tanto sus asimilaciones, como la incesante imaginación, perfeccionismo y sabiduría simbólica con los que el maestro Arreguín ha desarrollado su obra. Lo anterior lo comprobamos con la lista de sus exposiciones en museos y galerías, su presencia en importantes colecciones y los reconocimientos a que se ha hecho acreedor, todos los cuales confirman con creces su originalidad como pintor y la empatía que logra con quienes observan sus cuadros.

Alfredo Arreguín exhibió por primera vez y de forma individual en The Mexican Museum de San Francisco y en la Polly Friedllander Gallery de Seattle, en 1977. Pocos años después, en 1981, tuvo su primera retrospectiva en el Bellevue Art Museum de Bellevue, Washington. Asimismo entre otras muestras suyas destacan las efectuadas en el Museo del Barrio de Nueva York (1984), el Museo Regional Michoacano, Morelia, Mich. (1989), en el Fresno Metropolitan Museum of Art, Fresno, California y el Mexican Fine Arts Center Museum, Chicago; (ambas en 1990-91), a National Academy of Sciences, Washington, DC (1996), El Centro de la Raza, Seattle (1998). Su muestra: Patterns of dreams and nature, retrospectiva de 30 años, pudo verse entre 2002 y 2004 en museos de Bellevue, La Conner y Spokane, Washington y en Albuquerque, Nuevo México. Entre muchas otras muestras suyas, la última exhibición individual del maestro: Portraiture Now: Framing Memory tuvo lugar en la National Portrait Gallery, Smithsonian Institution, Washington DC. (2007-8).

Por lo demás, los cuadros de Arreguín han sido coleccionados por universidades y centros culturales, empresas, hospitales, hoteles, bancos y museos en Seattle, Denver, San Antonio, Washington, Portland, Tacoma, San Diego, Tucson, etc. Entre otras instituciones que disponen de obra suya está el National Museum of American Art, Smithsonian institution; el Washington State Department of Ecology, The White House, etc. así como el National Museum of Mexican Art y el Mexican Fine Arts Center Museum, ambas en Chicago; y el Mexican Museum de San Francisco.

Muchos han sido los premios y reconocimientos a su obra; entre los más destacados: el Premio-Palma de la Gente en el décimo primer Festival Internacional de Pintura en Cagnes-Sur-Mer, Francia (1979); la Beca para Artistas Visuales del National Endowment for the Arts (1980-85); el Premio de Arte del Gobernador del Estado de Washington (1986); el Premio OHTLI (1997) que otorga el Gobierno Mexicano en reconocimiento a quienes han contribuido a la promoción de la cultura mexicana; en el año 2000 la Universidad de Washington le otorgó el Premio a Alumnos Distinguidos; en ésta misma institución educativa la Sociedad de Alumnos, puso a funcionar en 2006 la Beca Alfredo Arreguín. En este último año, nuestro maestro se hizo acreedor al Premio Águila Azteca como reconocimiento a su solidaridad con la United Farm Workers of America.

Con una trayectoria de más de cuatro décadas, Arreguín siempre recuerda sus primeros años en México, el destino que le estaba esperando al conocer, en la ciudad de México, a la Familia Dam, pareja de norteamericanos que de visita en México con sus hijas, lo invitaron a vivir y estudiar en Seattle, ciudad a la que llega en noviembre de 1956. El camino que le lleva de la Arquitectura a la Pintura… Pero sobre todo, nunca olvida la noche en que se hizo uno con la selva; con el fin de analizar la posibilidad de dedicarse a la Ingeniería fue mandado al estado de Guerrero, México, como asistente de dos ingenieros quienes comisionados por el gobierno federal proyectaban un sistema de arrigación para la zona… Mientras aquellos se iban de vacaciones él se quedó solo en el pueblo de San Luis de la Loma que "en aquel entonces era un pueblo relativamente aislado, localizado a unos cincuenta kilómetros de la costa, rodeado por la espesura de la jungla guerrerense y más de veinte arroyos. La exuberancia del breñal y del follaje, que parecían henchirse a cada paso, espoleados por el clima tórrido y humedo, los brillantes colores de las flores y las aves y el resto de la fauna que abundaba entre el boscaje fascinaban y a la vez intimidaban al joven Alfredo. Las creencias de los habitantes del lugar, tanto indios como mestizos y sus leyendas acerca de la maleza que ellos percibían como una entidad viva, concreta y mágica, benéfica y maléfica a la vez también contribuyeron para que Alfredo percibiera aquel mundo de una manera totalmente distinta." [14]

Puede decirse que toda la obra de este maestro está marcada por esta revelación, por este descubrimiento, de ahí que la selva haya sido el centro irradiador de su pintura; es decir, sus recreaciones de aquella y todos sus motivos no son sino el reencuentro con ese paisaje total que como misterioso tesoro se le dio de joven.

VII

La pintura de Alfredo Arreguín nos muestra una admirable unidad estilística. Su diálogo inter-cultural ha sido plenamente enriquecedor. Con ello se demuestra que no sólo se conformó con la belleza de su lar nativo sino que salió al mundo a fin de tomar contacto con todo aquello que pudiera permitirle enriquecer sus visiones. Por paradójico que pueda parecer, es muy probable que su obra no sería la misma de no haber nacido en México y de no haber vivido y respirado de niño tanto el arte de su patria de origen como la riqueza de su paisaje.

Y es que en el arte mexicano hay, antes que nada, un extraordinario legado precolombino que da testimonio de la alta civilización desarrollada en Mesoamérica. Asimismo el arte colonial que se proyectó en conventos, iglesias, retablos, pinturas, esculturas, que si bien tuvo su origen en Europa, muy pronto fue adaptado a nuestras tierras, dando como resultado la creación de un barroco americano fraguado en el crisol del mestizaje. La conquista y el establecimiento del virreinato, que en principio fue un choque, nos llevó a ser partícipes de la cultura occidental. De ahí que es imposible abordar la historia, la filosofía o el arte mexicano sin integrar en el análisis "las relaciones cosmopolitas que se establecieron con todo el orbe; vínculos que han sido desde siempre característicos de la cultura de México, incluso remontándose al siglo XVI."[15]

Después de la Independencia el siglo XIX mexicano se definió con el Neoclasicismo, la pintura de historia y el paisaje académico; culminó con las primeras asimilaciones de la modernidad y ya en el XX, con la Revolución y la Escuela Mexicana de Pintura, misma que se dio a la tarea de recuperar nuestra identidad y de reencontrar el ser más profundo de la mexicanidad. El arte antiguo de México y las artes populares empezaron a ser vistas con otros ojos. Nos descubríamos y redescubríamos desde lo más profundo y ello conllevó una orgullosa comprobación: nuestra historia es milenaria y nuestras artes riquísimas.

14 Lauro Flores, op. cit. p. 17.

15 Luis Martín Lozano, Introducción curatorial, en catálogo: *Arte Moderno de México 1900-1950*, México, UNAM, Ciudad de México, Antiguo Colegio de San Ildefonso, 2000, p. 18.

Arreguín retoma del arte antiguo de México la síntesis de las formas y el sentido de lo sagrado; del arte colonial la categoría barroca; de la academia neoclásica el rigor en el detalle (recuérdese al paisajista José María Velasco); del arte popular el colorido; de la Escuela Mexicana de Pintura el afán de recuperar lo más genuinamente representativo de la mexicanidad. De ahí que sea tan importante en la multiplicidad de su obra la pintora Frida Kahlo, a quien ha dedicado cuadros memorables: *Images of Frida* (1978), *Kahlo's Garden* (1990), *Frida in Flame* (1992), *Coyoacán* (1995), *Diego y Frida* (1998). De suyo, creemos que entreteje vasos comunicantes con los maestros de la mexicanidad posrevolucionaria tanto como con pintores contemporáneos de la tendencia neomexicanista. Ello explica que se haya ocupado también de personajes o momentos de la historia de México en cuadros como: *Tehuanas* (1982), *Trilogía de la Independencia de México* (1988), *Zapata Stables* (1993), *La Malinche* (1993).

En fin, este hacedor plástico tiene sus raíces en México pero los árboles de su obra, con todas sus ramas han crecido en Seattle, Washington, desde hace poco más de 40 años. Aunque profundamente mexicano, la universalidad de su trabajo, lo ha convertido también en un artista "auténticamente americano, en el sentido real, hemisférico de este término" tal y como lo expresa Lauro Flores.[16] Entre más lejos, más cerca; entre más cosmopolita, más mexicano.

Y si como dice Fernando Benítez, "de hecho el mexicano sobrepone paisajes" [17]; nuestro pintor los ha inventado devolviéndonos el placer de la mirada que se mueve por entre sus cuadros con una delectación pocas veces vista. ¿Es verdad lo que vemos? Este espectáculo natural es una transfiguración y una comprobación de los poderes que tiene la pintura para enriquecer la realidad. Jardín de las delicias en el trópico, poética de lo maravilloso plenamente asequible, celebración de los sentidos y de nuestra conexión con el centro de la tierra.

Todo ello es posible porque, como expresa Pablo Neruda: "México, con su nopal y su serpiente; México florido y espinudo, seco y huracanado, violento de dibujo y de color, violento de erupción y creación, [nos cubre] con su sortilegio y su luz sorpresiva."[18]

Alfredo Arreguín pinta el alma de México y con ello pone a funcionar la música terrestre. Cuando eso sucede el cielo enrojece y las nubes son un abanico que se abre…

Ciudad de México

---

16 Lauro Flores, op. cit, p. 2.

17 Fernando Benítez, *Los primeros mexicanos*, México, Ediciones Era, 1965, p. 45.

18 Pablo Neruda, *Confieso que he vivido*, Memorias, Barcelona, Editorial Seix Barral, 1974, p.213.

José Luis Alcubilla

Alfredo Arreguín: the jungle and mosaic

Painting fabulous tiled display; painting: *Allegory of Wealth,* painting: praise of color, magnified in the images that unfold: A sight to behold that celebrates amazing paths of geometry... Painting thoroughly organized based on patterns that are masks, which are concentric circles, which are lines, arbors and unusual profusion of embellishments in the frieze, gorge and façade to the tree of life; right angles and vegetation that come and go, reproduce, be reborn or end only to start again in another game of the square, another mantra color to the horizon, another dream that wakes: Eve before Adam . . . This is the painting of Alfredo Arreguin, a teacher capable of staging in his paintings fragments of magical realism we are delivered only when we accept that poetry exists, that music is an essence of waves and breakers; the theater in the afternoon can be seen from the terrace and the architecture of the forest is under continuous rain, bountiful land delivered to your paradise imagined ... Unquestionably, then, tropicality of his work that certainly favors a true visual magnificence in his paintings he has matured into a style that draws attention given the complexity of their starting points and of course their results: unmatched port that grounds wisdom and feelings, reason and the free flow of fascination that very rarely a painter is able to raise . . .

How was this artistic proposal made possible? What are the ingredients that make it endure? In what way was projecting this work? Undoubtedly, in the creative consciousness of this master there are two defining ingredients: the culture of Mexico, the country where he was born and what he has learned over nearly sixty years living in the Pacific Northwest in the United States—more specifically in Seattle, Washington the state's largest city. Born in Morelia, Michoacan, January 20, 1935 he is educated in the house of his maternal grandparents. While still a child, his grandmother Pepita took him to the markets where he came in contact with Mexican folk art. What it taught him, along with other experiences, allowed him to begin contemplating, among others things, jewelry designs, blankets and pottery that reveal its imaginative and formal richness. Above all, its ornamental structures which he later integrated into his work amid a splendid fact that nature abhors a vacuum. AND: Curious predestination? His grandfather Carlos who enrolled him in the "People's School of Fine Arts, an institution linked to the Universidad Michoacana de San Nicolás of Hidalgo. That was his formal introduction to art. Thus, twelve years and during 1947 and 1948 he took several courses and among other things, the basic principles of drawing and painting."[19]

Some years later, this youth faced various expectations and hazards that were meaningful to his life. After the death of his grandparents he went to live with his mother, but she soon sent him to the city of Mexico—the time called for him to live with his father. Already in the decade of the fifties, the young Alfredo entered the vocational school Peralvillo. He learned various skills—carpentry and printing, electricity and other interlocking trades. His father conceived of a possible profession for him—engineering. To get his foot in the door, Alfredo became an assistant to a couple of engineers commissioned by the federal government. The task was to

19 Lauro Flores, *Alfredo Arreguín, Patterns, Designs and Nature,* Seattle and London, University of Washington Press, Second Edition, 2007, p. 10. (To amplify details of the life and work of this artist, look at the last book and also:Tomás Ybarra-Fraustro, *El universo de Alfredo Arreguín, en: Alfredo Arreguín, el universo vegetal, animal y humano de un pintor moreliano*, Morelia, Michoacán, México, Universidad Michoacana de San Nicolás de Hidalgo, 1989.)

build irrigation canals in the state of Guerrero and more specifically in the village of San Luis de la Loma. This isolated town is situated thirty miles from the coast—back then, surrounded "the dense jungle *guerrerense* over twenty streams" as Lauro Flores says. Arreguín was hosted in the front section of the town brothel, while his preceptors rested at the port of Acapulco. He, a young man, was impressed by the bustle and zafarranchos (rowdy crowds) that were heard all the time, including gunfire. Fearing someone might harm him one night he took refuge in an oven that was in the courtyard adjacent to the house. Upon waking he realized that the oven was overrun with scorpions and was amazed that they did not bite him. Lauro Flores also noted that for Arreguín, as a teenager, "this factinstantaneously produced startling results in him a sense of wonder that instilled a great respect for the forest and its inhabitants, feeling that preserves until today. From that moment the future painter perceived in nature an atmosphere of harmony. Your indebted to it is what motivated you to realize that long has been paying tribute in his pictures to this mysterious world, imposing and dangerous but extraordinarily beautiful . . . So did the first contact with the jungle Arreguín . . ." [20]

After his apprenticeship, he returned to the federal district and completed his education in vocational trades. He attended the National Preparatory School in the Antiguo Colegio de San Ildefonso. He spent his nights and days there until the summer of 1955. His twenties reflected a duality, like rolling two in a dice game—symbolizing a "dualism in which the whole dialectic supports every effort, every battle, every movement. The division is the principle of multiplication as well as the synthesis . . . The two expressed as an antagonism and reciprocity." One day he was driving and by chance met Alfred and Dorothy Dam and their three daughters—they were lost, and wanted to reach the Castle of Chapultepec. He led them to the door of the castle and they were so grateful they invited him to dinner. Days later, he accompanied them on a trip to Acapulco. The friendship quickly deepened and the Dam Family invited him to travel to Seattle where they reside in the district of Green Lake. Stars aligned, making neat records of what could be and was. In January 1956, he visited them on a two week trip. He expressed his desire to continue studying and his hosts offered the possibility of Alfredo moving to Seattle, living at home, and studying at the University of Washington. In November 1956, he decided to stay. Nearly sixty years later, the reciprocity, and synchronicity—Alfredo and the Dams disrupted the world with a generous bet; the promise of another land.

And the decision to settle in that city led to a Bachelor's degree (1967) and a Master of Fine Arts (1969). After some initial dabbling, he chose architecture and interior design. However, realizing that he did not want follow the conventions of a traditional profession, he took a great risk. He decided to be an artist. The American art scene at that time was characterized by Abstract Expressionism of the New York School and Pop Art. He was not influenced by them because his early works bear more reslemblance to German Expressionism. Certain variations were rendered in a manner that evoked thoughts of Edward Hopper. After his departure from the college, Arreguín experienced internal conflict, abandoning painting. Between 1971 and 1972 he only drew. However, according to Tomás Ybarra Fraustro, an encounter with the figurative painter Elmer Bischoff,his teacher and supporter, led Alfredo to develop an original vision. This encouragement to find his own voice would go to the foundation of Alfredo's imagined interior.

20 Cfr. Lauro Flores, Ibidem, p. 16-17

The daring plunge that cemented what he wanted. Approaching this mysterious process of getting a glimpse into his pictures during 1973 and 1974 we see a painter who begins to manipulate colorful geometric patterns and who, over the years, refines them to their maximum. The work *Emerald Island* (1970) reflects and important aesthetic, suggesting we seem to be seeing the bottom of a fountain in a Moorish palace. Definitive in this work, spanning over 40 years, we see Arreguín sieze ornament as a vehicle for pictorial expression.

What does that mean in the end? Unquestionably, the lexicon he interprets in architecture and applied arts are found already in ancient cultures and over the centuries in all civilizations. It is impossible list them all—filigree geometric or naturalistic Egyptians and Romans lining dance floors, the plasticity of plants, and ornamentation structurally influenced by Art Nouveau. Transcendant paintings emerge when the minor arts become magnified and validated it as an essential ingredient of great art. At this level, the work of Gustav Klimt can be a prototypical example of this operation. However, in the twentieth century, artists did not practice this integration. Instead, the world of painting and ornamentation remained estranged. It is only with artists such as Alfredo Arreguin that the accumulated wealth in the history of ornament is recovered and certainly becomes a fundamental part of the pictorial phenomenon. In this sense what draws much attention in production, is the set of plastic infrastructures that this artist was able to find and certainly portray in their work. Tess Gallagher is right to say that "Designs (patterns) Arreguin come from Mexican colonial art, baroque facades of churches, pre-Columbian decorative art, animal and floral motifs Pottery Tlaquepaque, but perhaps more handicrafts directly from Michoacan and Guerrero. Moreover, one can see there traces of Islamic architecture, painting Tantric India and the Far sources and environment Eastern as diverse as kimonos or sword handles. I used to look for books with wallpaper patterns and designs during my travels. Recently for his birthday I sent a volume designs used in Chinese gates ... "[21]

Every true artist has his fertile lands and clear skies, and calligraphers are housed in the mines of his brain; the problem is not in knowing that heritage but what is done with it. When sailing, one is always carrying luggage but the journey has to be conceptualized a new one; only then can we talk about authentic creation . . . This painter has solved an equation in which he claims the planetary value and timeless value of the Mexican artistic motifs, equating them with other art forms, as belonging to the universal culture. A blanket and a mandala are not so different. Here a tribute to the creative blood of a country but also a proposal for combination. This achievement is only surpassed by the continental stature of his work, by the assertion of the creative power that is received from the pure-water forest and perpetuo-growth in countries like ours. Indeed, forests—in all its exuberance—the Virgin that evoke and protect, other deep landscapes seen from within, portraits of liberators, poets and social activists; Frida, one two and many Fridas. Carpets, rugs or tapestries, tables, canopies inhabited by gods, the most intense guadamecí philosophy. Hers is a kaleidoscopic view of shifting layers of patterns that could be a precedent-twenty years earlier-than today offer computer programs for designing and editing of images. It is no wonder, therefore, that this artist's work spread through countless exhibitions, as well as prizes, awards and honors he has received, including important collections. Like Frida, Alfredo Arreguín is one of the most prominent painters of Latin American origin who today lives and works in the United States. And he, satisfied and energetic, always knew: the revelations of this country seen from near and far are always the same: a daily music, endless life returned fire, joy, galaxies in a line. "The ancient Mexicans left their embroidered story hidden in the jungle ..."[22]

21 Tess Gallagher, Preface to the book: Lauro Flores, Op cit., P. XXIV.

22 Pablo Neruda, *I confess that I have lived*, Memories, Mexico, Ed. Barral, 1974, p. 215.

Alfredo Arreguín: la selva y el mosaico

Pintura: fabuloso despliegue de mosaicos; pintura alegoría de la abundancia, pintura; elogio del color magnificado en las imágenes que se desdoblan: un espectáculo para la vista que asombrada celebra los recorridos de la geometría . . .Pintura organizada minuciosamente a base de patrones que son máscaras, que son círculos concéntricos, que son líneas, enramadas e inusitada profusión de barroquismos en el friso, la garganta y la fachada-árbol de la vida; los ángulos rectos y la vegetación que van y vienen, se reproducen, renacen o terminan sólo para volver a comenzar en otro juego del cuadrado, otro mantra de color para el horizonte, otro sueño del que se despierta: *Eva antes de Adán*. . . Esta es la pintura de Alfredo Arreguín, un maestro capaz de escenificar en sus cuadros fragmentos de lo real maravilloso que se nos entregan sólo cuando aceptamos que la poesía existe, que la música en una esencia de olas y rompientes; que el teatro de la tarde puede verse desde la terraza y que la arquitectura del bosque es el bajo continuo de la lluvia, tierra pródiga ofrendada a su paraíso imaginado. Incuestionable entonces la tropicalidad de su trabajo que sin duda propicia una verdadera magnificencia visual que en sus telas ha madurado dentro de un estilo que llama la atención dada la complejidad de sus puntos de partida y desde luego de sus resultado: incomparable puerto en el que encallan la sabiduría y las sensaciones, la razón y el libre fluir de una fascinación que muy pocas veces un pintor es capaz de suscitar.

¿Cómo se hizo posible esta propuesta artística? ¿Cuáles son los ingredientes que la conforman? ¿De qué manera fue proyectándose esta trabajo? Indudable que en la conciencia creativa de este maestro hay dos ingredientes definitorios: La cultura de México, país en el que nace y, lo que ha aprendido a lo largo casi sesenta años viviendo en el Noroeste del Pacifico en los Estados Unidos y más concretamente en Seattle, la ciudad más grande en el estado de Washington. Así pues, habiendo nacido en Morelia, Michoacán en 20 de enero de 1935 se le educa en la casa de sus abuelos maternos. Siendo todavía un niño, su abuela Pepita lo lleva a los mercados donde toma contacto con el arte popular mexicano. Lo que ésta la enseña y otras experiencias le permiten empezar a contemplar, entre otros, lo diseños de joyería, sarapes y cerámica que le revelan su riqueza imaginativa y formal y sobre todo sus estructuras ornamentales la cuales más tarde integra en su trabajo en medio de un espléndido horror al vacío. Y: ¿Curiosa predestinación? Es su abuelo Carlos quien lo inscribe en la "Escuela Popular de Belles Artes, institución vinculada a la Universidad Michoacana de San Nicolás de Hidalgo. Esa fue su introducción formal al arte. Así, a los doces años y durante 1947 y 1948 sique múltiples curso en los que aprende, entre otras cosas, los principios básicos de dibujo y pintura."[1]

Algunos años después su juventud le entrega varias expectativas y azares que serán muy significativos para su vida. Tras la muerte de sus abuelos va a vivir con su madre pero ésta pronto lo envía a la ciudad de México; en ella conoce por fin a su padre. Ya en esta última, inicia la década de los años cincuenta y el joven Alfredo ingresa en la escuela vocacional de Peralvillo. En ésta aprende varios oficios disímbolos, carpintería e imprenta, electricidad y trabar relación con esa carrera se le hace asistente de un par de ingenieros que comisionados por el gobierno federal, habrían de construir canales de irrigación en el estado de Guerrero y más concretamente en el pueblo de San Luis

1 Lauro Flores, *Alfredo Arreguín, Diseños, sueños, y naturaleza,* Seattle and London, University of Washington Press, Segunda Edición, 2007, p. 10. (Para ampliar datos de la vida y la obra de este artista, confróntese este última libro y también: Tomás Ybarra-Fraustro, *El universo de Alfredo Arreguín, en Alfredo Arreguín, el universo vegetal, animal y humano de un pintor moreliano,* Morelia, Michoacán, Universidad Michoacana de San Nicolás de Hidalgo, 1989)

de la Loma. Esta localidad, casi aislada, se sitúa a cincuenta kilómetros de la costa; en aquel entonces la rodeaba "la espesura de la jungla guerrerense y más de veinte arroyos" según nos dice Lauro Flores. Se le había alojado frente al burdel del pueblo y mientras sus preceptores se van a descansar al puerto de Acapulco, él, un jovencito, impresionado por el bullicio y los zafarranchos que en aquel se escuchaban incluyendo aledaño a la casa. Al despertar se da cuenta de que aquel esta invadido de alacranes y se asombra de que no le picaran. Al adolecente, "este hecho le resulta sobrecogedor produciendo instantáneamente en él una sensación de maravilla que le infundió un gran respeto por el bosque y sus habitantes, sentimiento que conserva hasta hoy . . . A partir de ese momento el futuro pintor percibió en la naturaleza una atmósfera de armonía. Su deuda a gratitud a la misma es lo que la ha motivado a concretar ese prolongado homenaje que ha venido rindiendo en sus cuadros a este mundo misterioso, imponente y peligroso pero extraordinariamente bello . . . Así se produjo el primer contacto de Arreguín con la selva . . ."[2]

Aunque esta última todavía tendrá que esperar su glorificación pues lares aguardaban (destino verdadero . . .) sin que él lo previera. Regresa al distrito federal y una vez terminados sus estudios en lo vocacional mencionada, asiste ahora a la Escuela Nacional Preparatoria en el Antiguo Colegio de San Ildefonso. Pasan las noches y los días hasta el verano 1955 en que el juego de sus dados coincide con su edad' la veintena, el dos como símbolo "del dualismo en el que se apoya toda dialéctica, todo esfuerzo, todo combate, todo movimiento. La división que es el principio de la multiplicación tanto como el de la síntesis . . . El dos expresa pues un antagonismo y también una reciprocidad . . ."[3] Aquel día va en su coche y por un azar conoce por un azar conoce a Alfred y Dorothy Dam y sus tres hijas . . . Estan perdidos, quieren llegar al Castillo de Chapultepec. Los llega hasta la puerta de éste y agradecidos lo convidan a cenar. Días después les acompaña en a viaje a Acapulco. La Amistad se enriquece rápidamente y la Familia Dam lo invita a viajar a Seattle donde residen en el distrito de Green Lake. Astros enfilados, pulcros registros de lo que podía ser y fue. En enero de 1956 les visita en un viaje de dos semanas y como él expresara su deseo de seguir estudiando, sus anfitriones le ofrecen la posibilidad de que se mude a Seattle, viva en su casa y estudie en la Universidad de Washington. En noviembre de 1956 vuelve a esta ciudad para quedarse. Hace casi sesenta años, la reciprocidad y todas las facilidades; la traducción del dos—él y ellos—trastocada en apuesta generosa; la promesa de otra tierra también suya . . .

Y de la decisión de establecerse en aquella ciudad a los grados que consigue en dicha universidad una licenciatura (1967) y una maestría en Bellas Artes (1969). Algunos balbuceos iniciales le llevan a la arquitectura y el diseño de interiores pero dándose cuenta de que no tenía porqué seguir las convenciones de una profesión tradicional toma su camino asumiendo todos los riesgos: decide ser un artista. La escena de las plástica norteamericana de aquel momento involucra prácticas creativas relacionadas con el Expresionismo Abstracto de la Escuela Nueva York y, el Arte Pop. No se ve influido por éstos pues sus primeras obras tienen que ver más bien con el Expresionismo Alemán y ciertas variaciones a un costumbrismo que podría recordamos a Edward Hopper. Significativo además que su salida de la universidad le provoque confusión; por esta razón abandona la pintura y entre 1971 y 1972 sólo dibuja. Con todo, en un reencuentro con el pintor figurativo Elmer Bischoff, quien había sido su maestro y mostrado interés en su obra, éste le insta- nos dice Tomás Ybarra Fraustro' a

---

2 Cfr. Lauro Flores, Ibidiem, p. 16-17.

3 Jean Chevalier y Alain Gheerbrant, *Diccionario de los símbolos,* Barcelona, Ed. Herder, 1999, p. 426.

desarrollar un visión original, lo cual tanto propicia que regrese a sus telas como igualmente que vaya al fondo de su imaginería interior. La osada zambullida que concreta en esa época le lleva a descubrir lo que era y lo que quería. Este misterioso proceso de conseguir una visión propia fructifica en cuadros de 1973 y 1974 en los que vemos a un pintor que empieza a manejar coloridos patrones geométricas que con el paso de los años refina a grados máximos. La obra *Emerald Island* (1970) es un importante antecedente dentro de su estilo pues desde los mosaicos que nos sugiere parece que estamos viendo el fondo de una fuente en un palacete morisco. Definitivo que en esta obra y las que ha realizado a lo largo de más de 40 años, nos encontramos con el reconocimiento del ornamento como vehículo para la expresión pictórica.

¿Qué es lo que esto último quiere decir? Incuestionable que los lenguajes de éste proyectados en arquitectura o artes aplicadas los encontramos ya en las culturas antiguas y con el paso de los siglos en todas las civilizaciones. Imposible hacer el enlistado que va de la filigrana geométrica o naturalista de los pisos egipcios o romanos a la danza de la línea, el valor plástico de lo vegetal y dicho ornamento concebido como símbolo estructural del Art Nouveau. Como parte de este último movimiento pero en el rubro de pintura se hace una traslación, es decir lo que otrora era dominio o espacio de las mal llamadas artes menores ahora se magnifica validándolo como ingrediente esencial de gran arte. En este nivel la obra de Gustav Klimt puede ser un ejemplo prototípico de esta operación. No obstante, en las artes del siglo XX aquella no se convirtió en una práctica que muchos cultivaran más bien, la pintura y los universos de la ornamentación permanecieron distanciados. Es sólo con artistas como Alfredo Arreguín que la riqueza acumulada en la historia del ornamento se recupera y desde luego se convierte en parte fundamental del fenómeno pictórico. En este sentido lo que llama mucho la atención en su producción, es el conjunto de infraestructuras plásticas que este artista fue capaz de encontrar y desde luego de proyectar en su trabajo. Tess Gallagher tiene razón al decir que: "Los diseños (patterns) de Arreguín provienen del arte colonial mexicano, de las fachadas de las iglesias barrocas, del arte decorativo precolombino, de los motivos animales y florales de la cerámica de Tlaquepaque, pero quizás más directamente de las artesanías de Michoacán y Guerrero. Más aún puede ver allí huellas de la arquitectura islámica, de la pintura tántrica de la India y, de fuentes del lejano y del medio oriente tan diversas como los kimonos, o las empuñaduras de espada. Yo solía buscarle libros de modelos con pape tapiz y diseños durante mis viajes. Recientemente para su cumpleaños le envié un volumen con diseños utilizados en las portones chinos . . ."[4]

Todo artista verdadero tiene tierras fértiles, cielos despejados y manantiales por doquier: el problema no está en conocer dicha herencia sino qué se hace con ella. Al navegar siempre se lleva un equipaje pero en el periplo ha de conceptuarse uno nuevo; sólo así hablamos de auténtica creación. Este pintor ha resuelto una ecuación en la que reivindica el valor planetario e intemporal de manifestaciones artísticas entrañablemente mexicanas equiparándolas con otras pertenecientes a la cultura universal. Un sarape y un mandala no son tan diferentes. Aquí un homenaje a la sangre de creativa de un país pero también una propuesta para el hermanamiento. Este logro sólo se ve superado por la estatura continental de su obra, por la afirmación del poderío creador que se recibe de la selva—agua pura crecimiento perpetuo—que en país como el nuestro marcan el ritmo del corazón y la temperatura del cuerpo. En su obra entonces selvas—en toda su exuberancia—y, las Virgenes que las evocan protegen, paisajes profundos vistos desde dentro, retratos de libertadores, poetas y luchadores sociales; de Frida Kahlo, una y dos y tantas Fridas. Y alfombras, tapetas o gobelinos-cuadros, doseles habitado

4 Tess Gallagher, Prefacio al libro: Lauro Flores, Op. Cit, p. XXIV.

por los dioses, la más intensa filosofía de guadamecí; la suya visión caleidoscópica de cambiantes capas de patrones que podrían ser un antecedente—veinte años antes—de lo que hoy nos ofrecen lo gráficos en 3D y los programas para diseño y edición de imágenes. No extraña por tanto la difusión de su trabajo a través de innumerables exposiciones, también los premios reconocimientos y honores que ha recibido, las importantes colecciones en las que su obra está presente.[5] Alfredo Arreguín es uno de los más prominentes pintores de origen latinoamericano que, hoy por hoy, viven y trabajan de cerca o de lejos siempre son las mismas; una música diaria, el gozo del color, galaxias en una línea, el fuego inacabable de la vida devuelta. "Los antiguos mexicanos dejaron su bordada historia escondida entre la selva . . ."[6]

5 Para conocer en detalle todo éstas, consúltese: http://www.lindahodgesgallery.com/#!alfredo-arreguin/c1806.

6 Pablo Neruda, *Confieso que he vivido,* Memorias, México, Ed. Seix-Barral, 1974, p. 215

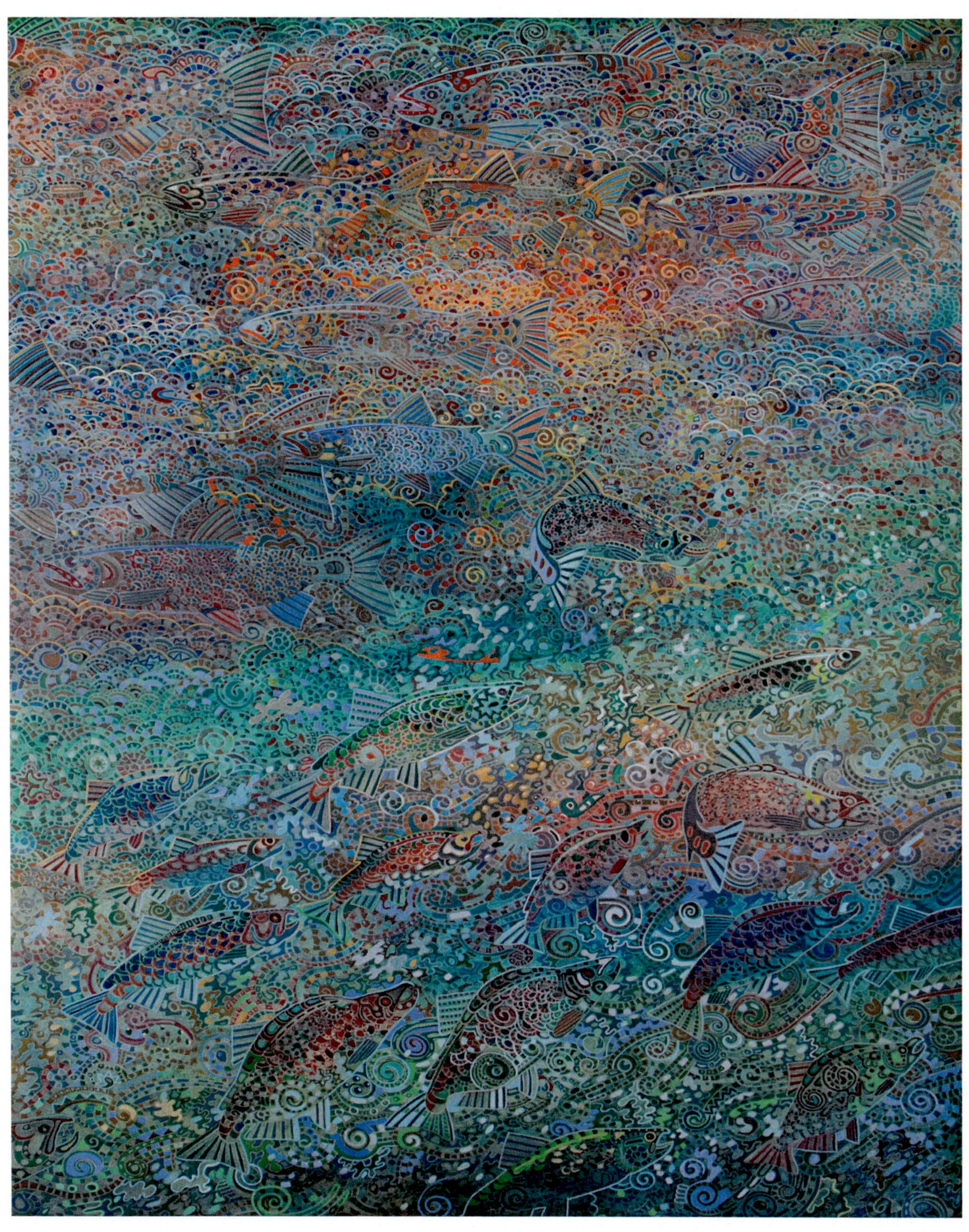

The Hero's Journey, 1994, 68 X 51 in., collection of the National Academy of Sciences

J.D. Talasek

For the Purposes of Rational Imagination

What is this object that hangs on the wall? Such vibrant colors.

Is it ornamentation? Decorative?

Or is it a portal? A bridge between ideas? A platform to inspire discussion and imagination?

Alfredo Arreguín's oil painting entitled *Hero's Journey* (1994) hangs in the halls of the National Academy of Sciences (NAS), located on Constitution Avenue in Washington DC. *Hero's Journey* depicts a waterscape of fish that fills the canvas from edge to edge. Arreguín's painting feels personal. Memories of Mexican culture inform his intricate and brilliantly colored canvas. It is also reminisces of the natural landscape of his home country as well as the flora and fauna of the Pacific Northwest, where he currently lives. The hypnotic and meditative patterns allude to pre-Aztec images, Mexican tiles, and geometric and optical patterns. The stylized way that Arreguín depicts the fish borrows from Mexican traditions and connects us with nature through a cultural lens. This raises a question about our relationship to the natural world. To what extent do we construct our perception of the natural world? Arreguín offers us a place to consider this question. Viewing the painting, one feels as if they are standing on a rocky ledge looking down into a glistening stream (or is it a dream?). Fish swim in the water's flow—dynamic, kinetic and full of life. This could be a river in Washington State where the artist lives, or perhaps it is a memory of a stream in Alfredo's birth place of Mexico. The depiction could be of any river in the migratory path of the fish or simply a conjured image from the artist's imagination. One imagines the sunlight reflecting off the scales of the fish bursting into a prism of colors.

In speaking of how culture constructs meaning in the natural world, it is not the intent to assign such a lofty aspiration or responsibility to the artist but rather to simply acknowledge the potential. To start answering the question about the impact of culture on perception one must interrupt the current cognitive patterns. It is not enough to simply chant, *c'est ne pas un pipe* about man-made objects with Magritte. A way of understanding a concept can take many forms and at many different levels. In the case of Arreguín's work, he offers a perspective on the environment that resonates with Native American attitudes on the subject. His paintings honor the land as a source for water, food and life is a core value. In keeping with that sentiment, his pieces offer a sense of the sacred. Even for those who are not religiously or spiritually inclined, Arreguín's work evokes the reverence for something bigger and more powerful than humans. When people look at *The Hero's Journey*, Arreguín gently helps them shed the viewpoint of humans as the conquerors of nature. He walks them, instead, to the edge of imagining oneself as part of nature, working within it and respecting it as both a resource as well as a deadly force. Furthermore, this does not remain a didactic work or modern moralist play, intended simply to perpetuate a given cultural value. The artist is able to make visual sense out of complex and contradictory ideas ranging from the pragmatic to the emotional. What countless range of ideas might this work inspire?

At the base of our cultural impact on perception is the fact that art and art making is transformative. For the artist it is the expression of an idea, emotion, observation or concern. That is why when encountering master artists, like Arreguín, people resist going, "Aha! I see what they meant." Rational faculties of cognition are constantly trying to decode patterns. That is why the geometric patterns of Arreguín go so far in offering us "rational imagination." They interrupt our natural impulse to decode. For the viewer, connecting with the art object may or may not be what the artist intended. How a viewer constructs meaning remains their own personal experience. It may be interesting and informative to know what an artist intended, but with Arreguín, he understands there are too many layers in each person's experience. Understanding that fact, he offers the viewer multiple layers to allow them a more enriched experience. He understands that his own intended meaning may or may not influence the viewer's connection to the work on a personal intuitive level. For instance, Simon Schama in his book *Landscape and Memory*, talks about the social, political, and personal meanings that are embedded into viewing a landscape. He provides a river as an example. Viewing a river may conjure memories of childhood afternoons spent swimming or sun bathing along its shore. However, he also points out that rivers, viewed in a historical context, represent sources of power as towns relied upon them for transport and commerce. Perceptions of rivers turn political in a pluralistic democracy as bargains and compromises take place. In the name of advancement, altering or even obliterating the natural landscape comes about and the group again becomes the conqueror of the natural world. Arreguín, in contrast, brings to bear a reminder of the cultural and personal relationship to the land and the flora and fauna around us. We are a part of the landscape through memory and experience. Therefore, in forcing us to admit that we are shaped by our personal beliefs, culture and biases, Arreguín's painting do not remain a passive experience. We filter our response to the fish in the waterscape. Our memory filters our perception of the river swirling.

There is yet another external layer of perception. We also form our perceptions within the context of the space where a painting hangs. *The Hero's Journey* hangs among other works of art in the NAS collection. A print of an eagle by naturalist John Audubon hangs around the corner. Ariel photographs by David Maizel's strip mines and a painting from Joy Garnett's *Strange Weather* series create a diverse constellation of ideas about the environment and our relationship to it. In the adjacent Great Hall, the dome of the ceiling is adorned with the iconography of Hildreth Meière's depicting the history and role of science in society as it was understood in the 1920s. This was Meière's first large commission and a ground breaking accomplishment for her as she learned to collaborate in the male-dominated world of engineers and architects. The bronze work of her contemporary Lee Lawrie, the foremost architectural sculptor of the time, can be seen throughout the building as well as on the exterior. As if asking the visitor to imagine the past and future of architecture, these historical works are juxtaposed by a document of Philip Beesley's *Sentient Chamber*, an immersive environment of responsive models that begs the question, "How do we imagine the spaces we want to occupy in the future?"

Art, especially, falls prey to the cultural perceptions of space. Paintings hang in museums. Paintings hang in galleries. Paintings hang in homes. Each location allows your mind to relegate them to the background of a pre-constructed set of values. Museums construct meaning from their history, prestige and wealth. Galleries construct meaning around the mercantile. Homes construct meaning around the intimate. Imagine, then, for a moment what it means for art to exist at a science institution-a space that has a history and context that differs from an art museum or gallery. Meaning for the viewer shifts and morphs in response to the setting—a constellation of ideas represented in art. The tradition of art at this distinguished building of science dates back to the original design actualized in 1924 by architect Bertrem Grosvenor Goodhue. Goodhue, along with the building committee, engaged leading artists of the time to adorn the building with imagery that would inspire thought of the history of science and its impact and role in society. Additionally, for almost forty years, the Academy has hosted rotating art exhibits that continuously introduces new ideas from artists to those who visit and work in the building. By continuing to introduce the work of contemporary artist in this way, reminds us that ideas evolve. Scientific discoveries and ideas intertwine with social and cultural norms in a dynamic system, one influencing the other.

The context in which art is displayed effects the viewer's perception and the interpretation of meaning. To reiterate, either on a conscious or subconscious level, visitors hold expectations and make assumptions. This is compounded by the practices of those in power positions; curators, directors, and historians. As Rudolf Arnheim points out in *Art and Visual Perception*, "No object is perceived as unique or isolated. Seeing something involves assigning it a place in the whole: a location in space...." Arnheim is referring to the elements within a piece of artwork, but the idea remains applicable even when a person steps back from the art object itself, redefining the whole. It is this process referred to by Arnheim—to intentionally include, not only the object, but the context in which it is placed.

In the case of *Hero's Journey*, as well as all of the work in the NAS collection, the original vision, or intent, is changed by the history and purpose of the building in which it is housed. The National Academy of Sciences was chartered by Congress, under Abraham Lincoln in 1863 to provide state of the art information on issues pertaining to science and technology. The NAS continues to serve both Congress and the public in this capacity. Although the institution existed for approximately the first sixty years of its life as a virtual institution under the umbrella of the Smithsonian, a physical building was constructed in 1924, giving the NAS a presence and a visible identity. Interpretation of the work within the building becomes intertwined with that history. The architecture of the NAS building and the art work within both reflect and participate in this history.

Although Arreguín did not, (nor any of the artists in the NAS collection, for that matter), intend that the NAS building end up as the final home for the work, Miwon Kwon's writings on site-specific art work has relevance. In her book *One Place After Another: Site-Specific Art and Locational Identity*, Kwon states there are three paradigms for site-specific work—phenomenological, social/institutional, and discursive. Phenomenology is a philosophy that refers to a method of inquiry based on the premise that reality consists of objects and events as they are perceived or understood in human consciousness and not of anything independent of human consciousness. In other words, a critical component of site-specific work relies on the viewer to react and respond in order for the work to be complete. Site-specific art was initially based upon the viewer's experience of a site defined primarily by the site's physical attributes such as the size of the room, ceiling heights, scale, texture, climate conditions, lighting conditions, and so forth. However, there also exists a social and political unction of the space in which art is viewed. Again, the modern gallery/museum space, for instance, with its stark white walls, artificial lighting, controlled climate, and pristine architectonics, is perceived not solely in terms of basic dimensions and proportion but "as an institutional disguise, a normative exhibitions convention serving an ideological function." The seemingly benign architectural features of a gallery/museum, in other words, were deemed coded mechanisms that actively disassociate the space of art from the outer world. It furthers the institution's idealist imperative of rendering itself and its values "objective," "disinterested," and "true." Sites of exhibition or display are culturally specific situations that generate particular expectations and narratives regarding art and art history. Institutional framing of art in other words not only distinguishes qualitative value, it also produces and reproduces specific forms of knowledge that are historically located and culturally determined—not at all universal or timeless standards. Intriguingly, viewers discovering this for the first time again peel back a layer of their cultural perception and react to Arreguín in a different light, when they view his work at the NAS.

This brings up an interesting juxtaposition of words. Does an art museum's coded architecture really imply they are "objective," "disinterested" and "true?" Have they then coopted the words traditionally associated with the sciences? Part of the answer lies in the following historical account bringing us back to a "rational imagination." It speaks to why both disciplines can share the words. In July of 1817, British patent no 4136 was awarded to Sir David Brewster for an optical instrument called "the kaleidoscope." He lived as a Scottish physicist, mathematician, astronomer, and writer. A kaleidoscope basically consists of a tube (often of wood or metal) that contains loose bits of colored material (glass, plastic and sometimes even liquids) held together with two clear plates on one end and an eye piece on the other. In between there are two plane mirrors placed such that reflect the materials in an endless variety of patterns. Variations of the kaleidoscope have existed since antiquity and have inspired several different types of inventions through the centuries. Nevertheless, Brewster's experiments with light polarization, reflection and refraction led him to refine a system of mirrors angled in relationship to the viewer and the "object box" (holding case that could contain a variety of objects —liquid, translucent and opaque) that would yield what Brewster felt were the optimum and most pleasing forms. Brewster thought that the instrument would be popular for the "purposes of rational amusement." However, he also felt that there was more to be had. He imagined the tool as an instrument utilized by artists to help imagine an "infinity of patterns." He envisioned the artists actualizing the patterns with the assistance of tools of the time such as a camera lucida or a magic lantern. He even wrote about the possibilities in his manifesto on the topic.

Brewster, in the end, helps inform our experience with *The Hero's Journey.* Breaking down the word coined by Brewster to its Greek origins, ***kaleidoscope*** simply means *observation of beautiful forms.* Like a kaleidoscope, Arreguín's paintings present the viewer with and array of fantastic unexpected colors and shapes. One may even have a similar sensation of awe and wonder. Like Brewster, however, we sense more purpose at play than "rational amusement." There is a shift in seeing and thus a shift in perspective in Arreguín's paintings that is a spark to our "rational imagination." The vibrant colors combined with the context of the building generates a kaleidoscopic experience that is both physical and mental.

Furthermore, like the kaleidoscope, artists change our perspective and challenge our way of thinking. They interrupt our normal patterns of thought with the unexpected. A noted example of this type of shift is when Don Ingber, a cell biologist from Harvard Medical School and Children's Hospital, found inspiration in a piece of modern sculpture. Kenneth Snelson's *Needle Tower* at the Hirshhorn Museum of Art—exists as a system of pipes and wires held together by tension wires that appear to defy gravity. The sculpture exemplifies a tensegrity building system, first described by Buckminister Fuller, the inventor of the geodesic dome. Such a structure gains its shape stability by balancing tension and compression between struts and strings. Snelson's sculpture inspired a scientific breakthrough in thinking for Ingber about the structure of molecular cells—a shift in thinking about cells as mechanical and structural, and not just chemical. Ingber, through further research and experimentation, showed that cells use tension to stabilize their structure. And that tensegrity not only gives cells their shape, but helps regulate their biochemistry. Ingber's breakthrough, inspired by Snelson's *Needle Tower*, was ground breaking in his field.

When Snelson created his work, he had no way of knowing its impact nor how it would catalyze threads of thinking that would inform other disciplines. It is nearly impossible to track the trajectory that leads to genius insight or where inspiration originates and equally impossible to predict. What triggers a *Eureka* moment? The subtle experiences, the chance encounters or subconscious moments that shape a person's mind along the trajectory of their lives can contribute to a moment of insight, yet these influences are typically impossible to determine direct impact. Ingber's awareness and credit to the work of an artist and architect is atypical. Nonetheless, it suggests the power of an artist to interrupt our thinking process and provide us with a new perspective. Not all inspiration is created equal and Ingber's example, of course, is an extreme. Yet, there are gradations of impact. Perhaps a work of art may reinforce a value or principle or spark a moment of inspiration. It can contribute to a trajectory of thinking that may prove beneficial even if unacknowledged. Such a process is not formulaic nor predictable. Creativity and discovery share moments by both the artist and the scientist. It is a phenomena of the creative process—not artistic nor scientific but intrinsically human—that is worth noting.

When Brewster coined the term kaleidoscope, he gave the English language a new word and a new concept. Something that is kaleidoscopic causes a shift of patterns, a dynamic succession of moments or a diverse collection of ideas. The kaleidoscopic nature of Arreguín's paintings run deeper than the canvas surface. It is a portal. It leads us towards a myriad of ideas that oscillates between painting traditions and the natural world shifting our perspectives and sparking our imagination. On the surface, it is a brilliant display of colors and shapes that practically overloads the senses. Housed in a building associated with science, it has the potential to shift our perception and ignite unexpected insight. Like the mirrors in a kaleidoscope, it alters our perspective and builds bridges between ideas. Arreguín's painting is a kaleidoscope of the imagination.

Amalia Mesa-Baines

Arreguín, the Master of his Universe

Alfredo Arreguín is a legend in Chicano art and his works are unique in their form and aesthetic power. Born in Mexico, his interest in art began when he was a young child and his family convinced the authorities of the School of Fine Arts in Morelia, his hometown and the capital of the state of Michoacán, to let him take classes there, along with the grown-up students. His early years in Mexico are key to his artistic production. Although he enjoys many influences in his work, his artistic stylistic foundation rests in the aesthetic of folk and traditional forms of art in Mexico. From pottery, weaving, and woodwork in the application of pattern, design and motif to intricacies in surface design in clothing and other folk forms, Arreguín has developed a practice in his paintings that creates a dazzling puzzle-like imagery. His integration of these patterns and designs has marked his work from the beginning. The complexity of the artwork is enriched by mythic elements and narrative meaning disguised in the layered surfaces. Unlike later Chicano work concerned with narratives of cultural resistance or affirmation, Arreguín has built a visual vocabulary that is rare and ever expansive.

Looking at the sources of his inspiration and the application of his process and the themes in his portraits and imagery helps us to see the exceptional place of his work in the larger Chicano and Latino art world. The historical presence of Arreguín and the Pacific Northwest is part of the larger world of masters of Chicano art. His works have been compared to tapestries that merge his varied aesthetic influences and concerns from the landscapes of his homeland and of the Pacific Northwest to iconic portraiture of Mexican and Chicano artists. A sophisticated world traveler his interests range form Japanese prints to Baroque European imagery and a love of masks and folk forms and textiles. He is a master whose paintings function much like a cabinet of curiosities that contain treasures of flora and fauna, miraculous meaning and historical artifacts and icons. He is a great collector whose imagery is discreetly disguised not within drawers in cabinets but within his paintings where they emerge and reveal themselves. His topography of images is often arranged in themes such as lush and verdant jungles, ultra baroque arabesques, repetitive geometric patterns and textually laden portraiture.

The artist describes these influences in an interview given for Artophilia in December of 2015:

"My inspiration comes from many sources. Clearly, Mother Nature has always occupied an important position in this regard, which is tied up to my early experiences in Mexico. In addition, the patterns used in Mexican arts and crafts—ceramics, textiles, tiles, masks, etc.—also have been present in the development of my mental and artistic imaginary from the very beginning. Other elements that I can mention are indigenous myths and legends, the expressions of other artists from various cultures, iconic historical figures, and the works of poets and other writers, some of whom are my friends. Obviously, my surroundings are also a big source of inspiration, as my series of paintings on the Pacific Northwest clearly show."

Strategy and source

Arreguín's paintings have become known for the patterns and layers of a mysterious intricacy that requires the viewer to search with visual observation like a cultural detective. Each layer is a dimension of information that is part of the whole and the act of discovery is part of the viewer's process. Like cabinets of curiosity the artist arranges the imagery with disguise and revelation hidden within the pattern of light and dark, within the foreground and background.

His use of nature to hide figures, portraits, flora and fauna, text and texture in an ever more complex palette is born out of his Mexican heritage including the traditional crafts of his native Michoacán and the cosmological and spiritual belief of the Mesoamerican universe. His emphasis on nature reflects his early life in Morelia, Mexico and his love of the landscape. Mexican folk art has long been connected to the terrain of each region. From pottery details to the woodworking of the folk artists, Mexican folk forms have interpreted the natural world of plants and animals and Arreguín's layers are part of the secret nature of his own folk topography. Like the wunderkammers of the age of discovery, Arreguín's work hold treasures of meaning arranged in grids and patterns almost like secret cabinets and drawers and we release them though our constant contemplation of the paintings. Layer after layer of leaves, flowers, butterflies, birds and natural phenomenon finally reveal to us the hidden gems of culture as masks and faces emerge. The complexities of his color choices are part of his skill and engagement.

The artist shares his vision and practice: (Artophilia)

"Colour and patterns are two fundamental elements in all of my compositions. In a certain way, many of the colors I use come from my cultural heritage. But I also use them to try to capture the mood of the particular subject I am treating at any given point, whether in a jungle or a portrait."

His works use a variety of techniques including those that merge flora and fauna, those that use text and portraiture and those that focus on iconic and mythic sources.

Flora and Fauna

Through much surveillance and observation, one is able to decipher emerging faces, in *Family Portrait* (1992). First, the eyes in the center of the format, then the smaller female face ¾ view, and then even smaller masklike visages. But in order to reach the individuals the viewer must move through a myriad of patterns reminiscent of Mexican tiles, arabesques, leaf like imagery, larger parrots and a patterned monkey. What the artist refers to as his Jungle works are influenced by his homeland and by the rainforest of the Pacific Northwest. In this painting the animal guardians guide us to the protected and minute features of the hidden family members by their positioning like arrows pointing the way and are often the key to the code of discovery. Facial features can be found in the center of flowers, butterflies, leaf structures, and eventually overlapping abstract designs. Each act of inquiry helps us discern the minute details concealing what the artist wants us to find. His works rely on both color and pattern,

"I guess that the manipulation of the patterns in combination with the use of color tones to create depth and perspective translates into a flatter view in the reproductions, thereby accentuating that mosaic or textile illusion."

Text and Portraiture

Arreguín's long friendships with writers, poets and philosophers are evident in his text portraits, which integrate language with image in meticulous synchronization. In particular his visual conversation with poet Larry Matsuda blends portrait in the language of loss and reconciliation as two old friends share family stories of struggle and healing in Masuda's poem, *Finding Morelia, Michoacan de Ocampo*. The portrait, *Mi amigo Matsuda* (2015) is a tribute to the overlapping autobiographies of their family and land. The portrait embodies Matsuda's life in the internment camp Minadoka with patterns of barbed wire, watchful faces and clasping hands.

Arreguín's painting memorializes this moment of internment, personal narrative and cultural resiliency. His portrait of Juan Felipe Herrera, the former poet laureate of the United States, *La Esencia de Juan Felipe* (2013), composed of names of other writers is an homage to the written word with the text surrounding the face composed of lines of a poem written for Alfredo by Juan Felipe Herrera and a roster of other writers. These word puzzles speak as both art and text in patterns of light and dark, color and line, like secret codes in a manuscript. As an erudite and cosmopolitan artist, he has created a visual vocabulary much as a writer of mythic texts hiding the code within the picture plane for the viewer to discover. The artist reflects on this (Artophilia):

'Other elements that I can mention are indigenous myths and legends, the expressions of other artists from various cultures, iconic historical figures, and the works of poets and other writers, some of whom are my friends. "

Icons and Madonna

His most constant companion in iconographic portraiture has been Frida Kahlo, Mexican painter and iconic figure in feminist art. Perhaps because they share a love of folk art and a devotion to Mexico's popular arts, Alfredo has found his way to Frida. Frida Kahlo along with Diego Rivera and other leading artists and intellectuals espoused the *Mexicanidad* movement, which sprung from the post revolutionary period and the public education models of Vasconcellos. This movement privileged the indigenous Mexican forms of craft, art and textiles. Frida, so well known for her dress claimed these textiles as a political statement as much as a fashion choice and her iconic image of braided hair and *huipiles* or Indigenous blouses became a marker of her love of the popular in Mexico. Alfredo Arreguín, more than any other artists, has repeatedly placed Frida Kahlo within the context of his multi-layered and pattered universe. Her love of animals is shared with Alfredo and her real life animal pets include her dogs, her deer and her pet monkey. Arreguín's paintings of Frida in tropical settings suffused with patterned leaves and foliage is a fitting ground for finding her image, which often emerges as a hidden mask and also as a central totemic likeness. Revealed in varying color and radiant design with repetitive pattern, Frida, like his Madonna becomes a sacred personage in the treasured universe of Arreguín.

Labyrinth and maze

Arreguín has continued to paint in his patterned model with evolutions along the way, in a sense remaining constant to his practice but also remaining innovative in this same practice. As his career has unfolded the space of labyrinth and maze has fluctuated in greater and lesser complexity in the paintings. It is as though he sometimes wants to make it easier for us to find the treasure hidden deep within the layers and at times is reluctant to reveal the private in the public space of the painting. The psychological nature of his work is often like a word play or riddle not easily solved. The mystery is composed of a combination of the geometric, the natural and the spiritual.

When categorizing his paintings we find the natural lies within the landscape and the spiritual with the sacred virgins and Madonnas. His pantheon and the mythic, within brilliant imagery of the Mesoamerican patterns much like mandalas and meditative spaces of abstract patterns and designs. The almost mathematical grids and overlays are part of the intensity of the pieces as practices of a visual cosmology. No other Latino artist has achieved such powerful and prolific production within the practice of this deep textured painting. In recent years, he returns to natural phenomena like water, oceans and waves, he traces our relationship to the organic world around us in minute detail, in the tradition of the great Japanese masters. As he has developed his oeuvre the palette has become a tool in changing mood and, like the decorative elements of the folk sources, has become a part of the mystery. Lighter palettes and all geometric patterns seem to rise in the latest paintings, with the exception of the ongoing studies of Frida Kahlo, whose portrait varies in headdress, jewelry and coloring of the layers, while her face remains the recognizable mask of an icon.

Alfredo Arreguín has created a universe for us that is part hidden history and treasure, and part natural mystery, and always carrying us to the heritage of his culture. He shares his vision of art with us.

"Art is life. It is a vessel that allows me to express my perception of the world, my sense of beauty and my social concerns—which, I believe, are shared by many other persons around the world."

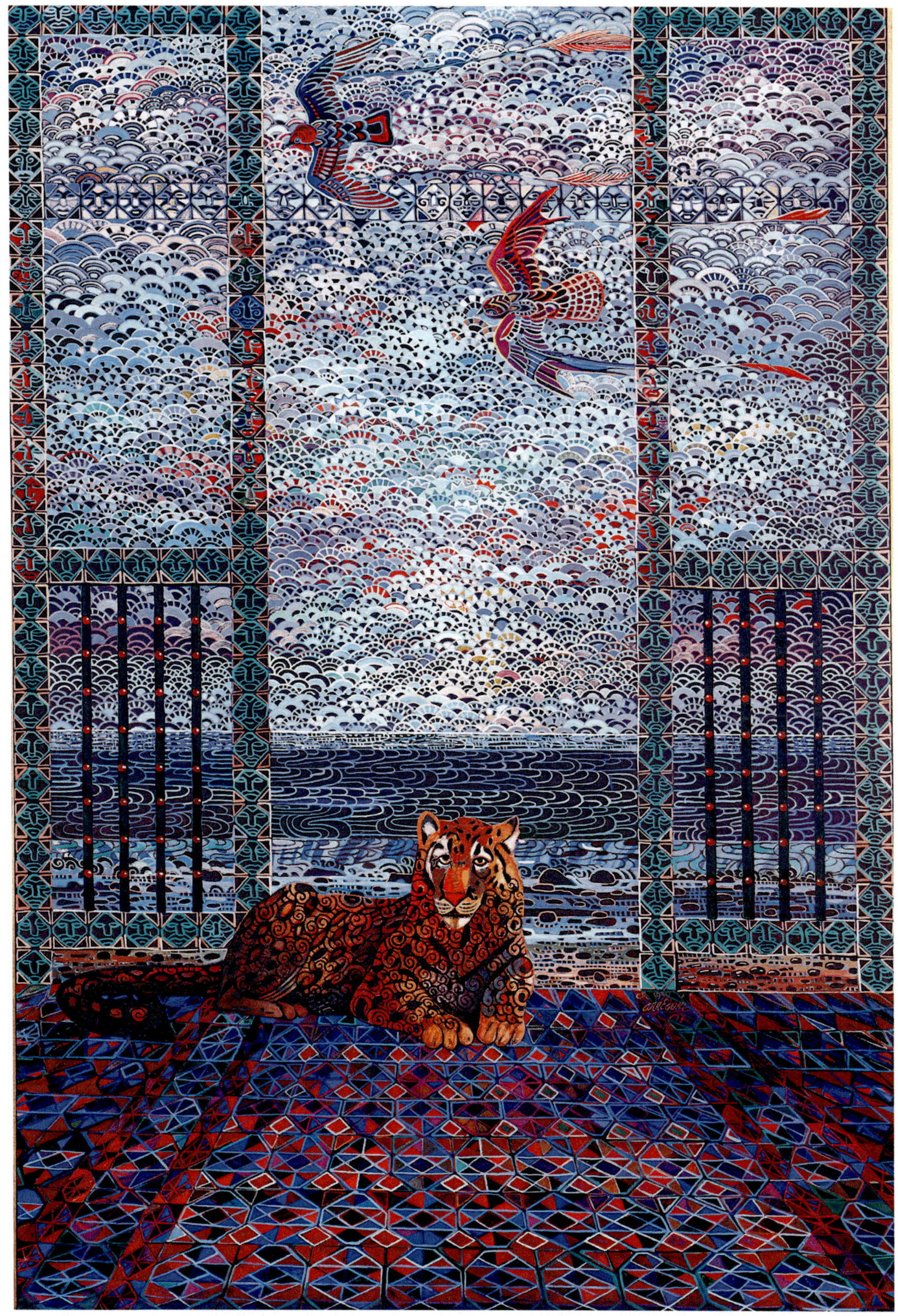

La Casa de la Paz, 1994, 72 × 48 in., private collection

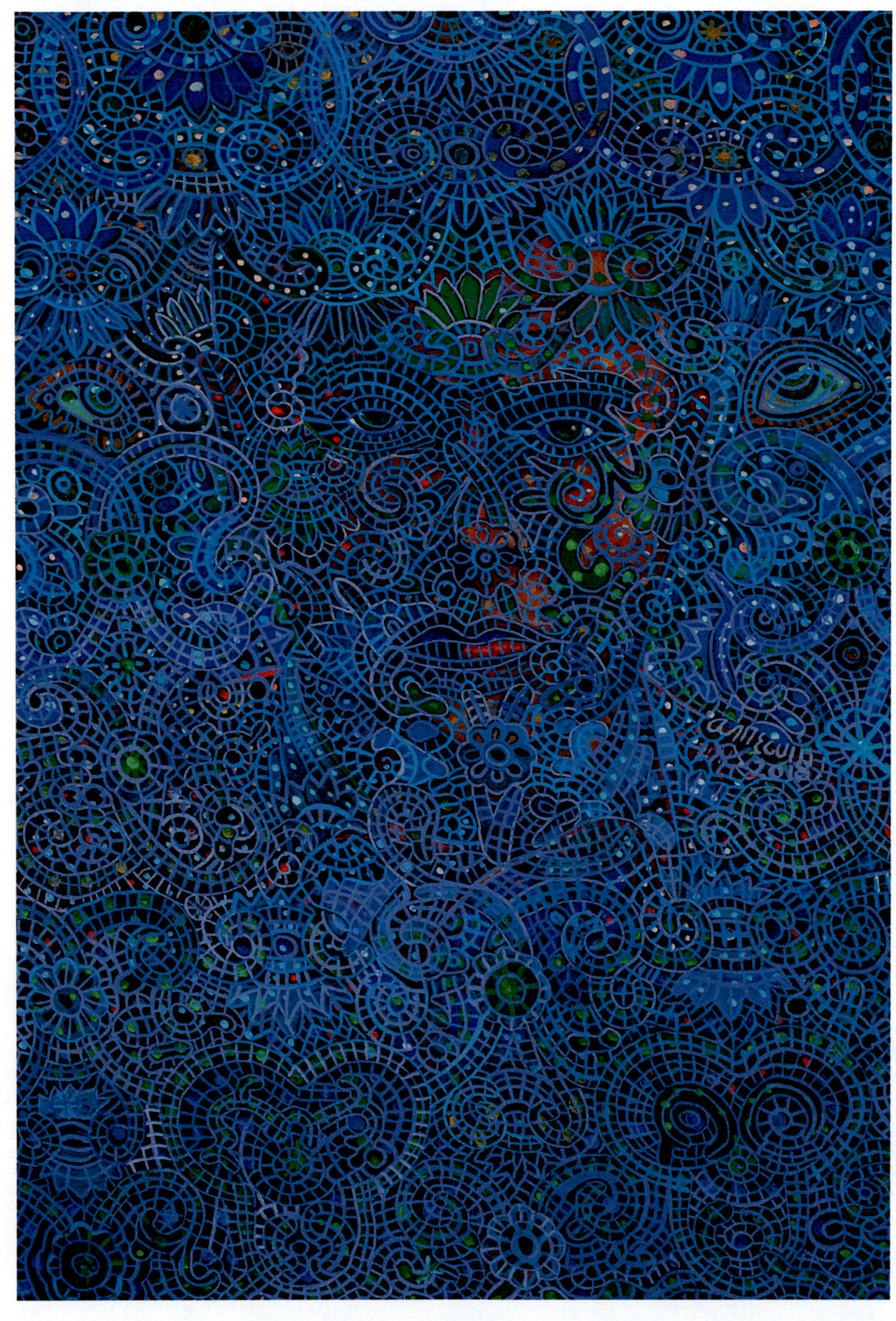

Blue Ray, 2017, 34 × 24 in., private collection

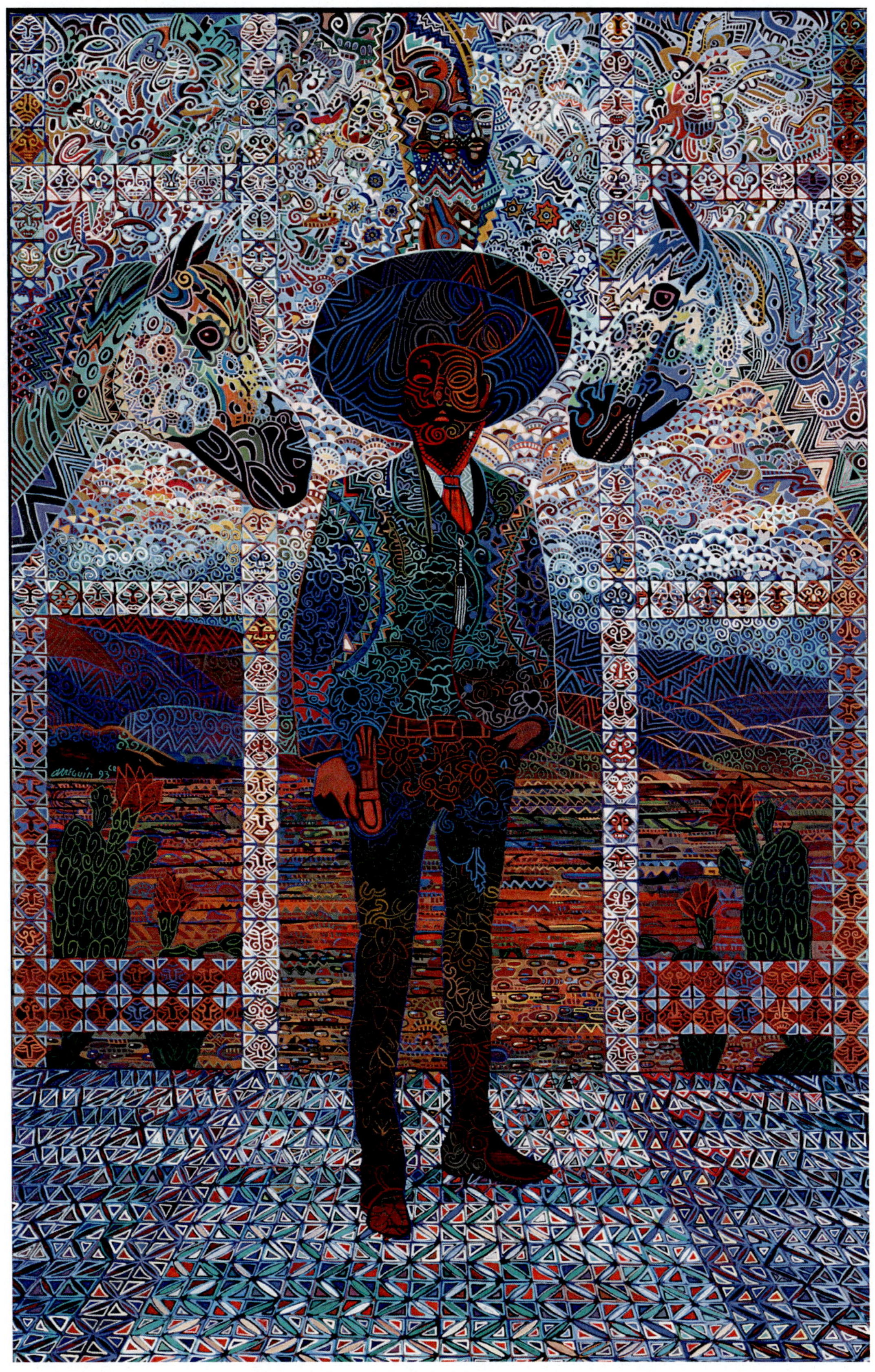

Zapata's Stables, 1993, 72 × 48 in., Sea Mar Community Health Center, Seattle

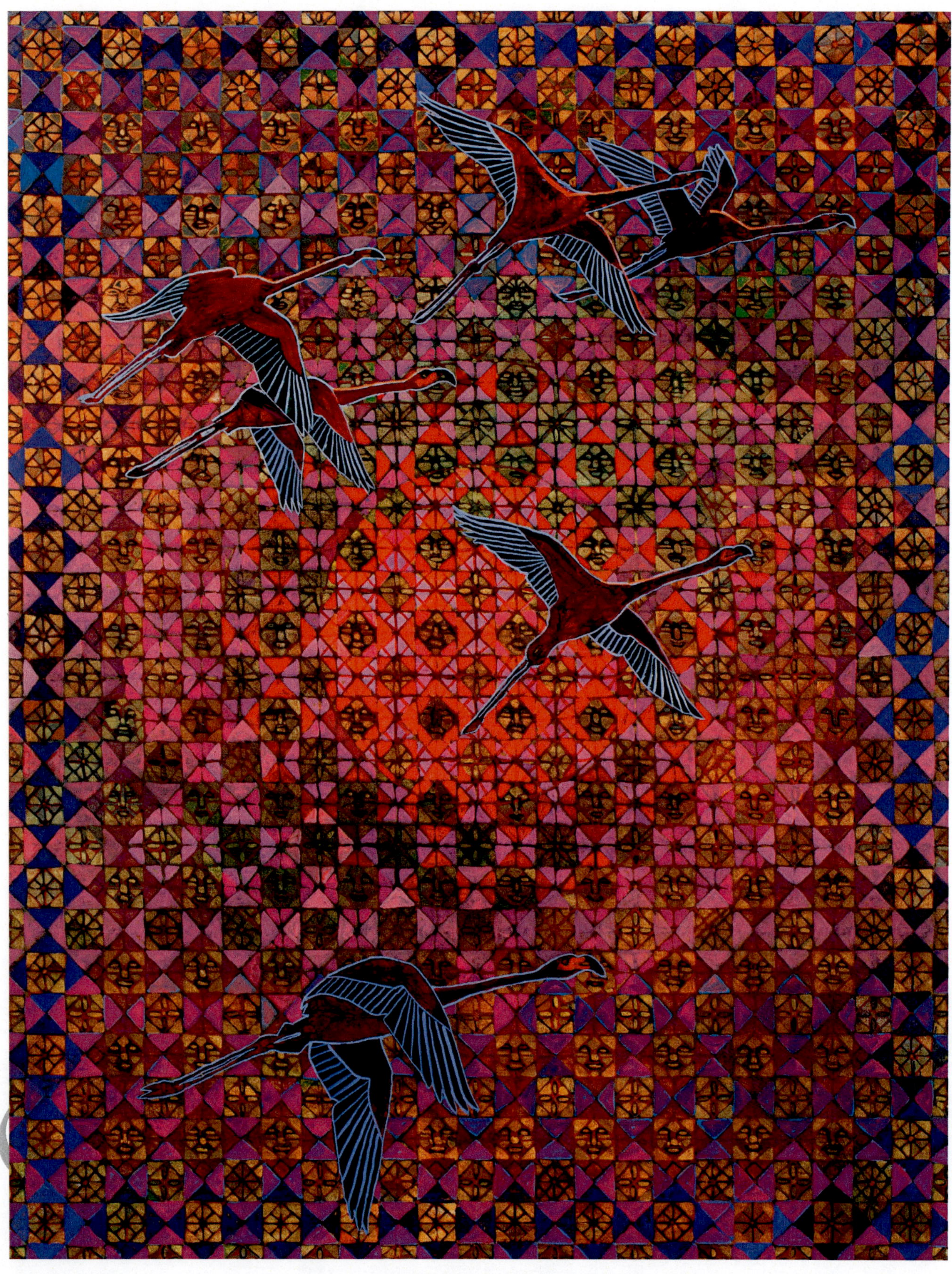

Florida, 2017, 60 × 48 in., collection of the artist

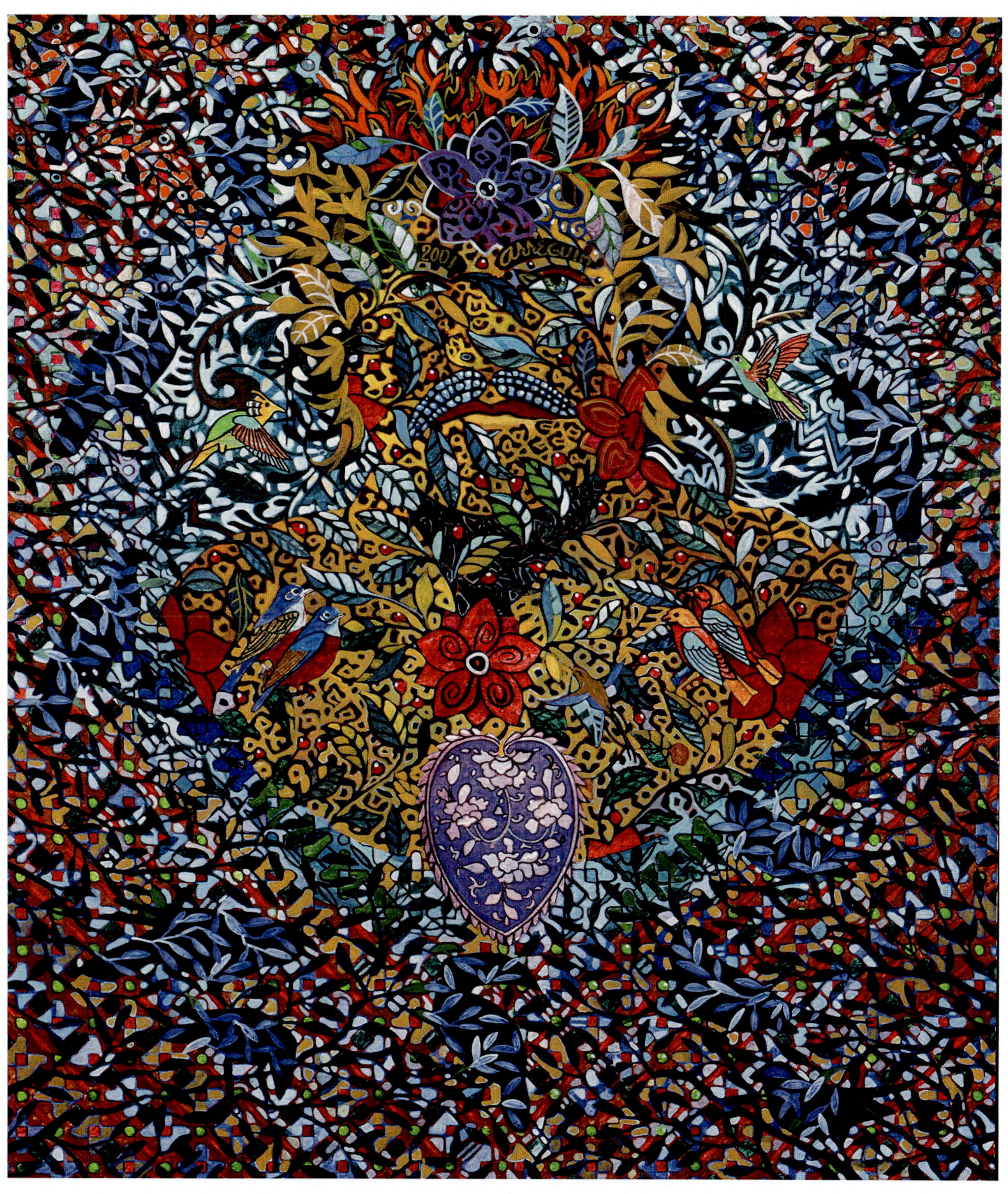

Jaguar Knight, 2001, 48 × 42 in., collection of the artist.

Juan Felipe Herrera

alfredo pinta pinta

en la casa

alfredo pinta pinta y suzy y el gatito chiggybutt y un emperador de

china en la pared limones y botellitas verdes mesa larga de caoba y

piña el lagarto de siglos de barro y las tortuguitas

el sol tejido

en estambres rayos y salsas diamantinas o son lucecitas o son

los mármoles nuestra amistad entre freeways y distancias de seattle

san francisco a fines de los 70 when I began again with

words el salvador centroamérica the streets marching poets my

mother lucha among them in her unconquerable brilliance in her

tiny room on the muni notice the city rush the mangos & guitars fly up

from the wars the women still calling liberation liberation &

wide flappy pants & love without the word love

it was fredo's brushstroke

at the end of the century the aromas

en la mesa de caoba alfredo's daring alfredo's arms

leaning into the ten thousand tlatoanis of the wide tall canvas

stare back infinite crying acrylic columns and halos thalos veridians

vermillions sit sit down pinta pinta alfredo says move the fiery arms

grayish clay dragons rising we are brothers & lauro too

walks in with paperbacks burning &

blue cerulean michoacán suzy paints a door in white kitchen light

again & the shadows again

stillness & light rain again

ten thousand faces are one

Juan Felipe Herrera

Tasmano

—For Alfredo, Suzy, Lauro & Cristina

Tasmano

tasmano

let me

hold you

& let me

bury myself

into your seasonalsalmon skin

ice disappearance

blackness lips

cabellera máscaras cholula culebra gold spattered spiral breasts la lumbre michoacana

de las cumbres brujas ripping spirit flesh blue madness locuras dentro

greener yellowness tehuana tehuanasalt storms arms i bow to

your tejido king kodiak spirit in your sacred belly egg

man woman flayed scales fins gone lives

gone face destroyed turquoise

azar albedrío

love will

love unto infinity

Doug Johnson

—After *Where I'm Calling From* in honor of Raymond Carver and Alfredo

When We Last Spoke

Amy and I are sitting in the day room. A diagnosis keeps you out of jail. You drive through the town of Pueblo to get here, so everyone else just calls this place Pueblo. Like the rest of us Amy is bat-shit crazy. But she's also Puerto Rican and from New York. Her English is okay even though she screams her sentences like we're always in traffic. It's my first time here, so I don't know what to think. She's back for a third time. Amy's real name is America, but she wants to be white so she blurts Amy at every orderly that tries to call her America Rodriguez. She's a couple of years older than I am and her blue eye-shadow is the color of the sky. Nobody knows the name of this place. We just know the name of the town. All I know is that we are in a red brick building. Everyone is in a haze at intake and all the doors lock from the outside. Amy is telling me how tonight was just like intake. I'm listening and she reassures me that I'll get used to it if I keep my head down and don't bother Frankie.

We've only been in here a couple of months. She said she's serving her sentence here. I asked her what for. She shrugs and says she has a multiple-personality disorder. She stabbed her roommate. Her eye-lid twitches and she rubs her neck, telling me it's a side effect of the meds but she hopes it doesn't stick. When I say that my mouth dries out, she nods. She tells me that she needs to rest her eyes and she'll get back to her story.

Right now, we're in group lock down because Juan killed himself a couple of hours ago. Hung himself in the shower room with towels. Paramedics yelled, "He's defecated and his lips are blue," thinking none of us could hear. It happened across from my room and I opened the doors for the orderlies with the crash cart. I saw Juan's glazed eyes before they yelled at me to get back into my room. Juan wore Western shirts that have fake pearl snaps on the pocket. His jeans were from Walmart and never quite fit, but he smiled quite a bit. They said he was a local who couldn't even out. Right before he killed himself Juan visited his family on the outside. A weekend pass is a big privilege. He was going to eat menudo and listen to corridos. It was the weekend before Easter and he planned on going to the barbecue. He promised no drinking. That was the plan. Yesterday he seemed fine and was waiting in line for his cigarette. Like most of the ward, he smoked. He lined up with the others right after breakfast. The only one who wouldn't line up was Mr. Foster, who smoked a special little cigar version. Mr. Foster didn't talk much, but he didn't wear underwear either, so he would cut in line before it was time for the break and mumble and gesture. He didn't talk. Just mumbled and gestured real loud so they would take him out earlier. He held his pants up with his left hand. When the left hand came up to beg for the cigar, the orderly would rush around the desk and hold it in front of him. He'd pick up his pants and mumble things. He got his own personal smoke break. Amy would laugh, but most people put their heads down because they didn't want to lose their smoke break. We should have been able to laugh more, but if it wasn't quiet the orderlies got irritated. I was at the table and it was after breakfast. I didn't smoke so I just pushed the powdered eggs around my plate. That was yesterday and Juan was happy with his smoke break. Juan had a pencil mustache and big Mexican hair like a movie star of the 1970's. We were both about the same height and he was even a little shorter. When I was trapped in my room while they used the crash carts, they yelled, "Clear!" like in the movies but they wouldn't let us out of our rooms even though we heard everything. There's only cinderblocks and even when they lock you down for isolation the ward hears everything. The click of the stretcher ratcheted through the walls, as they grumbled more things about his suicide.

They let us out of the rooms, and announced to us what we already knew. There aren't enough neon lights, so now it's dark on this couch, here with Amy. Juan mentioned that he was Catholic so they asked if someone in the group wanted to say a prayer. We didn't care. I muttered a prayer and sat down next to Amy. Amy said she wanted to ask Juan what pushed him over the edge but Juan never talked to anybody. Amy said it wouldn't matter. They were going to ask her more questions than the rest of us. No matter how many times she told the group that she was Puerto Rican and that Juan was Mexican, the orderlies would ask her more questions.

In the lime green chair at the breakfast table, Amy looks herself up and down in a compact mirror. I draw roses and use a tissue. I listen to Amy rattle on about New York and how much the Mexican food sucks here. It's nine o'clock in the morning and they are going to make us go swimming this afternoon. Group happens at ten and we all try to stay mute until the therapist threatens to keep us the rest of the day. Right now I watch Amy. We all want to be in group with Gretchen who loves to talk about her hallucinations and turn them into some hot date in the back of a 1959 Buick. The leader stops her when she wants to count the orgasms but most of us are happy to listen because it fills the time. There's more pressure in group now because of Juan. They all want us to talk about our feelings. Some guy just went through intake. He's in lock-up, screaming. What is Amy talking about anyway? She's talking about how when she was fifteen her mom made these elaborate plans for her quince and she invited all of her friends. Then, unlucky for her, she got locked in the janitor's closet at school because Joey shoved her in there instead of the locker and she screamed and screamed all day. She already didn't like tight places. Being locked in there might be the reason she's locked in here. Amy is popping her gum and painting on extra mascara. She has freckles on her chubby cheeks. Today a red striped sweater wraps around her bust. All her clothes look too small, but she's a pretty big girl anyway and not really shy. When she was trapped in the closet she finally stared up at the vent to the outside and noticed that the light was shifting back and forth when clouds passed overhead. She said that's what she thought at least. She was tired of screaming. She smelled bleach and other cleaners for the school. The yellow mop bucket had a crack at the top. She leaned up against the shelf and fell asleep dreaming that she was at the bottom of a well in one of those farm stories with the princess and the frog. When the keys rattled in the lock she screamed and decided that her life was never going to be the same. The nightmares from when she was five started to get worse. She wouldn't let them close the bedroom door for weeks. She was happy that Pueblo didn't allow doors closed except at night. After the janitor let her out, she went to her quince but squealed when a van backfired in front of the Mason's hall.

"Keep on going. What happened next, Amy?" I show her the rose I'm drawing. She shrugs. When she was seventeen or eighteen she dropped out of high school and started hanging out with her friend. Not the one she stabbed. They didn't have anything to do and smoked weed most afternoons and talked about Ruben or Benito. One day, they decided to get something to eat and went down to Pietro's Pizza. Pietro's eyes crossed and he was big as a house, but the pizza was good. Amy and her friend were sitting there when some guy with a jackhammer came up, sweating and blasting away. They couldn't hear and quit talking, deciding to watch his yellow hard hat and red suspenders instead. A white t-shirt was tucked into his jeans tight enough to advertise his package. When he was done, he tipped his hat at them and started to walk away. Both girls giggled. He was hot. Amy's friend rushed outside to get his number. She smiled and wrote it on her hand. When her friend showed her the number Amy wrote it on the napkin. Amy's friend bolted outside again. He laughed out loud when she bumped into him and Amy saw him kiss her friend. He wrote on her hand again. He waved and kept walking. His name was Tony. Amy said it was short for Antonio. Her friend was squealing when she got back to the restaurant. Amy wished she had the courage to get a kiss, but she was shy. Not like now.

They went back and lit up again and her friend dreamed about the yellow hard hat and they made jokes about his package. Her friend always wrote down numbers. She never had the courage to call. When they got busted for possession, it was their first time and the judge said that if they got a job, then he would dismiss the charges, since they still looked young. Amy didn't know what to do, so she called Tony and asked if she could have a job. He said they needed someone to hold a road sign and flip it around. Amy said she put on an orange vest and that's where she learned to talk so loud. Tony didn't care if she smoked, as long as she flipped the sign. Tony squeezed her butt on the way out of the trailer. He was good with cement and they got a job on a paving crew upstate. Tony asked her if she wanted to go, and she shrugged, even though she was squealing inside. The boss griped about paying for another room and Tony said she could bunk with him, so the boss let her go on the job.

"Then what?" I say. "Where next, Amy?

I was drawing. I was listening, but with the echoes of Juan in my head, I would have listened to her talk all day about painting her nails. They made us sleep with the doors open, last night. The sun is shining. Amy pulls out a nail file and squints out the window. Then she keeps talking. Nothing happened at first with her and Tony on the road, but she was getting louder and louder. Pretty soon they were crawling out West, paving roads, and patching potholes. In case Tony wasn't around, Amy learned to fight with a knife for when she couldn't talk her way out of jam. Tony jacked up a local pretty bad when he tried something on Amy and the boss cut them loose with some cash. The local did a fair number on Tony and Amy nursed him back to health. They found a new crew in Prospect Kansas and were doing a pretty good job steering clear of trouble until they got on a crew near Cody Wyoming. Amy said the work was fine and Tony was great but that trapped version of her would pop up. Sometimes they almost got fired. Sometimes she got fired. She said the weed wasn't helping most days and the only thing to do in Cody on the weekends was to listen to the wind and drink. Tony took to drinking and she started feeling paranoid. They were loaded one night and the paneling in their hotel took a beating. They took to hitchhiking out of Wyoming toward the coast. Tony heard that there was work in California, but they needed to hold up in Denver for a bit to see if he could score some union work on the down low. Amy accused him of all sorts of shit and pretty much screamed at him like a jealous whore every day he came home. She couldn't work anymore because either she insulted the bosses or accused someone of stealing. Tony got it good in a knife fight, she said. That really meant he got good at disarming her. Finally, one night there were bright lights outside their apartment. Someone called the cops on them and somebody had to go to jail. Since Amy sliced Tony pretty good on the arm, they cuffed her and led her out of the room. When she heard that door slam to the cell, she went ape-shit on the other lady and they locked her down in solitary. The closet incident never quite went away. Without any meds or weed about three versions of Amy would appear. Thanks to Tony, they started with a 72 hour hold and here she is all these years later, waiting for Mr. Foster to get his cigarette. Amy sighed and looked at the pinky she was filing. After that it was a haze. She hooked up with a guy who worked at Coors. He worked the graveyard and brokered enough uppers and downers to keep his shift going without the brewery catching on. Amy said they got along. His name was Zach. He had a brother who went Wiccan and the whole family used. Zach pulled his younger brothers out of a burning house when his mom passed out, drunk on the lawn. He understood the darker versions of Amy like a warm blanket and shrugged most of the time she screamed at him for sleeping with another woman. With only the two of them in the house, she couldn't screw with the storylines. Even when she did shift around his story and blame it on him, he just told her she was high. Then one day he woke up and wanted to be sober and wouldn't let her rope him into a fight with some thug she met at a bar. Amy said the state still had her in the system and so she applied for food stamps and housing promising she would go to treatment.

Amy stopped talking. She just shuts up and stares out the window. What's up? I'm listening. It distracts me, from the meds that aren't working. After a couple of minutes I lean over and whisper, "Then what, Amy?" "What the hell!" she yells at me. An orderly looks up and she glares over her shoulder. "Don't you every sneak up on me!" Two months in, I know to wait her out. When the cloud clears the window, I clear my throat and ask, "Then what?"
Tony found Amy and they took up where they left off. Except now they were having some knock-down, drag out fights. Amy points to a scar where he got her with a beer bottle. "Look at this," she says. "Right here." She pulls her hair back from above her ear. The top was missing. She tucked it back behind her hair. She left scars on his back from boiling pasta water. Things got out of hand again. One black-eye too many. The state was asking too many questions and was going to put her in one of those safe houses, or worse yet, a place like this. Amy yanked her thumb at the bars covering the window.

Amy gets real quiet again. She pulls out lipstick and then a lip liner with a darker color. Juan called her a chola. The orderly grabs the phone when it rings and they start to file in from the smoke break. We both look for Juan, knowing he isn't there. Amy stays real quiet. Junior tries to sit down and make conversation. Amy threatens him in Spanish and he gets up with his hands in surrender. Junior doesn't speak Spanish. Nobody messes with Amy. "Come on, Amy" I say. "I'm listening." She shrugs and looks at the orderly. Then she looks out the window again and reaches into her purse for her compact mirror.

Tony tried to fix things by taking a break and getting his own apartment. He still looked really hot. Working in cement made him look even hotter, so women were always throwing themselves at him. He said he wasn't having an affair. The therapist, in group, tells Amy she tends to shuffle three or four words around in every conversation to make it the other person's fault. The therapist is full of shit, Amy says. Amy went to all the local bars and found him chatting up a blonde at the end of a bar. Two beer bottles and a broken pool cue later, Amy was tossed out on her butt. Mumbling off her meds for three days they picked her up on Colfax. The bar owner pegged her in the brawl. Amy was convinced the bar owner was lying and Tony's girlfriend started the fight. Now Amy is at Pueblo on reduced charges for stabbing Tony. The therapist said Tony did not have a girlfriend on the side. Tony called Amy his girlfriend. The therapist was lying but at least Amy kept her mouth shut long enough to get her privileges back. That way they would let her use her make-up. After they picked Amy up this time, the judge ordered her convicted with probation. She ended up at Pueblo. The day she chased Tony to the bar she missed her job interview at the cement company. She said she didn't care and adjusted her lip liner.

* * *

Amy was at Pueblo to try and figure out how to live life on the outside without getting locked up again. The state put us all on a 90 day program, but we all knew that they would extend it if we were a danger to ourselves or others. Like I said, this was my first time at Pueblo. My parents brought me down and checked me in. Nobody knew what to expect. My parents looked at the bed in my ward and we didn't say much. They said they would visit on the weekends. The sun was out. The doors locked from outside and clanged against the door jamb when it shut. They left. Amy looked out the window. When my parents dropped me off, Mom had the same look as Amy does right now. Not crazy. Just empty. That first day I sat on the broken down sofa. Some little guy in a hoodie told me that it was his spot. I moved to the chair. There was a lady with knitting needles, who never let anyone change the T.V. channel. It was mostly static but she muttered things at the reporter like he was her husband or the cat. Now Amy lets me sit next to her and listen while she puts on her make-up. That's my spot. There's an ashtray on the table even though nobody is allowed to smoke in the building. Sometimes it is raining and they let Mr. Foster smoke so his pants stay on at the front desk. Amy pulls out a nail file, again, and sighs like we are two old women talking about the price of milk at a grocery store. That's when Amy keeps going with her story.

The orderly wears a cowboy shirt with the pearl buttons. It's blue. Not like Juan's. He has a small gut. Amy calls him Tex because of the big belt buckle. A crease circles his head where his cowboy hat sits when he isn't at work. He's marking things on a clip board and walks by to look at Amy, like he knows what she has in her purse. She has cosmetics in her purse. I've been watching her all day.

Amy gets quiet again but she glares out the window. She knows not to glare at Tex because she wants to keep her make-up. She will do anything they say to keep her make-up. She starts to pull out her mirror, eye-liner and mascara to dig for something at the bottom of her purse. Tex stops to look at what has her so upset. She finally smiles and pulls up a bag of peanuts. The kind you get on an airplane.

Tex cleared his throat. "You two read that book *100 Years of Solitude*? Gabriel García Márquez used to ask my dad if it was better to fish Six Mile or Wild Horse Creek. Dad would just steer clear. Gabriel knew his fish but he just couldn't keep his shit together. Him, Juan and Hemingway, they're all the same. People think García Márquez died of old age. I don't believe it. Read his book. You'll understand. Just keep your shit together, America." Tex snapped his clipboard to finish his little lecture and moved on. Amy didn't say a word. Tex knew saying her full name pissed her off. "Just 'cuz my parents named me that doesn't mean, nothing. Name's Amy." She went back to staring out the window.

My parents brought me up here and they were hoping it wasn't the end of the line. They stayed here an hour or two, Before, at St. Joseph's, they dropped me at the E.R. That's what the doctors said they should do. The first nurse said, "You have to take this." When I refused, she said, "Suit yourself." She said that four times until she forced me to take it. She said I needed to calm down. My ex-wife didn't bring me. It was my parents. At the time she wasn't my ex-wife. Now she is gone because the shrink said most of the time spouses leave. So they made me take the pill and said it would make me calm down. Sometimes my ex-wife I would just go take a walk. They wouldn't let me take a walk. One night I couldn't calm down and she said take a walk. I was afraid I would get lost so I called 911. They said to calm down and gave me directions. I walked to that E.R. He had me lay down on the table. Nobody was there. It was two in the morning. I laid there counting the dots in the Armstrong ceiling tiles. He gave me a Valium and told me not to take it until I got home. I walked home and took the Valium. They said I couldn't take that all the time.

We lost the apartment job and our place to stay. I tried to call the seminary students who got us the job but they stopped answering. We got a new place and it was still close to where I could walk and look at the ducks. I guess my ex-wife is okay but I don't know anymore. After that my parents started driving me to the different hospitals. I was transferred to this one after St. Joseph's when my parents tried to take care of me but it didn't work out.

Amy is still staring out the window. Some people are in here to detox. The new guy is still screaming. Some people are in for other reasons. Frankie is sitting on the couch but the kid with the hoodie isn't claiming it is his spot. Frankie's a head taller than me and has hair the shape of a toilet brush. He doesn't talk. One day he decided to kick the shit out of another patient. When I body slammed him to the ground, Tex got mad at me and sent me to my room. Another patient tried to strangle her doctor in the hallway and I body slammed her, too. Tex yelled again but I didn't get sent to my room.

Today, me and Amy are doing okay and nobody is sending us to our room. She isn't yelling. Now she's just staring out of the window. She put everything back into her purse. Even the peanuts. Finally she says, "Tony is coming next week. I'll introduce you." She says it in a faraway voice. "I'd like that." Amy gets up and I know not to follow her because I don't want her to yell at me again about being a puppy and to get a damn life. I'm starting to think about her working on the construction crews and directing traffic and when nobody knew how much trouble she was causing when she wasn't on her shift. It made me wonder about that first day. I remembered before my ex-wife told me to take a walk by myself all the time. She worked in a mall and there was an art gallery there. In the front window it had a huge painting of Frida. They must have been putting up the new show. I was just standing there watching the painter. He saw me and waved and I waved back, just looking in the window and staring. He was a Mexican guy with wild hair and suspenders and laughed at something the gallery owner said. The window had nice letters on it. Clean white letters. The Art of Alfredo Arreguín. Somebody was bringing in a heavy box and I opened the front door of the gallery. "You want to see some more paintings?" Alfredo said. I blinked a couple of times and nodded yes. I looked around the room. The paintings didn't know where I was from or why I was walking. The gallery owner frowned a bit but Alfredo didn't seem to notice. I smiled and held the door for somebody else carrying a box. Then I wandered out so they could keep setting up the show. Alfredo nodded and smiled. There was a little step ladder he started to climb, and I took one last look at Frida in the window.

Frida reminded me of *The Lacuna* and about this character who does the cooking and cleaning for Frida and Diego. I used to cook and clean. Maybe I could try and phone my ex-wife and remind her of the walks. Our walks. She'll remind me of when we last spoke. She will ask about Amy and I'll tell her we broke up. She won't believe me. Amy won't either. Not because of where I'm calling from but from when we last spoke.

Lisa Alvarado

Alfredo In the Bardo and Frida in the Cut

In the Bardo

In some schools of Buddhism, ***bardo*** (Tibetan བར་དོ་ Wylie: *bar do*) or ***antarabhāva*** (Sanskrit) is an intermediate, transitional, or liminal state between death and rebirth.

Milam bardo (*rmi lam bar do*): is the second bardo of the dream state.

I chose this as part of the title of this essay. Essay, rumination, love letter to Alfredo Arreguín.
I will talk about Frida in the cut a bit later. I first found Alfredo's work several years ago, chatting with people of Facebook, of all places. Whether it's portraiture, landscape, or still life, Alfredo's work is all at once representational, and symbolic.

In his paintings, the key subject is at first "hidden" against a patterned background, just like the emerging images in a dream. And like a dream, the background stays suggested, while the central image gradually comes into focus, capturing your attention. Liminal, you see, in the bardo, Alfredo takes you to the borderland of what exists in the "real" world and what we see in our mind's eye, in our dreams.

Speaking of dreams, Alfredo's intricate patterns, his ingots of color, precise in placement and repetition, remind me of Huichol beaded worship—animals, icons—all painstakingly built and layered bead by bead. Alfredo shapes his work, I think, in much the same way. Huichol beaded work, their yarn work, is an expression of the bardo; a present-time bridge from this world, into the real world of the spirit, of what exists in a shared vision quest.

Alfredo invites you to see, and see past this world, into the tangible realm of the deeply felt, the perfect spirit. It is specific, in that the imagery springs from the roots of Mejicanismo, and by implication Chicanismo. It is universal, in that it assumes the viewer, from whatever background, understands the longing, and the revelations of the borderland.

And like the art and living message of our indígena brothers and sisters, Alfredo's work call us to reconnect, to re-construct from a borderland/bardo of Pan-American experience, something I truly understand. Alfredo was born in Mexico, and I am the child of immigrants, and the idea of border/ bardo is one that constantly shapes my self-definition, and I suspect shapes him as well. I want to share this poem about the power of the bardo, specific and universal. I hope it also serves as the introduction to my reaction to Alfredo's re-creation of Frida.

Reclamo

En este sueño
estoy completa.
No tengo que guardar
las historias de otra gente.
No tengo que buscar y escudriñar
a través de los restos de sus palabras.

En este sueño
paso mis dedos
através de la cabellera de Frida
Con esa cabellera,
tejo flores obscuras
del color de la sangre.
Y me dice
que el jaguar viene a traerme
su poder.

La medicina que calma este dolor
es como comida para
calmar esta hambre.

En este sueño
hago magia
con el lodo del Río Grande.
Arropado en corridas y música ranchera,
que son el hechizo y el encanto
que anula la edad
del olvido y el adoctrinamiento.

En este sueño
tengo un amante
cuya cara es de piedra,
como el antiguo marcador del templo.

Su boca es carnosa,
sus ojos están entrecerrados y
murmura:

"Ven conmigo mi ndia,
mi pequeña perdida.
Recuerda quién eres.
Recuerda quién eres."

Reclamation

In this dream,
I am whole.
I am no longer
saving other people's stories,
scavenging their words;
sifting thru their remains.
In this dream,
my fingers run
thru Frida's hair.
In this hair, I plait
dark flowers
the color of blood.
She tells me
the jaguar comes
to bring me power.
The medicine
to end this pain,
the food for this hunger.
In this dream,
I have made magic
from the mud of the Rio Grande.
Wrapped in corridas and ranchero music;
are spells and incantations
to undo
the age of forgetfulness
and indoctrination.
In this dream,
I have a lover
whose face is stone;
ancient as a temple marker.
His mouth is full,
his eyes half closed.
He whispers:
"Come to me, mi India,
mi pequeña perdida.
Remember who you are
Remember who you are."

In the Cut

Agency is the ability to express you true self on your own terms. It is the power to think for yourself and act in ways that shape your experiences and life trajectories. Alfredo's portraits of Frida reveal his root understanding this essential truth. It utterly rejects the common trope in the most recent cult of Frida expropriation—Frida as victim— with the artist and the viewer indulging in the voyeurism of pain. Alfredo never stoops to that. In every painting depicting her, she is vibrant, aware, her gaze resolute and self-aware. This is the greatest homage and the deepest understanding of one of the twentieth century's most important artists

I tried to capture that agency in writing about her, and perhaps, strengthening the agency in myself.

Bashert

I am the catch
in your throat;
the wordless cry,
unexplainable.
I am the cloud
that follows you;
raining
at the slightest provocation.
I am the scar
that has
become a flower.
I am the pilgrim
you brought home;
the Jew you hid
from the fire.
I am your dark sleep.
I am your dream
of finding someone
whose arms
will hold you
when daylight comes.

Frida was never her wound, her physical limits, her crushing disappointments in private life. She takes her life and as alchemist, transforms it into art, into awareness, into a psychic rebar stronger than any back brace. She gives all comers as good as she gets. I chose the phrase "in the cut"—a hip hop term meaning hidden in the 'hood, but also someone at the top of their game, their quintessential self.

Frida will always be the foundation for Latinx artists of all persuasions, as we emerge from the 'hood., as we gather onto ourselves our own rebar, forge our own agency.

Matthew Kangas

Alfredo Arreguín: Painter from the New World

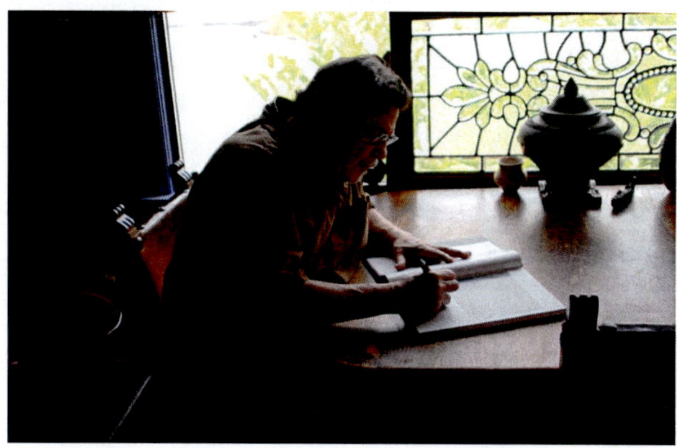

FIGURE 1. The artist at home, Seattle, 2006.

I. *Crucible of the Academy*

The American painter Alfredo Arreguin has attained a stature that reflects a bi-cultural—not to say intercontinental—status within the Americas and, recently, Iberian and Latino art communities, all overlapping. While Arreguin's early years as a virtual artistic child prodigy in provincial Mexico have been extensively discussed and analyzed[1]—often without agreement—examining various cultural, archaeological, mathematical[2], art-historical and even paranormal[3] roots in both Mexico and Spain (actually, Basque), there has been little, if any, discussion around the formative crucible of his advanced art training at the School of Art of the University of Washington in Seattle, where he received both his undergraduate (B.A., 1967) and graduate degrees (M.F.A., 1969). An important historical note: this institution's art department was founded in 1919 upon the arrival from Paris of the Australian-born Post-Impressionist painter Ambrose Patterson.[4]

Arreguín's attendance at the University began in the College of Architecture, at his builder-developer father's urging, but quickly shifted to the adjacent interior design section (where he met fellow classmate Dale Chihuly) and thence to the School of Art proper, at the northeast corner of the main campus quadrangle. He quickly became comfortable in the basement student café, Parnassus. Embarking on a rigorous two-year array of painting and drawing classes in 1963, along with liberal arts and humanities requirements, he graduated in 1967, a product of the GI Bill after his US Army service in South Korea. It is important to note that despite the honored alumni's dismissive comments to interviewers about faculty and students, there existed highly competent faculty and students, steeped in a French atelier teaching system which emerged as an alternative to the École des Beaux Arts in Paris Their perspectives combined with a Bauhaus-based, tolerant attitude toward design—stressing the equality of the fine arts and decorative arts or crafts. Arreguín benefited considerably from this curriculum and from the documented encouragement he received from faculty, as well as his witnessing the living examples of their working methods as artists. Several were full-time studio artists, exhibiting widely beyond the Pacific Northwest in New York, San Francisco and Los Angeles. Seeing their careers, Arreguín soon realized he did not want to teach but to make art—all the time.

Furthermore, the tiresome canard about some tyranny of a hegemonic, New York School style, Abstract Expressionism, has also been exaggerated and overstated by writers discussing the artist's student years[5]. More pertinent, as we shall see, were the precepts of teachers embracing Cubism and Surrealism, in several cases, at first hand or at least, once removed. In addition, this course of study, building on the curriculum of long-time School director, Walter F. Isaacs (who had trained at Columbia and in Paris where he exhibited with Picasso in the 1922 *salon des indépendants*), stressing several aspects of art that would become engrained in Arreguín's aesthetics: the perfect placement of dispersed elements in any composition; the significance of color theory to balance impulse; and the solid construction of any art object whether oil painting, ceramics, jewelry or weaving, all of which bear substantial traces in his art made in the years to come. All these arts flourished within the School of Art.

Less than a decade after leaving the bohemian allure of Parnassus and the tall sun-filled classrooms upstairs, Arreguín confessed in an interview published in a neighborhood newspaper, *The Outlook*:

> I'm basically dealing with the pattern. . . the interrelationships between patterns [and] shapes. . . the subject is not as important as how everything fits together.[6]

Old Professor Isaacs could not have put it better. Before his death in 1964, while Arreguín was an undergraduate student, Isaacs had hired two of his former pupils whom he had sent to study in Paris with a warm personal recommendation to his close friend Cubist master Fernand Léger, Spencer Moseley and Wendell Brazeau. Besides them and the others Isaacs had recruited from back east, artistic meccas such as Yale, Harvard, Howard and the School of the Art Institute of Chicago, the painting department within the School of Art (with as many as 22 full-time instructors at one point) offered a wide range of courses including introductory night-classes covering basics as well as more advanced, frank studio critiques *à la façon de Paris*, frequently attended by important visiting professors. Fortunately for Arreguín, the co-founder of the San Francisco Bay Area Figurative Expressionist painting movement, Elmer Bischoff, was spending one semester and summer of 1968 at the School of Art. Coming from the University of California at Berkeley, Bischoff was no doubt already comfortable with Latino art students (Arreguín was the only one at the UW), and helped guide the eager, but older, pupil away from typical grad student imitations and experiments back toward a re-encounter with his roots. He had been gone from Mexico for over ten years. Bischoff suggested looking again at the folk art, architecture, and landscape of southern Mexico, around the student's home town of Morelia, in the state of Michoacán. This eventually led to a breakthrough series of crowded, often erotic, figurative-narrative compositions that were playful, imaginary and distantly reminiscent of the dream logic of French and Spanish Surrealists in early 20th century art. Arreguín was now channeling Europe as well as Mesoamerica.

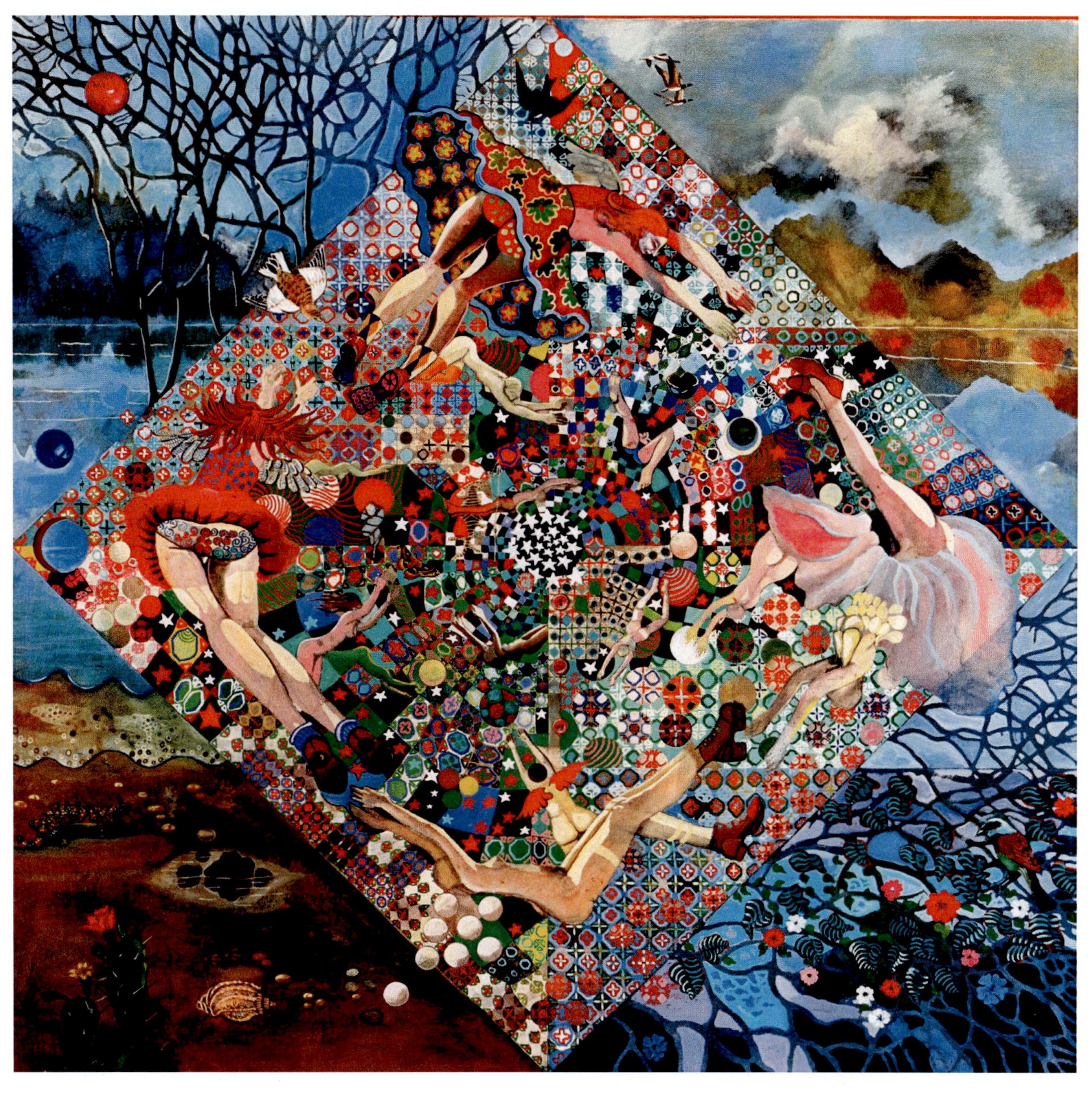

FIGURE 2. *Remolino*, 1974. Oil on canvas, 48 x 48 in. Private collection

The riotous, explosive paintings such as *Remolino* and *Floating* (both 1974), were akin to similar works by another visitor, British artist and fellow graduate student, Michael Lawson of Liverpool, and former student at the Liverpool College of Art and the Royal College of Art in London, where he studied printmaking but was more influenced by tabloid political cartoonists.[7] Having been invited by Chihuly (who met him at the University of Wisconsin where Lawson was a foreign exchange student) to Seattle, Lawson's hectic, zany tableaux, such as *Department Store* (1969) shared qualities with Arreguin's work of the period. They became close friends and shared: a tilted-forward, nearly aerial view perspective; a sharp separation of colors due, in Lawson's case, to the enamel paints he preferred to use; and a propensity for hallucinatory imagery, perhaps the result of Lawson's use of LSD-25, a popular psychoactive drug of the day. It was, after all, the Summer of Love, 1968. This was cut short by Lawson's nervous breakdown after hospitalization in Seattle before he "self-deported" in 1970 back to Liverpool.

Two other friends and fans of Lawson, whose work may have been an indirect inspiration for the Beatles' *Yellow Submarine* (1969), Professors Fred Anderson and Alden Mason, had encouraged both Lawson and Arreguín in their funny, cartoon-like paintings (which the teachers also expressed in their works). Commenting on Arreguín's earlier student work, Mason noted:

> They were large, broadly painted, with lots of emotion. . . and very passionate and intense.[8]

Bischoff was not alone in telling Arreguín to find his own path rather than follow trends such as Abstract Expressionism. Michael Spafford, a professor who had also lived in and travelled extensively in Mexico, conceded that the young naturalized citizen was "like a fish out of water," but added that "he was stubborn—like all good students. He was very focused on being an artist.[9]"

Amusingly, Arreguín's comment about art teachers and students in 1992 echoed director Alfred Hitchcock's remark comparing actors to cattle:

> Teachers are like cattle drivers and we are the cattle, all in a stampede and we don't know why. I don't feel that teachers really teach you anything.[10]

Seen many years later, this attitude can be discounted in view of the strong connections he maintained with a number of former teachers and fellow students over time.

Surprisingly, among the instructors whom he did credit were realist painter Norman Lundin and gestural abstractionist William Hixson, admired by their student for their teaching methods rather than any affinity he had to their art. Along these lines, it is important to draw attention to the artist's non-Hispanic sources as well as any such other influences on this bicultural artist. As Richard Andrews, long-time director of the university's Henry Art Gallery and former head of art in public places for the National Endowment for the Arts, put it in his foreword to *Re-encounters*, a survey of Pacific Northwest Latino artists that included Arreguín:

> These are artists who move freely within two cultural traditions: Latino and Euro-American. Truly bicultural, these artists represent in their work the combinatorial possibilities of twin cultural histories and perspectives.[11]

Looking through binoculars at both aspects of Arreguín's cultural hybridity—his Mexican and Euro-American touchstones—leads us to further suggestions about his art as one with global origins, too many to mention here, but thoroughly researched and analyzed elsewhere.

One faculty member who did not arrive at the School of Art until 1970, the year after Arreguín graduated, Jacob Lawrence, concludes our brief sketch of how the School of Art affected the "fish out of water," an artist who later painted a picture of isolated growth and evolution in interviews, as he told Deborah R. Huacuja in 1992: "I never had any painters who were my heroes.[12]" Lawrence, the most prominent member of the University of Washington School of Art after his arrival, was long a major figure in Seattle, whom Arreguín met shortly after his arrival. Both shared personal stories of success and struggle as minority artists in 20th-century America as well as qualities true to Mr. Isaacs's dictum—separate color areas with meticulous placement and composition, something continuously apparent in Lawrence and the mature art of Arreguín. Add to that the African-American's commitment to social and political subjects blended with his modernist approaches such as the ambiguous, shallow picture plane of Cubism, oscillating between flatness and deep space, and an appealing, directly accessible technique that was instantly recognizable as his own. Arreguín created his own pantheon of historical figures, as Lawrence had, and built a pictorial space every bit as unique and identifiable as Lawrence's.

Thus, arriving in Seattle in 1956 with a thorough artistic academic background, both in folk art and the fine arts, thanks to the vast array of fine art and vocational schools in Mexico, Arreguín was perfectly poised to take advantage of the rich scholarly and academic creative environment in Seattle.

European cultural influences, transmitted by Paris-trained intellectuals such as Isaacs, Moseley and Brazeau, along with the others mentioned above, prepared the young man for a journey that would lead him to a parallel world, similar to one repeated in 20th-century France and Mexico: the painter who gravitated toward poets and the poets who were stimulated by the company and example of painters they met in bohemian cafes and bars, restaurants and clubs in European capitals. Leaving the campus in 1969 at the age of 34, Arreguín headed for the nearby Blue Moon Tavern, not quite the Café Deux Magots or the Café Flore, but the lair of more than one Pulitzer Prize-winning poet and of several writers who would become literary celebrities, long after they changed the young man's life and art more than he could imagine.

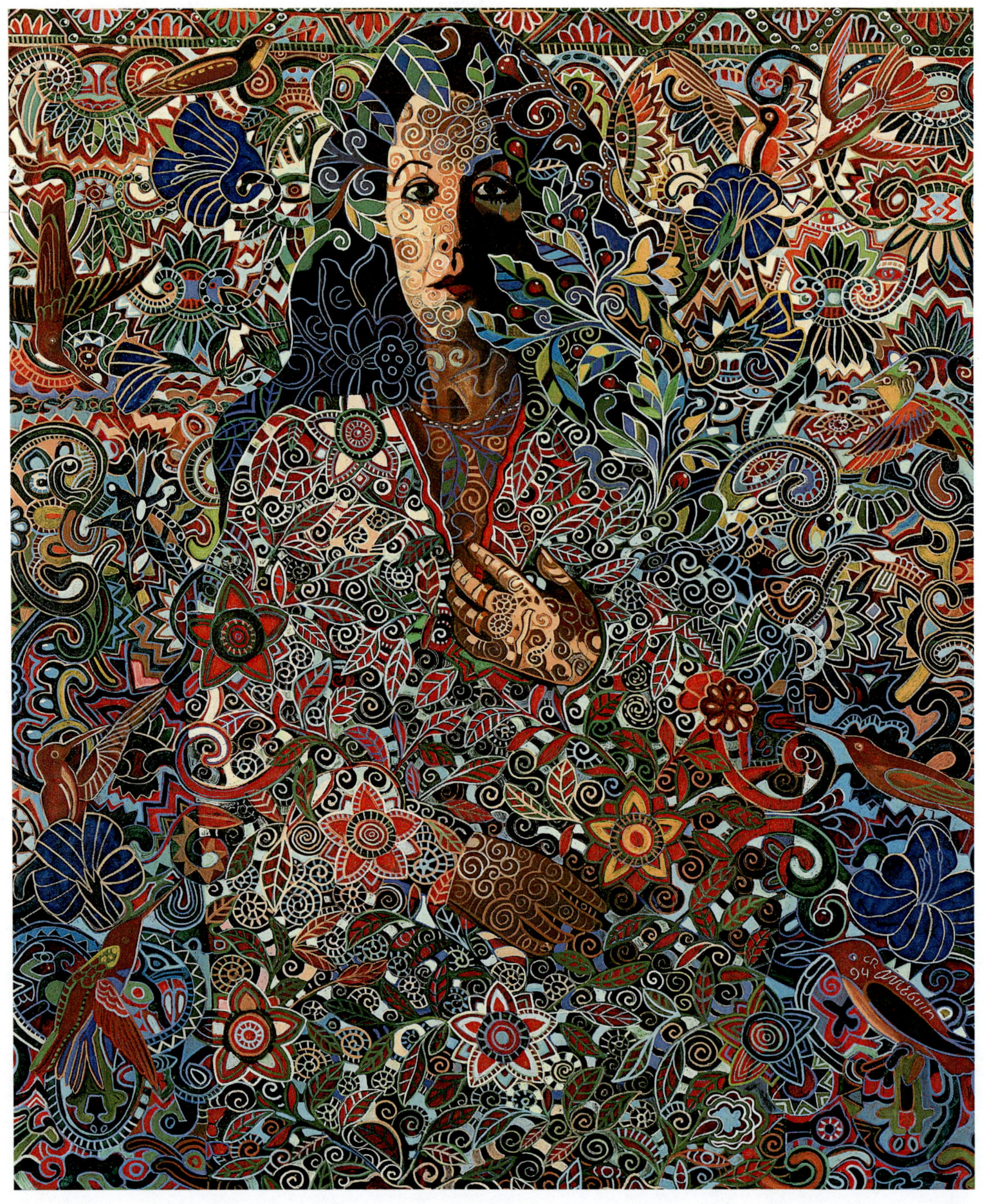

FIGURE 3. *Nuestra Señora de la Poesía*, 1994. Oil on canvas, 44 x 36 in. private collection

II. *Painter Among the Poets*

Two major 20th-century poets, Guillaume Apollinaire[13] and Frank O'Hara,[14] are referred to as "poets among the painters." Apollinaire was befriended by Picasso and others who found an affinity to Cubism in his poetry. O'Hara, also an art critic for *ARTnews* and a Museum of Modern Art, New York, curator, is associated with the New York School and Abstract Expressionist artists such as Willem de Kooning, Michael Goldberg and Larry Rivers, among many others. His poetry shared a spontaneous informal quality with Abstract Expressionism.

For our purposes, understanding Alfredo Arreguín's precise cultural matrix requires flipping the analogy: he became the painter among poets. The reversal is crucial. Rather than Arreguín emulating or imitating the poetry of the writers with whom he became associated, poets have responded warmly to the metaphorical, narrative and other seemingly literary potentials of his painting and as a result have been demonstrably influenced by him.

Before we examine those close friendships and aspects of symbiotic creativity between Arreguín and the poets who love him, it is necessary to mention two other Pacific Northwest painters who also formed close bonds with significant literary figures during the 1960-1980 period: Paul Havas and Joseph Goldberg. Havas, a New Jersey-born painter who attended the graduate School of Art (M.F.A., 1965) moved to the Skagit Valley north of Seattle in 1970 and became an ardent landscape artist, falling in with a coterie of pastoral poets equally inspired by the area's dramatic climate and topography. They wrote poems about his art and he, in turn, benefited from their camaraderie. Goldberg, who also wrote poetry, was picked up in Seattle by a conclave of local poets associated with the UW, like Michael Rust, James Wright, and John Logan, the latter two visiting professors with substantial reputations. All shared Goldberg's interest in dark lyric poetry, growing out their collective admiration of Theodore Roethke, a Pulitzer Prize-winning poet who taught at the UW before his untimely death in 1963.

Poets surrounding Havas in La Conner included Jeanne Heuving, Rust, Robert Serpa, David Horowitz and Jeffrey Gray. They favored a more loose diction, growing out of a different tradition than the poets on campus or in the University District where Goldberg lived.

The Blue Moon Tavern was a popular watering hole for students, faculty and alumni alike. Arreguín was drawn to the bohemian atmosphere not that different from New York's Cedar Tavern or the Flore or Deux Magots in Paris. At one time or another, Havas, Goldberg and Arreguín were regulars or frequenters of the bar about a mile from the campus.

Arreguín found writers gravitating to him. Although they did not influence the look of his art, many of them wrote poems and short stories about his art and personality. In a few telling examples, poems would arrive in the mail from complete strangers, such as Marit Bockelie, whose "Studying Alfredo Arreguín's Painting" singles out his 1989 veiled portrait of murdered Amazon rain-forest activist Chico Mendes. Her six couplets conclude:

> In the distant foliage Chico's dark prophetic face
>
> falls on this shadowed habitat ruled by waters.[15]

Earlier, another unexpected letter came from Kaija Berleman who was moved by the artist's canvas *Sonora* (1980) to write 24 lines, a poem of the same title that announces a long, single sentence, ending with an observation of her own physical engagement with the artwork while standing before the canvas:

> butterflies rise
>
> from her shoelaces, turn
>
> to flowers weaving
>
> through the tireless
>
> webbing of dappled jungle, defying any boundaries.[16]

A decade later, poet Jim Bodeen identified with an exhibition of the artist and his wife Susan Lytle's two- person show in his poem, "After Looking at Paintings by the Married Artists." Part of it read:

> A man from Michoacán goes to the market.
>
> His mother never sees him again.
>
> But every time he loads his paintbrush
>
> There she is again on the canvas.[17]

The two poets most central to Arreguín's life and bolstered creativity are Raymond Carver and Tess Gallagher. He met Gallagher long before her subsequent literary accomplishments and acclaim while she was a fellow UW student who became a poet, translator, novelist, and essayist, and introduced her boyfriend (and later, husband) Carver to Lytle and Arreguín in 1978. Gallagher has written extensively about "Alfredito" (as she calls him in her letters). Two poems in particular were reprinted in an 80th-birthday volume celebrating the relationships between the artist and writers, *A Arreguín: Correspondencias.*[18] "Reaching: For Alfredo Arreguín" and "I Never Wanted to March" conflate memoir and autobiography with art commentary. Both Gallagher and Carver were painted by Arreguín, portraits that are discussed below. In each portrait, words from their writings surround the figures, assembling a protective nest of language. In "Reaching," Gallagher reaches out to her friend to claim him as a fellow poet:

> Your poetry—of strokes,/of line and color—un-words me, stammers me/into myself like laughter in the rain, so I am/lifted out of myself by your intensity, by/gratitude.[19]

Carver's relation to Arreguín is more widely known, not to say equally fabled. Many readers may be aware of "Menudo," the short story that refers to "Alfredo" by name. On the surface, a tale about the Mexican hangover cure, tripe stew, "Menudo" contains the line delivered to Carver: "You listen to me. Listen to what I say, man. I'm your family now."[20] Bearing in mind that both men had already given up alcohol by the time the story was written, and that they then became able to produce their greatest achievements, "Menudo" exists on several levels: valedictory drunken revel aftermath; cautionary tale; sad, Carverian plaint. More expansive, "My Boat" is a joyous celebration of friendship with Arreguín, Lytle, and the others of their circle of poets, painters and writers. "There'll be a place on board for everyone's stories," Carver proclaims in "My Boat." "For my painter friends, paints and canvases will be on board my boat," is surely directed to Lytle and Arreguín.

The author Lauro Flores set the artist's entire oeuvre in perspective for the first time in his 2002 bilingual monograph, *Alfredo Arreguín: Patterns of Dreams and Nature.*[21] For Flores, Chilean writer Pablo Neruda is the poet he alludes to most often in relation to Arreguín. The two share references to the jungle, the ancient pre-contact past, and sensuality. Flores's poem, "A Arreguín," in *Correspondencias*, written in Spanish, is an elaborate invocation of the artist's youth near the jungle, among other things.[22] Another Spanish-language poet but living in California, Juan Felipe Herrera, an American-born writer of Mexican parentage who became Poet Laureate of both California and the US, contributed a poem that combines Spanish and English, appropriately reflecting the painter's bicultural background and widely admired spoken-word poetry performances. Suggesting the quality of light and darkness in Arreguín's paintings, he concludes:

again & the shadows again

stillness & light rain again

ten thousand faces are one.[23]

Like Arreguín discovering America, Japanese-American poet Lawrence Matsuda, another close friend, recaptures the painter's hometown of Morelia, and his reconciliation after many years with his father. In addition, Matsuda stresses his west/east bond with Arreguín who visited Japan during his U.S. Army service and undertook a study of Japanese woodcuts, especially Hokusai, whose great wave prints influenced him. Together, Matsuda and Arreguín:

We scale the white claw-shaped crests

of Hokusai's blue Tsunami waves,

descend into troughs and rise above Fuji

the eternal mountain.[24]

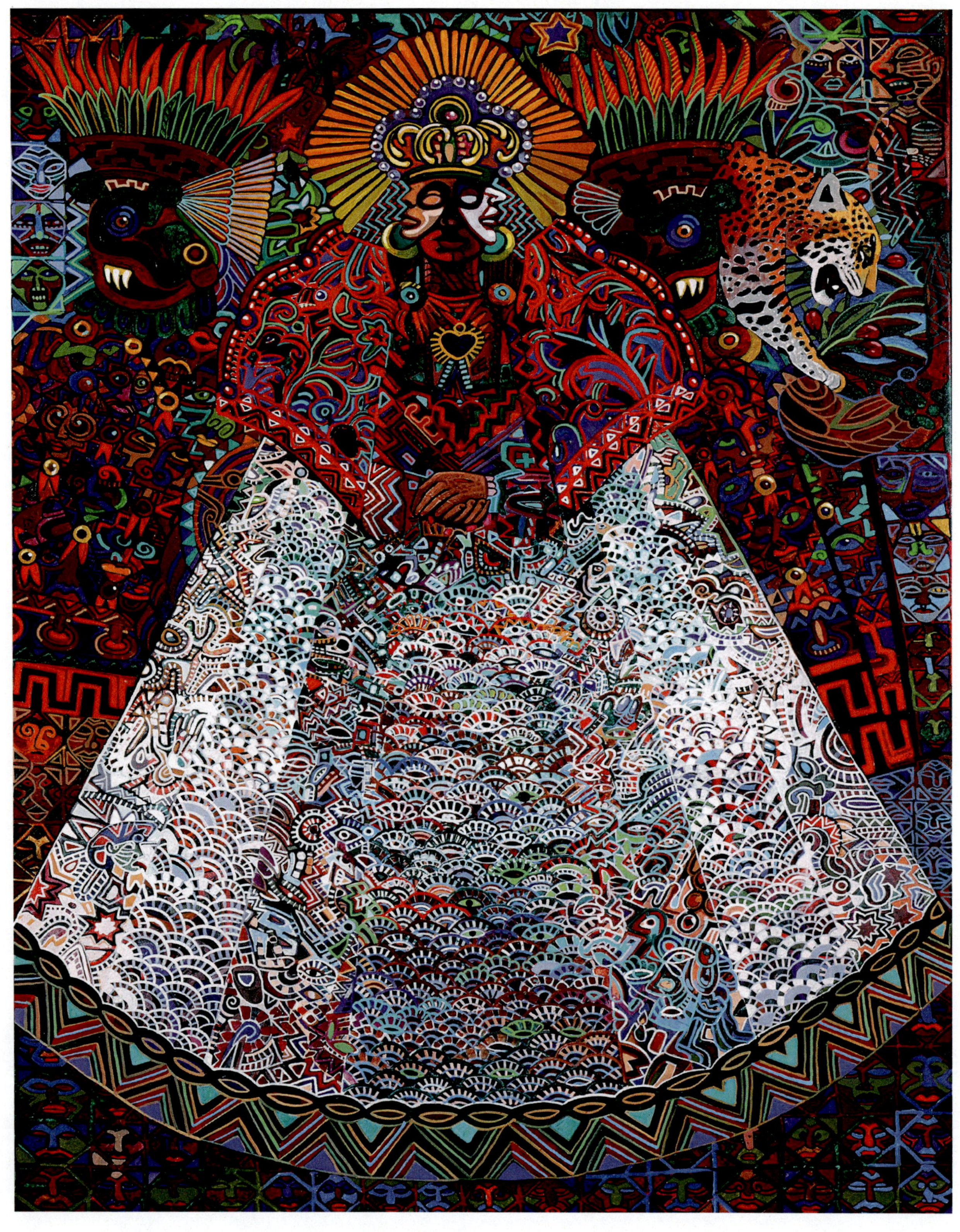

FIGURE 4. *La Malinche,* 1993, 48 x 36 in. collection of the artist

We have briefly examined the painter among the poets, although space does not permit a more thorough examination of other Spanish-language poets (and critics) inspired by the Seattle resident. The links and results reinforce Arreguín's stature as a figure of cultural influence, spreading across the visual arts into poetry and prose. The personal ties to Gallagher and Carver led to a series of portraits of them, as well as of Arreguin's family members.

III. ***Painter From the New World***

> I paint [the *Madonnas*] not for religious purposes, but to convey a spiritual feeling about saving the rain forest.[25]

These early portraits opened up a whole new world of commemorative and memorial portraits, not drawn from live sitters, but based on photographs. Arreguín's decisions about whom to honor or eulogize comprise a turning point, one that now embraces global issues of concern to him such as ecology, human rights and regional and community activism. With these portraits of Latino worthies and others, Arreguín was finally bestowed the title or category he had previously resisted or rejected: Chicano artist.[26] In this sense, the portraits depict participants in historical events, playing off an entire Hispano-European tradition of large paintings about historical happenings.

Frida Kahlo, perhaps the younger artist's most favored portrait subject, has also been a topic in many interviews with him.[27] The dominant Mexican woman painter of the past century, Kahlo's struggles and triumphs, her ties to folk art, and her construction of inward-looking dream worlds are an aesthetic plan Arreguín strongly identifies with.

However, the Frida portraits have obscured the wide range of cultural and political figures that make up Arreguín's most specifically Chicano artistic legacy. To engage in the community, to make a difference, to help children to have a healthier environment tomorrow: these were all commitments on the part of the artist before he embodied them in formally staged, i.e., full-frontal views common to the whole history of Spanish court painting and historical tableaux, from 17th-century Velázquez, through the Colonial portraits of the elite immigrants to the New World, to the so-called "crowned virgins," to whom Arreguín made several tributes. A few of the social activists and religious figures are of most interest here. They move backward and forward in time simultaneously, like an Aztec calendar.

It is one thing to "recover" such images for Latino cultures in North America and Mexico. However, when the artist's works were shown in a series of travelling exhibitions of his work in three cities in Spain, he brought the images back from the New World, a fact that was not lost on Spanish critics and media commentators.[28] In this sense, he became a re-conquistador, that is, a returning conqueror from the New World to what began as the world of Isabella la Católica, the Queen of Spain who underwrote the discovery journeys of Christopher Columbus. What did Arreguín bring? In the portraits, he has combined the presence of the jungle of Mesoamerica with the representations of sainted figures from Mexico, as well as those from South and Central America, so they could re-visit their country of religious origin, Spain. Bridges to Europe, Arreguín's pictures emphasize not only the bicultural nature of his oeuvre, but its universality and portability as well.

As he told Thomas Hubbard,

> I identify with humanity and nature, rather than with a particular race or nationality.[29]

The portraits, which are not really portraits, fall into three categories: family members and friends; artists and cultural figures; and historical and political heroes from the past and present. Beginning with portraits of his wife and daughter, the artist continued with his meditations on the life and art of Frida Kahlo, Diego Rivera and others, including poets such as Gallagher, Carver, Herrera, Flores and Matsuda.

Perhaps most important for the Spaniards to see were the political and activist figures, coming so long after the country's repressive dictatorship of Francisco Franco. Thriving in free countries, Mexico and the US, Arreguín's heroes are openly activist, if not to say revolutionary as well: Hidalgo, Zapata and Morelos from Mexico's history of revolutionary struggle; Chico Mendes, Hazel Wolf, Paulinho Paiakán, veteran protectors of the environment; Cesar Chávez, the Chicano labor activist; and even Marxist guerrilla leaders Che Guevarra and Subcommander Marcos. Exulting in the freedom to rebel and express oneself in both the US and Mexico, Spanish audiences embraced the artist's blend of mysterious, beautiful jungles and forests, magical constructions of shifting spaces of land, sea, water, mountains that enclose and people who once lived, walked on the earth, and changed the lives of many.

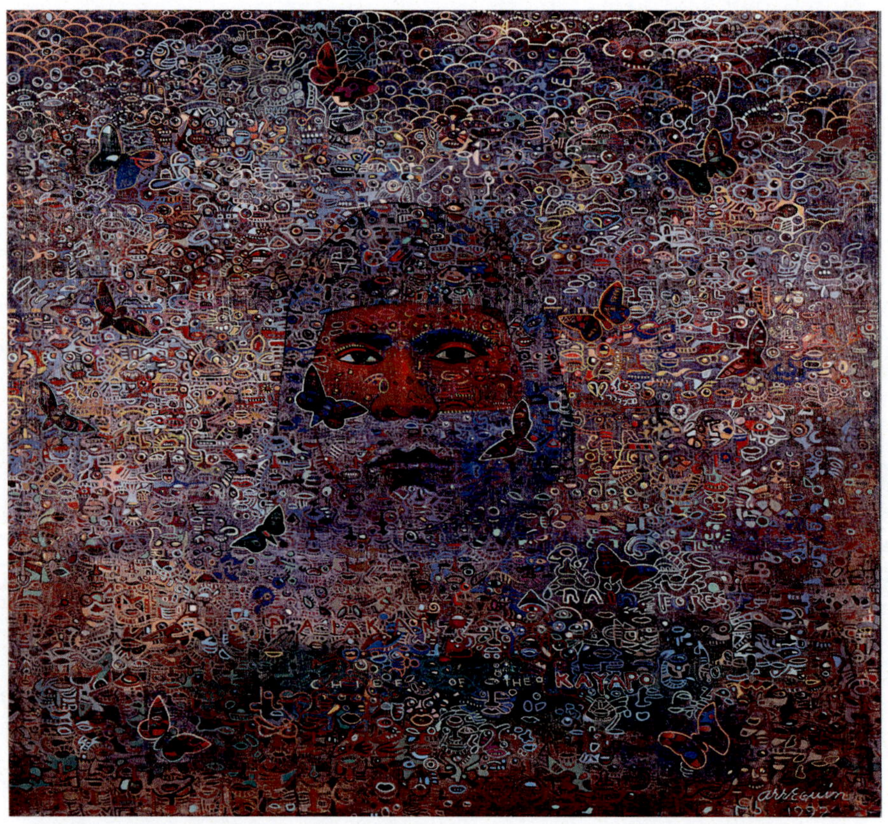

FIGURE 5. Chief Paiakán, 1992, 48 in x 48 in. private collection

Arreguín commemorates and honors their lives, reminding us, as well as audiences on other continents such as Europe and Asia, that art can be a vehicle both for subjective fantasy and social-political commentary. As such, he provides a model for an art that fuses both without recourse to rigid ideology or external plans for re-orienting society. Beginning with a luxuriant beauty of landscape, viewers may engage with issues, stories, histories and icons relevant to their lives.

Endnotes

1 Lauro Flores. *Alfredo Arreguín: Patterns of Dreams and Nature*. Seattle: University of Washington Press, 2002.

2 Douglas P. Johnson. "Mathematics, Magic Realism and the Mayans: The Paintings of Alfredo Arreguín," *Alfredo Arreguín's World of Wonders: Critical Perspectives*. Yakima, Washington: Cave Moon Press, 2018: 156-177

3 Jacquie Witherrite and Shirlee Teabo."Alfredo Arreguín Layered Images Send Intuitive Message." [Tacoma] *Morning News Tribune*, n.d.

4 See my "University of Washington School of Art 1920-1988: Three Curator's Notes." In *Relocations: Selected Art Essays and Interviews*. New York: Midmarch Arts Press, 2008: 107-115

5 Matt S. Meier. *Mexican American Biographies: A Historical Dictionary 1836-1987*. New York: Greenwood Press, 1988: 17.

6 Dee Dee Arrington. "Artist Lives On Fantasy." *The Outlook*. May 25, 1977.

7 See my "Michael Lawson." In *Relocations: Selected Art Essays and Interviews*. New York: Midmarch Arts Press, 2008: 274-291.

8 Jon Marmor. "The Magic Realist." *Columns*, September 2001: 25.

9 Ibid., 26.

10 Deborah R. Huacuja. "A Talk with Alfredo Arreguín." *Reflex*, November/December 1992: 8-9.

11 Richard Andrews. Foreword to *Reencounters: Expressions of Latino Identity in the Northwest of the USA*. Seattle: Washington State Trade and Convention Center, 1993.

12 Deborah R. Huacuja. "A Talk with Alfredo Arreguín." *Reflex*, November/December 1992: 8-9.

13 Francis Steegmuller. *Apollinaire: Poet Among the Painters*. New York: Farrar, Straus, 1963.

14 Marjorie Perloff. *Frank O'Hara: Poet Among Painters*. Chicago: University of Chicago Press, 1998.

15 Marit Boecklie. Unidentified source. Alfredo Arreguín Papers.

16 Kaija Berleman. Letter to Alfredo Arreguín, February 11, 1981.

17 Jim Bodeen. Letter to Alfredo Arreguín, October 20, 1999.

18 Lauro Flores, Ed. *A Arreguín: Correspondencias*. Seattle: Lucia/Marquand, 2015.

19 Tess Gallagher in Flores, Ed. *A Arreguín: Correspondencias*. Seattle: Lucia/Marquand, 2015: 12-13,

20 Raymond Carver in Flores, Ed. *A Arreguín: Correspondencias*. Seattle: Lucia/Marquand, 2015: 10-11.

21 Lauro Flores. *Alfredo Arreguín: Patterns of Dreams and Nature*. Seattle: University of Washington Press, 2002; Second edition, 2007.

22 Lauro Flores in Flores, Ed. *A Arreguín: Correspondencias.* Seattle: Lucia/Marquand, 2015: 19-20.

23 Juan Felipe Herrera in Flores, Ed. *A Arreguín: Correspondencias.* Seattle: Lucia/Marquand, 2015: 22-24.

24 Lawrence Matsuda in Flores, ed. *A Arreguín: Correspondencias.* Seattle: Lucia/Marquand, 2015: 29-30.

25 M. Nélida Mendoza. "Alfredo Arreguín: A Silent and Colorful Homage to Mother Nature." Poetasdelmunco.com. June 24, 2010: 4

26 M. Nélida Mendoza. "Alfredo Arreguín: A Silent and Colorful Homage to Mother Nature." Poetasdelmunco.com. June 24, 2010: 4. "I don't paint Chicano-style. . . But at the same time, I try, because everything is connected in the world—nature and politics--. . . Therefore, my connection with the Chicanos is that I cannot deny the time I've remained here, in which I've assimilated many things of this culture."

27 Thomas Hubbard. "Alfredo Arreguín, the Artist, Talks with Raven Chronicles." *Raven Chronicles,* date undetermined.

28 Virginia León. "Recorrido didáctico por la obra del mexicano Alfredo Arreguín," *Diario de Cadiz,* February 4, 2015.

29 Thomas Hubbard. "Alfredo Arreguín, the Artist, Talks with Raven Chronicles." *Raven Chronicles,* date undetermined.

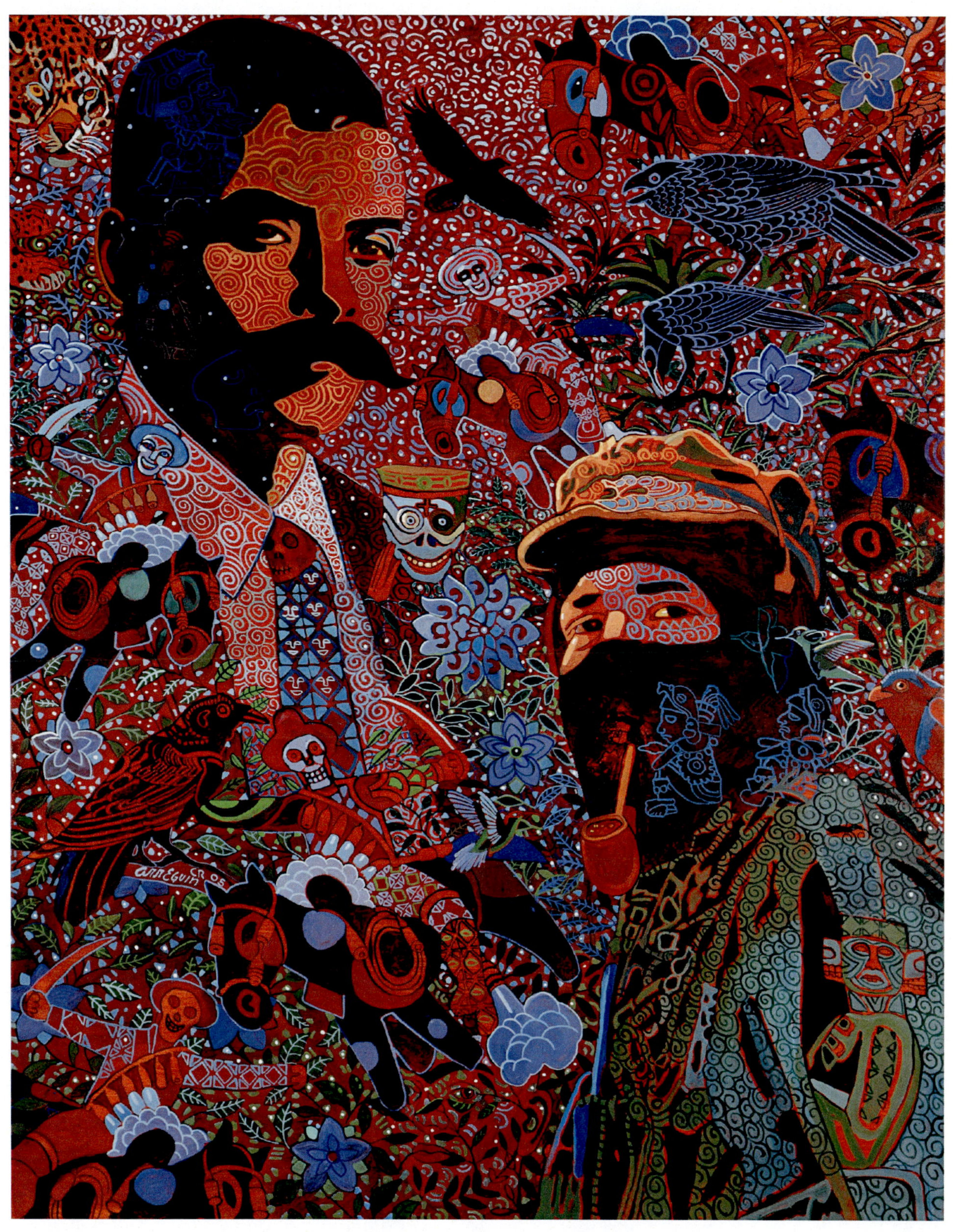

Herencia, 2005, 60 × 48 in., collection of the artist

Lauro Flores

The Eyes of Arreguín

Praise [...] for their magic lantern ...
for their huge eyes with six optical nerves!

César Vallejo

Labyrinths are puzzles that challenge us to find a way out, and nothing causes greater anguish than the labyrinths traced in dreams or life. But it is pure pleasure to get lost in Arreguín's labyrinths. Being inside his paintings, his jungles, who would want to leave?

Eduardo Galeano*

In the course of a conversation held at the University of Washington on May 16, 2006, the late Eduardo Galeano remarked, as he had written before, that "the universe must be seen through the keyhole: the largest thing seen through the smallest one." On that same occasion, the brilliant Uruguayan also said he wished that he had many eyes and could see things from many different angles at the same time.

This profusion of eyes Galeano longed for is a haunting leitmotif in many of Alfredo Arreguín's canvases, especially in his Jungles where, paraphrasing one of Pablo Neruda's poems, eyes and leaves become confused and entangled with each other. If the eyes are the windows to the soul, as it is sometimes said, it is precisely the soul of the rainforest that Arreguín attempts to capture in his paintings. From there, the enigmatic gaze of Mother Nature seems to invite us to enter her realm, her luxuriant mazes, and, as Galeano suggested, get lost there for a while in a symbolic if fleeting act of communion and reconciliation with her. However, one cannot help but wonder about the real significance of those eyes that lurk from behind the foliage. Is Mother Nature beckoning us to rejoin her, or rather issuing a warning? Is she returning our gaze, watching us and silently reproaching us for our disregard, intrusions, abuses, and rampant destruction of her realm?

Displaying his extraordinary ability to alternate between landscape painting and portraiture, and frequently fusing elements of both figurative and decorative modes, Arreguín has successfuly developed a distinctive, powerful, and highly recognizable aesthetic expression. With a vast body of work and countless exhibitions and recognitions under his belt, his reputation has grown over the years, and his artistic genius is now fully cemented and broadly acknowledged. In 2007-2008, for example, he was invited to participate in the *Portraiture Now: Framing Memory* exhibition organized and hosted by the Smithsonian National Portrait Gallery, in Washington D.C. The five pieces selected for the exhibition were: *Good Harvest, Herencia, Kahlo de Coyoacán, The Return to Aztlán*, and *Zapata's Messenger*—all included among the new illustrations added in the second edition of my book, Alfredo Arreguín: *Patterns of Dreams and Nature* (2007).

About ten days before Galeano's talk at the University of Washington, on May 5, 2006, during her latest visit to Seattle, I took the eminent Mexican writer and cultural critic Elena Poniatowska to visit Arreguín and view a small sample of his work, including some of the portraits he was preparing for the aforementioned show at the National Portrait Gallery. After our impromptu and hasty visit to the artist's studio, Poniatowksa commented to me that she did not find in the eyes of Arreguín's subjects—Emiliano Zapata and Frida Kahlo, specifically—the glimmer and intensity that the real persons seem to have had, at least as we perceive it in the extant historical photographs and video recordings.

Poniatowska's insightful observation was correct, of course. A pensive quality, almost a certain aura of sadness, permeates the gaze of these and other iconic figures portrayed by Arreguín. For example, in *Sacrificio na Amazonia* (1989), Chico Mendes, the rubber tappers union leader who fought valiantly against the wanton destruction of the Brazilian rainforest, and who was ultimately murdered in 1988, seems have been reabsorbed by Nature, to have become part of that organic and ghostly entity that watches us impassively from that eternal realm, which is the same timeless zone occupied by the soul of the jungle. In similar fashion, Zapata and Frida, also re-appropriated now by Nature, seem to observe us with an air of remoteness—perhaps curious to learn what we are going to do, which path we are going to take. Nevertheless, at the risk of incurring into a paradox, I must say that it is almost as if they were peering from the distant past into the future, which is our present, into the current situation in which we live: a world riddled with abuse, violence, injustice, hunger, and war—and seemingly doomed by the accelerated destruction of the environment. How could the regard of those souls be different? How could their eyes be devoid of sadness and apprehension? "Is this what I fought and died for?", the meditative Zapata seems to ask.

The artist is the oracle, the visionary who has the ability to look beyond the immediate reality, to apprehend the universe by peeking through the keyhole and then depict it on the canvas or in the poem. Thus, he becomes the voice of conscience that opens our eyes, that nips, bites, and zings urging us to reflect upon our common human condition and the organic place we occupy within the order of the cosmos. As the great Spanish bard Rafael Alberti wrote in his poem, The Eyes of Picasso:

He's always all eyes
he doesn't take his eyes off you
He eats words with his eyes
He is Seven Eyes
The One Thousand Eyes in two eyes
The great Peeping Tom
like one brown button
and another button.
The keyhole
through which you eye the painting so.
The one who opens wide your eyes
when he nips you with his eyes

Ultimately, it is through Arreguín's eyes, through his soul and artistic sensibility, that we are able to perceive our human condition and share that vision of a common legacy. He leads us to ponder our individual location and quotidian interaction with Mother Nature, and also our role in determining the quality of the world we'll be leaving behind for future generations. In that unfathomable future, will our faraway eyes show the twinkle Poniatowska would like to see in the eyes of Arreguín's portraits, or will they display the malaise stored in the soul of those who feel they did not do enough, or that what they did was all in vain?

As Galeano observed, the lush labyrinths Arreguín creates in his paintings are a delightful refuge—especially when one considers the current state of affairs of our planet. Once we enter his jungles, we never want to leave.

*I want to thank Eduardo Galeano once again, now posthumously, for giving me this quote for the publication of the second edition of the volume Alfredo Arreguín: Patterns of Dreams and Nature (2007). Our mutual friend Tony Geist, who translated Alberti's verses included in this piece, also helped me with the translation of Galeano's epigraph into English. The last sentence, however, "Being inside his paintings, his jungles, who would want to leave?", is Eduardo's rendering of his own words.

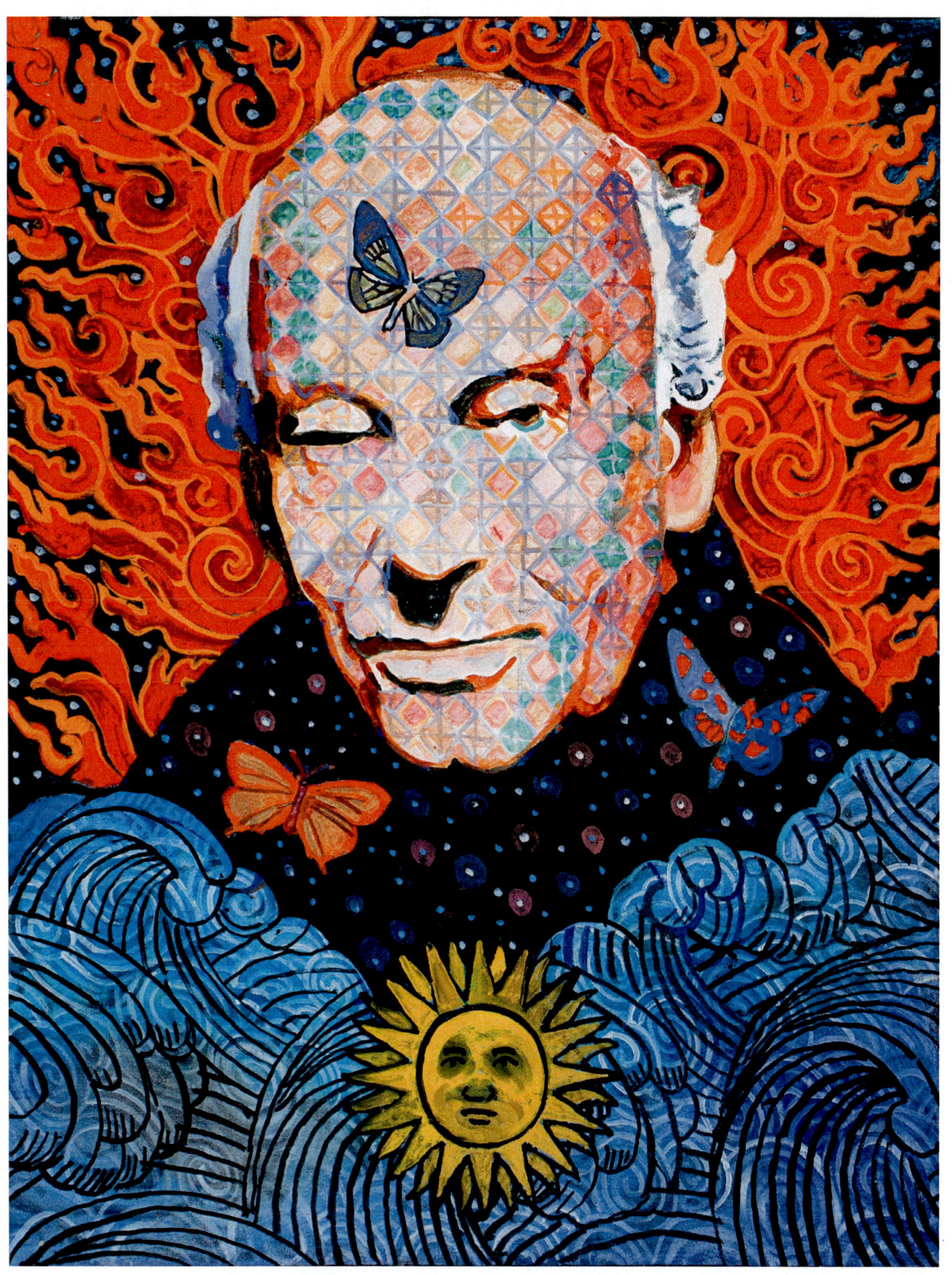

Galeano, 2015, 28 × 22 in., collection of the artist

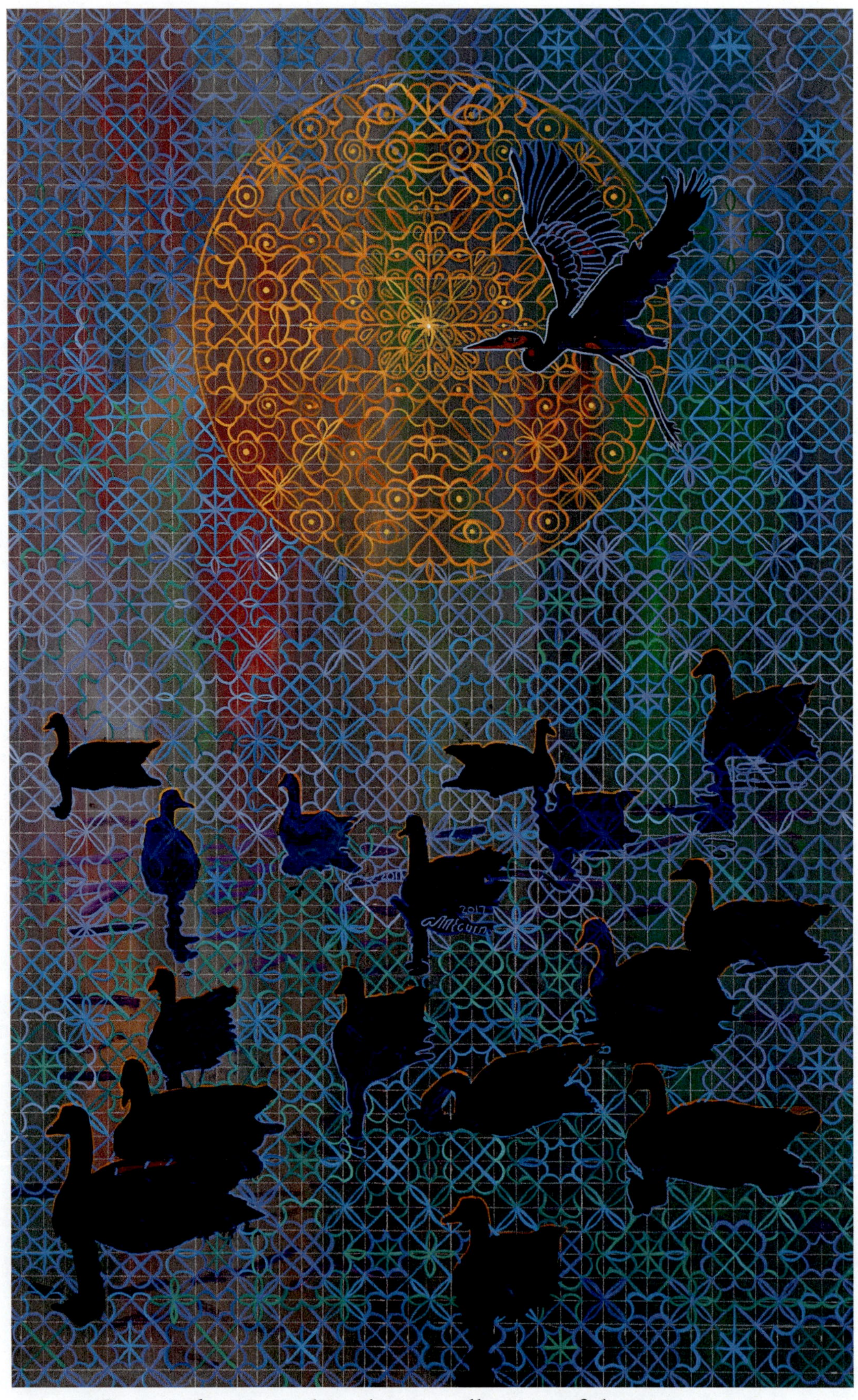

Green Lake, 2017, 60 × 40 in., collection of the artist

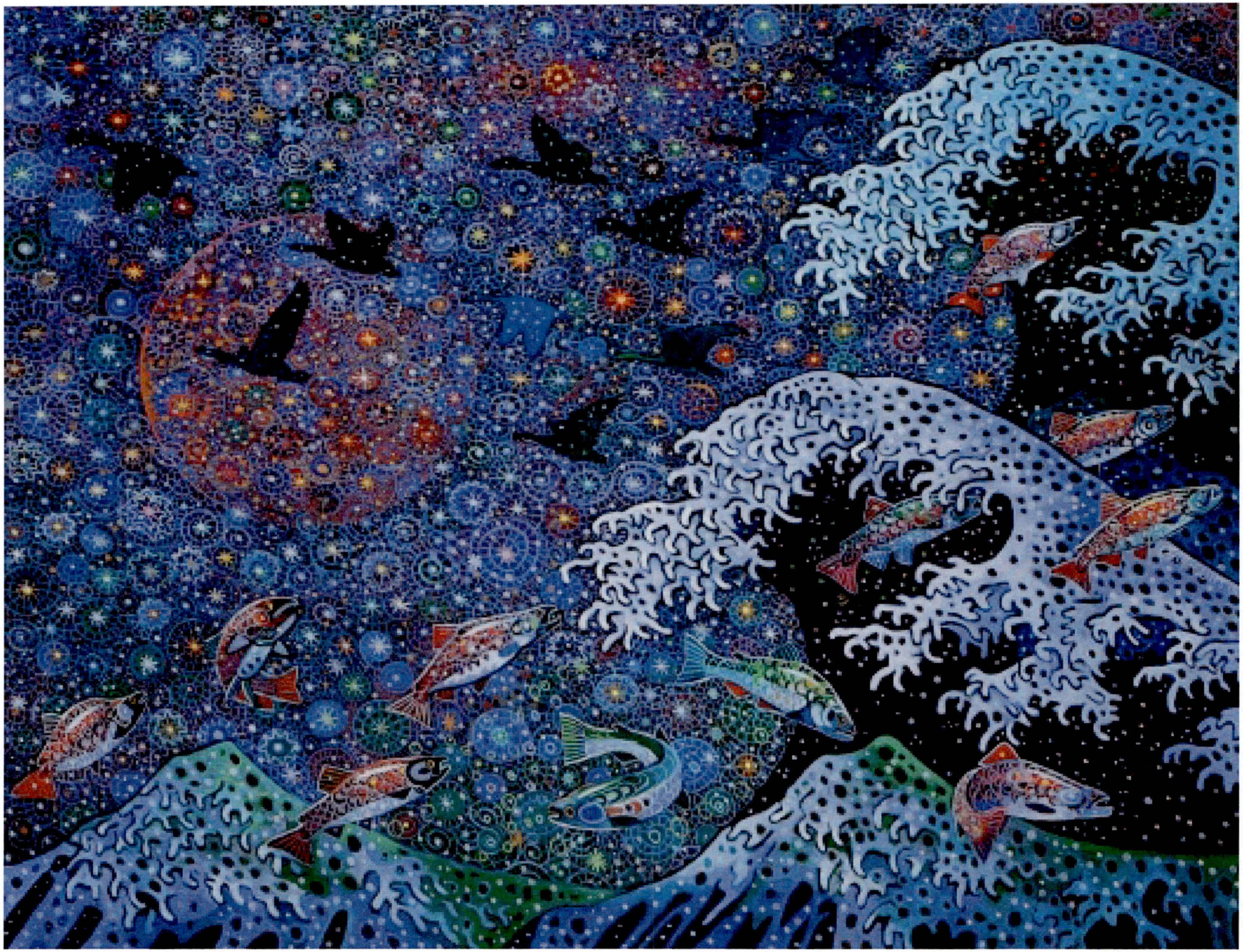

Dancing with The Stars, 2016, 48 × 60 in., collection of the artist

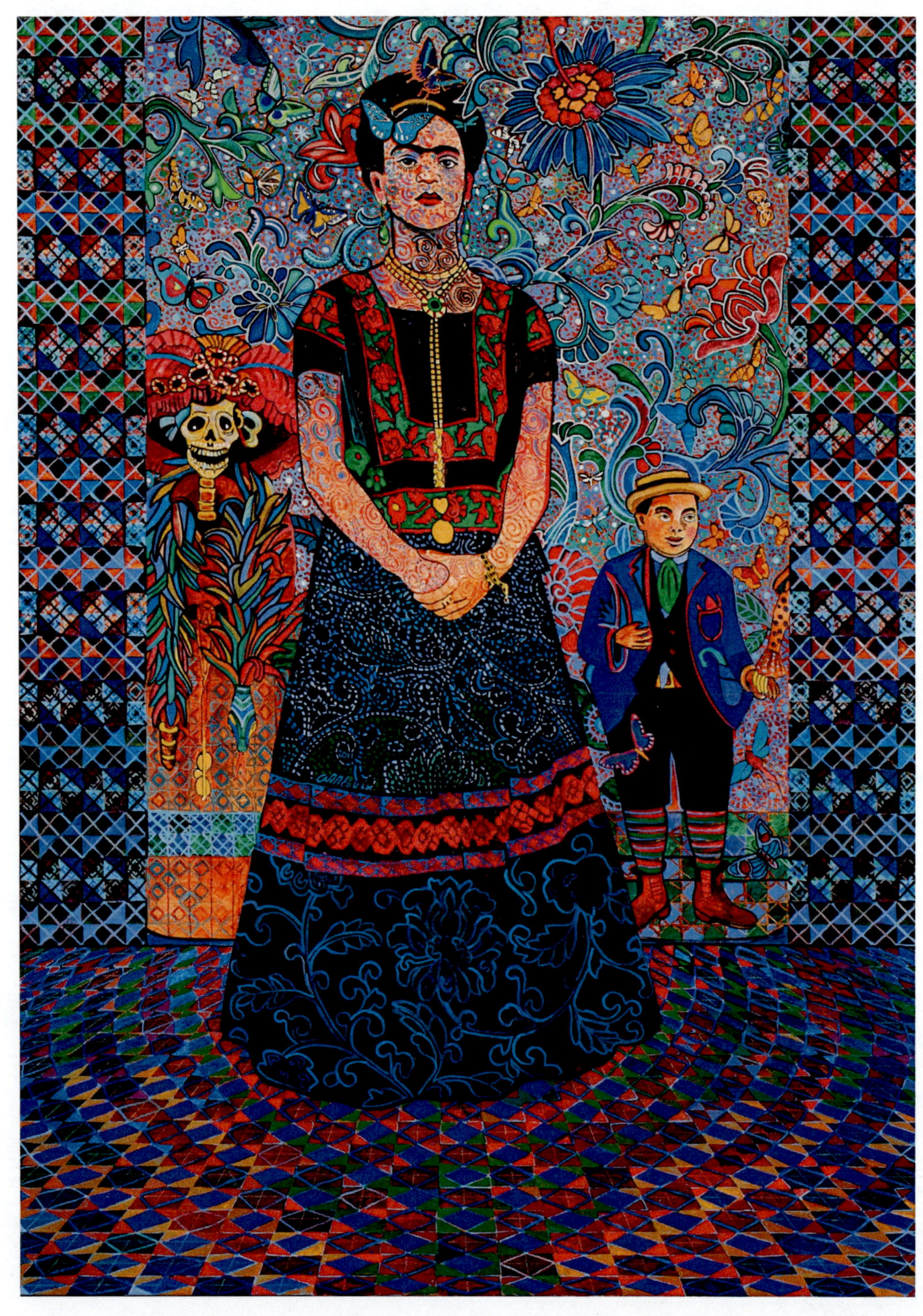

La Alameda, 2012, 58 × 42 in., collection of the artist

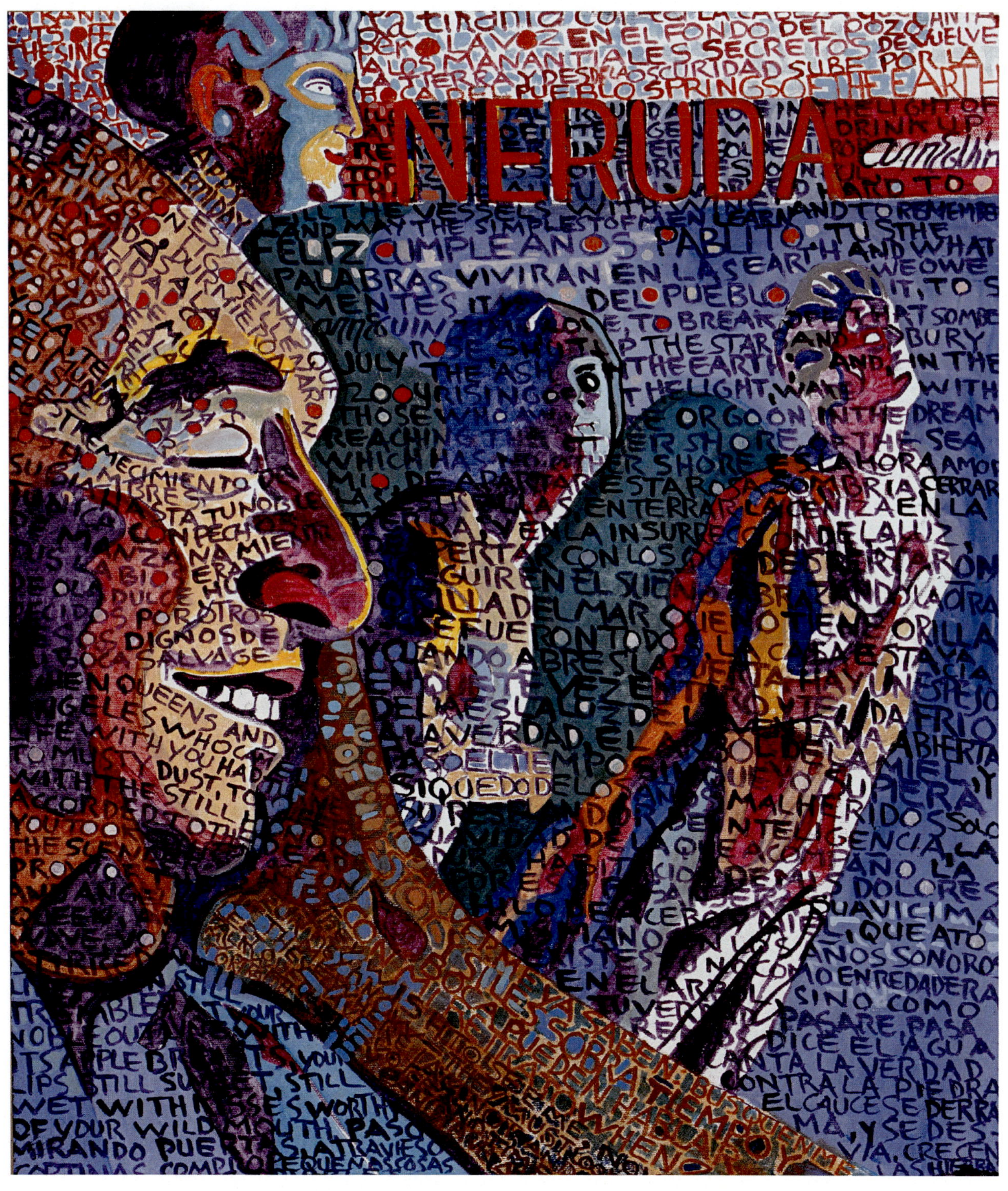

Sirenas, 2003, 24 × 18 in., collection of the artist

Lawrence Matsuda

Finding Morelia, Michoacan de Ocampo

—for Alfredo Arreguín

Wine glasses purple to the brim
sooth the restless soul.
Alfredo no longer the aspiring artist who
swings on Blue Moon Tavern chandeliers.

Tonight he holds court,
remembers his childhood trip
with his grandfather
to Morelia, Michoacán.

Family, he says, *means more than fame.*

His English words ripe –
smooth and luscious,
in their Mexican precision
launch like fireworks: skyrocket
to the ceiling, explode into ever-expanding
bursts of colors, then cascade as embers.

Alfredo recalls peering through train windows
beyond clouds of sooty smoke that yield
to a lush countryside, purple mountains.
Thick forests and billowing seas of dried grass
emerge. Pintos gallop with abandon
to the chunking rhythm of the train from Morelia,
place of his birth, home of Conquistadors.

A majestic city glows golden in his paintings,
surrounded by green jungles teeming
with red-orange toucans
and yellow-eyed jaguars.

Alfredo dances barefooted in the town square,
l'enfant terrible, a fatherless orphan of love.

Love means more than fame.

Morelia becomes a dream,
an imaginary place
only children remember
and adults never find.

Memories materialize on canvas:
thin contours, shape-lines,
filled in with layers of brilliant colors
trap thousands of pulsating
swirls, ovals and hidden faces.
Every molecule sparkles
as if held in the Madonna's arms.

His blue eyes explained in Mexico City:
eyes of the Conquistador set in Alfredo's Michoacan face—
his blue-eyed father, appears
to claim his son and embrace his art.

Absorbed by his paintings,
falling through their looking glass,
his testimony, his cauldron— colors
envelop, transform me
into a blue-eyed child. Like him
I search for that protected
place of belonging where ripe
mango clusters grow iridescent.
Where fathers embrace their sons.

Listening to his story of reconciliation,
the love of his lost father—
the mental shackles of my internment shatter
into a thousand coral snakes
twisting on the ground.

I kick them aside like a wild pinto
and sprint through frothy waves
of green to the golden heart, Morelia,
cradled between purple mountains.

Alfredo, descent of conquistadors and Indians,
chases schools of spawning King Salmon with me, the samurai.
Adventure is our compass to the essence of all living things.
We scale the white claw-shaped crests
of Hokusai's blue Tsunami waves,
descend into troughs and rise above Fuji,
the eternal mountain.

Rose City Vacation (Excerpt)

In Portland, Oregon I rise in my hotel room,
pillows strewn helter-skelter,
scene reminiscent of marshmallows floating
in a hell's broth. I recall our mutual friend, Alfredo,
who lands in Portland like a shanghaied sailor
unable to remember anything beyond
his Blue Moon Tavern binge in Seattle the night before.
Alfredo's adventure rivals the night he stacked
two unsecured paintings on the roof of his car,
navigated hills under the influence
and pin-balled down Ravenna Avenue.
His canvases must have sprouted Edvard Munch-like
expressionist arms and hands to grip their extraterrestrial
mosaic faces in fear as they screamed all the way home.
I discover Portland is a carnival wonderland where
bacon drapes maple bars and pretzels impale chocolate
voodoo-doll donuts oozing raspberry blood.
Food-cart shantytowns sprout in downtown parking lots,
gypsy chuck wagon villages, magnet for hordes of lip-smacking,
khaki-clad office workers and itinerant street musicians.

Lauro Flores

A Arreguín (cartouche libre)

tout ce que le
soleil entoure

La luz te vio, y tú viste la luz
—halo invernal, azul y primigenio—,
en un lugar erigido con piedra
y primaveras: flores labradas,
aves labradas, libélulas labradas
en canteras rosáceas—suaves y
bellas pero, a fin de cuentas, piedras.

El milagro ocurrió sin magos ni pesebres:
la piedra vuelta flor en alegres relieves.
Mariposas posadas en arcos aún sin triunfos,
en nichos y balcones, en las vides de hierro.
Suave aleteo del abejorro por los verdes
vergeles, y el canto plurilingüe del cenzontle,
¡pájaro bicolor de cuatrocientas voces!

Llegó la primavera con una flor de lis:
aquel rayo febril—¡soles de abril y mayo!—
cayó a plomo sobre campánulas y nardos
(varas de San José), dragonarias tarascas;
margaritas y mirtos, rústicas chalihuescas
y albos alcatraces—monoicos embudos,
¡flores de pato! ¡petálicos cartuchos!

Allí te iluminó en cada ocaso
el rojo resplandor del sol poniente
—agonizante, herido, taciturno—
En aquella ciudad hecha de piedra
—cantera suave pero, con todo, pétrea—
aunque rosada y bella. Flor encendida,
ángelus cárdeno, ¡crepúsculo escarlata!

Y en los pasillos, en claroscuros perfilados,
una fila de tiestos de helechos atestados,
de malvas, de geranios, flores especulares
de aquel diseño azul de añejos azulejos.
Firmes custodios del corredor, ¡celosos guardias!,
persistentes serenos en constante vigilia,
tu infancia vigilaron con ojos sigilosos.

Al interior, ceñido por esbeltas columnas,
un vergel habitado por seres vegetales:
limoneros, higueras, un hermoso naranjo;
dos nísperos nipones y una guía de estropajo.
Una esencia de azahares perfumaba las tardes
y endulzaba tus siestas en faldas de tu abuela,
tus tías y tu madre, María la *più bella.*

Los sutiles susurros del colibrí sagrado,
atávico emisario del reino de Tzintzuntzan
(de Las Canoas vecino ¡antónimo del duelo!)
y el zumbido fugaz de los nupciales zánganos
delirantes de polen (¡ambarinos! ¡profanos!),
pausaban la cadencia de tu impúber sueño,
y alentaban el ala de tu onírico vuelo.

Pero un día el azar y una mágica bala,
pérdida y encontrada, te llevaron en vilo
al altiplano padre—a la urbe de asfalto,
de edificios en ciernes y altos rascacielos.
Rodeado de volcanes coronados de hielo,
de guerreros humeantes y mujeres dormidas,
vislumbraste tu estrella: tu sino adivinado.

Pensativo, inclinado sobre el atlas del cosmos,
el padre Hado empuñó astrolabio y sextante;
buscó con telescopio el astro inexorable,
dedujo las distancias, midió las situaciones,
y con pulso templado dibujó tu trayecto,
hacia el mágico bosque, pluvial, interminable.
¡De donde sale todo!—dijo, con voz tronante.

Las henchidas simientes de aquel recinto verde
entraron en tu esencia por las puertas azules
de tus imberbes ojos y esparcieron en tu alma
sus feraces semillas, sus pólenes dorados.

*

Años después, el trazo de la diosa Fortuna
te condujo a otros lares por ti insospechados:
topografías afines de volcanes nevados,
valles, pluviales bosques y lagos argentados.

Allí adquirió forma cabal—redonda, entera—
aquel, el leve balbuceo inicial de tu pincel.
Germinaron, por fin, los núcleos que la selva
plantó en las hendiduras de tu substancia fértil.

Allí brotaron, al final, flores y hojas,
pájaros y jaguares, mariposas, iguanas;
toda la fauna y flora de tu primera infancia,
de tu dual juventud en Guerrero y Anáhuac.

Paul McVeigh

Hollow

1.

A couple lived on a farm far away from the rest of the world. They had land to grow vegetables, chickens that gave eggs, and a well for water. Nearby, there was a stream jumping with fish and, right at the edge of their land, a wood with trees to chop for the fire.

The couple had everything they needed except for one small thing.

On their wedding day, to mark the occasion, the couple had planted an apple tree at the entrance to the wood and, exactly five years later, it bore fruit for the first time, as though celebrating their anniversary.

"Surely, it's a sign," the wife said.

The husband patted her stomach and smiled.

The years passed and the woman's belly showed no swell, and though deep love slept within them, the couple stopped lying with each other.

The man took to going to the edge of the wood at the end of his working day to sit underneath the apple tree. At times, when he hadn't come home for supper, the woman would go looking for her husband only to find him sleeping against its trunk.

"See what you've done," she said, one evening, while helping her husband to his feet. "You've worn a dent in the tree with your back."

She smiled through a sting of jealousy. Being of a sensible nature she shook her head and laughed at herself, returning to the calm she knew.

One day, when the man was tired from his work and felt the cool of the setting sun in his bones, he went to the wood and sat, leaning in the nook he had worn in the trunk of the tree. This groove his body had made over the years seemed to welcome him. Before long he drifted off to sleep.

In his dream, he was exactly where he'd sat to rest but the day was unbearably hot. He took off his shirt, then the rest of his clothes, and lay naked at the foot of the tree. Despite the heat, a blanket of cool damp leaves covered the earth beneath the shade.

I wish there was a breeze, he thought, and closed his eyes.

What felt like a cool breath, ran over him, making the fine, blonde hair of his stomach stand and his skin bump and tingle. When he opened his eyes, the five-flowered blossoms on the apple tree waved. The branches swayed. He knew it wasn't the wind but the tree itself fanning him. The branches came toward him, wrapping around his body and pulling him up and in until he was pressed against the trunk of the tree.

He placed his hands on the bark and looked up at the dance of the branches above.

"How beautiful you are," he said, then kissed the tree tenderly. "How I've ignored you all this time. Have I been blind?"

The groove he had made with his back was now hip-height as he stood, and it yielded as he pressed against the tree. Leaves whispered in his ear and the smell of apple blossom filled his head and he became aroused. He made love to the tree in way that dreams allow. As he came, the tree caved, and he sank deep inside the damp, darkness of the hollow.

When he woke, he found he was lying naked on the earth. He tried to piece together what had happened, grasping at images from his dream, but, like snowflakes, they disappeared the instant he touched them. All that remained was a feeling of deep shame. He was cold and became self-conscious. Dressing quickly, he hurried home, his head thick with fog and full of fear and the sense of something very important lost.

2.

The tree waited for the man to return. Every day, as the sun rose, the tree unfurled its leaves to the cottage in the distance. Every afternoon, the tree waited, hoping to see the man appear walking towards it through the long grass. But he was never again to rest himself on its bark.

As the days grew hotter, apples burst from its branches, tiny and sore. One, sprouting from the tip of the highest branch, caused the most pain. Within a week it had grown ten times the size of the others. It weighed down the branch until it rested on the earth. As the summer had its way, while the other apples matured and fell, the huge fruit stayed and did not stop growing.

One morning, as the tree opened for the sun, something was different. The large apple had disappeared. The branch that had held it now led inside the hollow that had been made the last time the farmer had come. The tree pulled to bring the fruit out, bark cracking from the strain. It called upon its deep roots to help. And with the strength of the earth itself, it strained until there was a cry. A human cry. Now the branch came easily. It rustled out from the hollow and with it a baby boy, the tip of the branch attached to the boy's belly.

The tree slid some branches under the baby and lifted it off the ground. The tree wept leaves and blossoms of joy at the sight of the boy. The boy screamed and cried. The tree curled a branch around a rock and bashed its trunk until its bark split. It brought the boy to the split and he drank the sap.

The tree was devoted to the boy. It shaded him under its branches when he was hot and sheltered him in the hollow when he was cold. It let him drink his fill of its sap, held and rocked him till he slept. And the boy was content, playing among the roots. The farmer never returned.

When the boy had been with the tree for seven years, and the autumn had painted them both brown and orange, a tiny figure appeared in the horizon and came towards them. The tree became frightened for the boy, ushering him into the hollow and concealing it with its branches.

A little girl emerged from the grass swinging a small basket. She sat on the ground and picked the apples, throwing away the bruised and wrinkled but keeping the golden and shiny for herself. The girl began to sing. Clear, high and pure, her voice hung in the air like a sweet smell.

The tree resisted as the boy pushed at the branches to escape the hollow. The boy growled, a sound he'd never made before. The little girl jumped. The growling became a whimper. The girl looked at the tree, glanced back at the cottage in the distance, then stood. Flattening down her skirt, she tiptoed towards the tree trunk.

"Hello," she said, tugging at the branches that covered the hollow. The boy struggled on his side, too, and soon the two of them were standing face to face.

"Who are you?" she said.

The boy reached out and touched her hair then touched his own. The girl spat on the hem of her skirt then wiped the earth from his face. The tree shivered at this, its leaves rustled a warning.

"That's better," the girl said.

The boy glanced back at the tree and then at the girl.

"I'm not supposed to come here," she said. "It'll be our secret."

She held her finger to her lips.

"I have to go, but I will come back." The girl smiled, picked up her basket, and off she skipped.

The boy run after the girl until the branch that led from his belly to the tree snapped him back. He pulled at the branch. The tree felt those tugs deep in its sap. As the girl disappeared over the horizon, the boy dropped to the earth with a thump.

The boy didn't return to the tree straight away but sat watching the sun grow tired and heavy until it sank from the sky to rest. When the chill of the dark came to rouse him, the boy stood and, with his foot, made a circle of turned-up soil around the tree, mapping his boundary.

As the autumn darkened, the girl came to the tree every afternoon. She brought books with drawings inside and taught the boy about the world beyond the field. Even after he understood her talk, he would not speak back. He was ashamed of the rustling whispers that came out of his mouth when he practiced alone. The girl didn't seem to mind that he was always silent – except when he laughed. He couldn't keep the wet, sticky clacking sound inside. The next summer, while the tree was busy bearing fruit, energy low, busy with so much life, the girl came all day, every day. The children started whispering. They were keeping secrets. When they did this, the tree would tickle them with leaves or drop apples on their heads. They'd laugh then move further away.

One sticky, late summer's day, under the pale blue sky, the boy ran to greet the girl. This time they lingered at the very limit that his branch allowed. The summer had been a hot one, and the apples on the tree had grown heavy and begun to drop before their time.

When it happened, it was like an explosion. Every branch shook, every apple fell. When the surge passed, the tree saw the girl and the boy running across the field, hand in hand. In the girl's other hand, an axe glinted in the sun.

3.

The boy's bony fingers felt crushed by the girl's hand, he was sure he heard a snap, but he didn't mind. He barely touched the ground, pulled with such force by the girl, as she ran through the field, down and then up the hill. He'd never been outside of his little circle around the tree and the further he went the more frightened he became, but excited too. The girl didn't seem to notice. She pulled, dragging him on.

Ahead he saw a cottage, just like the pictures the girl had shown him. It was where people lived. People like him. At the door, the girl said, "Wait here," and kissed him on the cheek. He nodded and watched her go in. The door clicked but didn't catch and remained slightly open. The boy was left alone for the first time in his life, he felt light headed and wondered if he had made a terrible mistake.

He watched through the gap in the door.

"Daddy! I've brought my friend home," the girl cried.

"A friend? Where?" The father squinted at his daughter. "Don't leave the child outside."

"It's the boy I've been telling you about," she said, "the boy from the tree."

"The apple tree at the edge of the wood?" her mother asked. "That's your father's tree."

"I've told you to stay away from that tree," her father scolded. "And it's not my tree!" He glared at his wife. "No wonder her head is full of nonsense."

The girl ran out the door and grabbed the boy by the hand. He was stiff with fear, but she dragged him in and helped him onto a chair.

"See," she said, pointing at the boy.

"Oh yes, he's a lovely boy, isn't he?" the mother said. "He looks a little familiar." She winked at her husband.

"Can we get him some clothes?" asked the girl.

"You're not dressing a piece of wood," her father snapped.

"When I start school, he can come too," said the girl. "We can say he's my brother."

The father slammed his fist on the dinner table.

The mother laughed. "He does have his father's eyes."

At that, the girl's father jumped up, lifted the boy from his chair, snapped him in half over his knee, and threw him on the fire.

As he burned, the boy saw the little girl cry on her mother's lap while the father picked up an axe, walked out the door and headed for the wood.

David J. de la Torre

Alfredo Arreguín: From the Mexican Museum to the National Portrait Gallery

Alfredo Arreguín's astonishing patterned artwork - referencing ancient culture, tropical habitats, exotic creatures, and historic portraiture - has engaged and delighted audiences for over fifty years. Arreguín was born in Morelia, Mexico, in 1935 and traveled to Seattle, Washington, at the age of 21 to attend college. He went on to pursue life in the United States as an artist and also served in the US military. His journey to success as a Mexican immigrant represents an inspiring and timely achievement, and I am fortunate to have witnessed the artists' rise to importance and recognition.

I first became familiar with Arreguín's work and its amazing capacity to engage viewers in September of 1976 while working as an intern at The Mexican Museum in San Francisco. Museum founder Peter Rodriguez had mounted one of the first exhibitions of Alfredo's work at the museum's original venue on 1855 Folsom Street in San Francisco's Mission District.

Alfredo recalled, *"Living in Seattle, I saw a newspaper article mentioning that Peter Rodriguez was opening the country's first Mexican Museum on Folsom Street in San Francisco. I wrote asking him to consider showing me. After sending him slides of my work, he was very enthusiastic to offer me my first show in a Mexican Museum."*

Rodriguez brilliantly paired Arreguín with masterworks by Dr. Atl (Gerardo Murillo, 1875-1964). I recall Peter's proud, enthusiastic attitude toward Alfredo's work at the time and with reason – his paintings immediately captivated everyone who walked into the new museum. The pairing of the two artists, one emerging and one well known, also helped draw visitors in during the museum's formative days.

The bond between Peter and Alfredo continued to grow during the 1970's. This was a time of Chicano activism and advocacy as community-based ethnic arts organizations, struggling to achieve recognition and appreciation for minority artists, continued to emerge and proliferate in most major metropolitan cities across the country. Alfredo became part of a national movement for inclusion and visibility for minority artists through his involvement with alternative arts organizations such as Plaza de la Raza, Los Angeles; Intar Gallery, El Museo del Barrio, Museum of Contemporary Hispanic Art (Caiman Gallery), New York City; and Mexican Fine Arts Center/National Museum of Mexican Art, Chicago.

Recently, René Yañez, co-founder of the Galería de la Raza in San Francisco reflected on Alfredo's early career *"...Alfredo was a hustler.* He was always sending slides to us and updating his resume." Alfredo was just one of many up-and-coming visual artists who dedicated themselves and their work to pressing social and political themes facing the nation and the world. However, Alfredo became a leader and an example of a highly skilled, savvy artist working for the common good as he propelled his career forward.

Peter continued to nurture Alfredo and his work, offering Arreguín two exhibitions, a one-person show in 1977 and a retrospective in 1983. Peter wanted to provide opportunity to Latinos, particularly Mexicans, for exhibiting their work in a world where larger institutions at the time seldom recognized minority artists.

Alfredo acknowledged the significance that his first museum exhibition was organized by The Mexican Museum and the opportunities that were presented to him as a result, stating, *"The Mexican Museum was very important in my career as an artist. Because of Peter's recommendation, I was chosen to represent the United States at the International Festival of Painting in Cagnes-Sur Mer, France, where I won The Palm of the People's Award. With Peter's collaboration I was part of CARA (Chicano Art: Resistance and Affirmation), a major national touring exhibition organized by UCLA that landed at the Smithsonian's National Museum of American Art, and, later on, a curator, Andrew Connors came to Seattle to ask me to submit slides for consideration to purchase a work for the museum's permanent collection. They acquired my triptych, Sueño Dream: Eve before Adam), in 2004."*

One of the milestones in Alfredo Arreguín's artistic career was exhibiting at the National Portrait Gallery, which acquired his painting *The Return to Aztlán* (2006). Alfredo explained how the Smithsonian's National Portrait Gallery became interested in acquiring his work:

"When I was being celebrated at a Smithsonian party that Andrew Connors organized, the woman sitting next to me at the table was the Smithsonian Secretary of Education. She asked what my opinion was of the National Portrait Gallery. I told her that it was too white and gray and that it needed COLOR!, a suggestion that I thought would carry the message that we needed more artists of color in the museum. Then I was offered, not only that they wanted a painting of mine for their collection, but also to give me a show. Agreeing, I had the exhibition of my work and at the opening night, as I approached the gallery where my paintings were being exhibited, I noticed intense hues shooting out of the gallery. My suggestion of allowing more color to be part of the museum was taken literally!"

I eventually succeeded Peter Rodriguez in directing the Mexican Museum, from 1984 to 1989, and returned for a second tenure from 2013 to 2015. When I returned, I made a trip to visit Alfredo in his studio. We had been in communication about a portrait Alfredo had painted of Peter Rodriguez. Alfredo related that Peter had commissioned the portrait in the early 1970's. Peter provided the artist with some photographs of himself as an artist and as a museum director that ultimately became themes for the finished work. Peter planned to make payments for this work but the sale was never completed. Many years passed while Alfredo kept the painting in his studio.

On the occasion of The Mexican Museum's 40th anniversary, I asked Alfredo if he would consider donating the painting to the museum in the founder's honor. Peter was very ill at the time and Alfredo agreed to donate the work without hesitation. The painting is one of the only formal portraits of Peter Rodriguez in existence. Peter Rodriguez passed shortly thereafter, in 2016, and the painting has become an iconic piece in the museum's permanent collection.

Over the years, as museum director, curator and educator, I have had many inspiring moments watching people view Alfredo's work. From frequent patrons familiar with Alfredo's work to novices viewing his art for the first time, all are captivated by Alfredo's imagery.

Much has been written on the content and style of Alfredo's work that has been described as magical, surrealistic, and evocative of ancient culture. For me, the shear technical and aesthetic genius of Alfredo's work is what impresses. The detailed, geometric patterns, at first glance hidden within the content of the overall theme, become a fascinating and consistent visual language. Once the eye is allowed to linger, to delve deeper, the complex nature of Alfredo's work hold the viewer's gaze and imagination.

Alfredo's personal style and demeanor complement the beauty of his work and have contributed to his success which includes exhibitions, recognition, awards, and most importantly the collecting of his work, thanks to his loyal dealer, Linda Hodges Gallery in Seattle.

Kind and caring, Alfredo's is the embodiment of the Spanish word, "simpático". Though he has received many impressive honors, including the Keys to the City from his hometown, Morelia (a rare honor he shares with Pope Francis), Alfredo Arreguín remains humble. We are fortunate that this man and his art continue to delight and inspire all of us.

Doug Johnson

Mathematics, Magic Realism and the Mayans: The Paintings of Alfredo Arreguín

Don't just practice your art, but force your way into its secrets. Art deserves that, for it and knowledge can raise man to the Divine—Ludwig Van Beethoven

Arreguín explores the injection of mathematics into aesthetics and the philosophical expression of the divine. He especially explores the transcultural nature of that injection in Mesoamerica that has blended with but not been dominated by Western traditions. Some artists do this to an extent, but he strongest examples of this blend are found in the paintings of Alfredo Arreguín. Arreguín, like daVinci, seamlessly uses mathematics to strengthen his compositions. The key difference is that Arreguín is much more overt about his insistence that mathematics remains the servant of art in his compositions. daVinci saw the Golden Ratio *phi* Φ as the foundation or even backdrop for the figure or object in art. He even illustrated one of the first treatises trying to connect *phi* Φ and its mathematical properties to divine beauty (Livio, 2002, 2005, 2009). "The sense of gratification provided by the Golden Ratio's surprising emergences probably comes as close as we could expect to the sensuous visual pleasure we obtain from a work of art." (Livio, 2002, p.230) Mathematics for the artists of this era was raised to the status of gravitational pull on the earth by astronomers. The patterns of mathematics were assumed overlords and invisible. DaVinci explored this idea in multiple formats. An artist in any epoch is partially defined by their peer group proficient in other disciplines. Arreguín, like DaVinci is no exception in this current generation. To begin with, a background of how deep the connection between mathematics, culture and definitions of beauty need to be explored. These connections have developed a distinctive Western epistemology.

Mathematics

Cultural context goes a long way to explaining the inspiration of the different thinkers, whether they are philosophers or artists. The first thing to note is that this epistemology is notably a Western idea, with the exception of Schopenhauer, who studied the first English translations of the Upanishads (Wickes, 2011). These studies informed his attempts to refine the ideas of Kant and the German Idealists such as Fichte, Schelling and Hegel (Wickes, 2011). Prior to Schopenhauer the ideas revolve around tensions between a cosmology where mathematical reasoning rules society and a cosmology where faith in a divine being rules society. Who will determine what is true and beautiful? Increasingly, one of those answers becomes the mathematician. It isn't because there is more value in the cardinal number system over colors and shapes. Succinctly it is because the mathematician is able to acquiesce and state, "The mathematician's patterns, like the painter's or the poet's, must be beautiful." (Hardy, as cited by Livio, 2002, p. 230.)

The caveat to that expression is that in the past the discoveries in mathematics have taken somewhat of an ethnocentric bent, much analogous to Columbus 'discovering' the Americas and ignoring the fact that people were already here. Diamond (1997) explores the variables around why the Euroasiatic peoples dominated other cultures. He documents what trends occurred on various continents that led to abstract reasoning and mathematics. He does not offer causation due to a tribe's prowess or origins.

"...the striking differences between the long-term histories of peoples of the different continents have been due not to innate differences in the peoples themselves but to differences in their environments." (Diamond, p. 405) Put succinctly, if the Fertile Crescent gave rise to agriculture somewhere in the Americas then the matters would have reversed in any of these cultural collisions. In fact, Cortés must have been quite shocked to come upon the complex civilizations of Mesoamerica. The Mayan system of mathematics developed (independently) the same notion of the zero that was only made popular by Fibonacci in the 13th century in Europe after he integrated the works from mathematics he learned from Arab traders (Aczel, 2014). In fact, the Mayan use of the zero is the only known example where, while used for mathematics, the concept did not spread past its own culture. The number zero is a must in any mathematical system to express nothingness or how to reset the cycle of a season. Mathematical discoveries are transcultural and deserve equal attention. That is the key concern in viewing Arreguín's work and whether or not it belongs in the canon alongside daVinci's *Benois Madonna.* What follows tracks through the traditional Western philosophical ideals of how mathematics intersects with the divine or mystical portions of human beings.

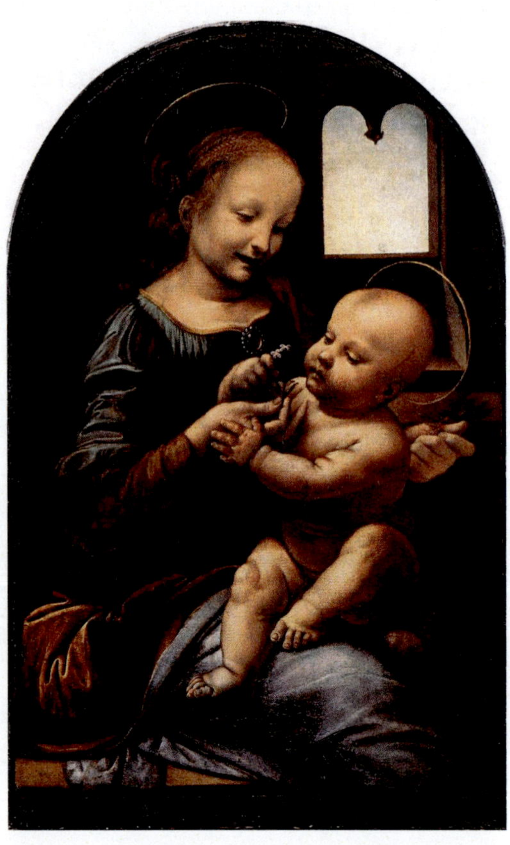

Benois Madonna (1478-1480)—Leonardo daVinci

Plato

How do we define the human interior? For Plato it is placing mathematics at the foundation of all that is true and beautiful that drives this question. That comes around definitions of the soul and the parts of us that express our humanity as more than just an exterior representation of skin, hair and eye color. Artists have always been the people to express a culture's set of these definitions. Those definitions did not always come from the robes of a priest. Those definitions came from artists and depending on the cultural values those definitions include mathematics. Al-Rasisi (2005) and Livio (2005, 2009) offer that for Plato anything said about the mechanisms of consciousness should be well aware of geometry. Euclid, and his axioms laid out for deductive reasoning, became the standard for any abiding theory in geometry. Further, the appeal of immutable patterns discovered by Pythagoras with his formulas took on a larger definition than just how a person could figure out the last side of a triangle in math class. All of these theorists saw the grand patterns discovered in geometry as having great balance and beauty (Livio, 2002). The rules of the human interior, therefore were assumed to have similar immutable laws that could be reasoned. All the ideas of the soul were ruled by reason. Plato and Aristotle impacted how the West has forever viewed consciousness but they were surrounded by thinkers such as Euclid.

> "One, thus, observes that, in Plato's view, mathematics has a philosophical importance. Mathematics is a tool that helps and trains the mind to think. This process of thinking will then help the mind to understand and acquire the idea of good, which is the ultimate aim of philosophy. Plato did not deny the important applications of mathematics in people's daily life. But, to Plato, the philosophical importance of mathematics is more important and more rewarding as it may affect one's understanding of his being." (Al-Rasasi, 2005 p. 2)

For Plato, speaking of the soul fits into a larger discussion about the deals of truth and beauty. The scope of topics in Plato's *Republic* and his attempt to codify the dynamics of the soul are daunting. His definition of the soul was fully intended to fit into an idealized model that covered everything from the laws of physics to the political state of government (Lorenz, 2009). Plato thus offered three parts to the soul. He saw them as *governing* different areas of our consciousness, going as far as to compare this level of government to types of people within the borders of Greece. He saw that there was a part that operated our *Reasoning*. There was a part that operated our emotions, or in his term *Spirited* and a part that ordered our physical desires such as the need for food and sex. He applied the term *Appetitive*. Society was simply a reflection of the individual. Large, complex societies still reinforce this and charge the artist with the task of reinforcing these group norms (Diamond, 1997). Plato writes this idea.

> "Is it not, then," said I, "impossible for us to avoid admitting this much, that the same forms and qualities are to be found in each one of us that are in the state. They could not get there from any other source. It would be absurd to suppose that the element of high spirit was not derived in states from the private citizens who are reputed to have this quality, as the populations of the Thracian and Scythian lands and generally of northern regions; or the quality of love of knowledge, which would chiefly be attributed to" the region where we dwell, or the love of money, which we might say is not least likely to be found in Phoenicians and the population of Egypt." (Plato, Book IV, p. 379-381)

Thus the three pieces integrated and depending on how an individual chose to order his life, they would live well (be good) or live poorly (be bad). The entire idea of ethics, justice and crime were held in this analogy of the soul as a micro reflection the collective of citizens or cities Livio (2002, 2009) noted that he didn't just use the word reason or rational in a cursory manner. He believed that truth could be directly reasoned and the person that lived the best life did so through a series of well-argued steps, most notably, like Euclid's theories and postulates revolving around geometry.

What becomes lost to the modern mind is that this pursuit took on religious proportions (Gould, 1996, 1999; Livio 2009). Plato, although criticizing the Pythagorean cult, did not disagree that mathematical reasoning was the highest form of philosophical discourse (Gould, 1996, 1999; Livio, 2002, 2005). When the ideas of Plato's Forms enter the discussion, he is speaking as if the geometry of Euclid describing planes, rectangles and solids could be equally applied by extension to these ideas of the human interior. For the modern scholar, where different branches of study have taken on their own distinct body of work, Plato sought to capture it all under one cosmology ruled by reason. The elegance of Euclid's rules appealed to Plato, and thus the soul had to fit, simply and elegantly into a proof format. As a government has a hierarchy of power, Plato reasoned that the soul had the same hierarchy with Reason being at the top, much like the rulers of city were at the top of the political order. They were the philosophers and kings. Spirited emotions were thus regulated and guided much the same way as a standing military is regulated. Spirited in the discussion quite often simply meant anger and rage, as would be seen on a battlefield. The Spirited guided the Appetitive or the workers (slaves) and in Plato's culture.

Crucial to the discussion later becomes how he viewed slaves. Slaves were deemed to not have higher intelligence. In the political system they were simply brutes of labor (Gould, 1981). Through the ages scholars debated as to whether or not a fellow human being had a soul at all when they were enslaved. It eats at our modern sense of equity, but a caste, and especially a slave caste, was common for all of these ancient civilizations. All of these conceptions come into play later in history when others grapple with the idea of consciousness and how far the implications of those definitions play out in the rules of society (Gould, 1981, 1996, 2003). Mesoamerica had risen to the same heights as ancient Greece but it was isolated, much like dynastic China, from these philosophical frameworks. Plato's lines of logic and mathematics are one path. Mesoamerica was discovering similar paths in isolation.

Aristotle

In agreement with Plato on many levels, Aristotle also requires that the philosopher have a keen mind for mathematical reasoning (Livio, 2005). Geometry was at a base level an abstraction of reality given through a set of proofs. For the philosopher therefore, describing those patterns constituted its own reality apart from the observed object. A tree trunk is a tree trunk but the mathematical proofs that prove the existence of a cylinder are not held in the material world. Aristotle, however, varied with Plato on a key point when it came to consciousness. Plato saw the soul as a separate entity and capable of finding its own perfection (Plato, 1932). This perfection would be found as elegant as a geometric proof. The body was of its own world. Aristotle, however, consciousness or the soul is what gave the body its inherent definition. A person is human because of their soul (Shield, 2010). Without it people would be a collection of molecules, undifferentiated from wood or dirt.

Aristotle also had a three part hierarchy of the soul, but different than Plato, he was attempting to develop a comprehensive philosophy of all living items when he defined soul (Shield, 2010). The hierarchy defined the stages of the soul by the capacity of the systems it demonstrated in nature. His three parts, therefore, included plants (nutritive or vegetative) non-human animals (sentient cognition and sentient appetite) and humans (intelligent cognition and intelligent appetite) (Freddoso, 2014; Lorenz, 2009; Shield, 2010). In this hierarchy, Aristotle used capacity of function as the framework for describing the activities instead of the political metaphor for beauty and perfection offered by Plato. A plant can only gain nourishment, while a person can think about highly complex abstractions. The person is placed at the top of the hierarchy. In the end Aristotle's ideas were one of the first attempts at creating an inclusive taxonomy of consciousness that included other life forms that were observable in nature (Shield, 2010).

Aquinas, Neoplatonists and the church

Mathematics as the underpinning of cosmology fell off the map for a while. Gould (1996, 1999, 2003) asserts that as Europe started to wrestle with the ideas of Aristotle and Plato a distinct schism emerged. While Plato and especially Aristotle were trying to demonstrate that consciousness was part of a larger rationalized system of philosophy, the Catholic Church had a different agenda. (This will be detailed further in chronological sequence.) In the face of Hellenistic ideals emerging in the art and architecture, the church had to grapple with which portions Plato and Aristotle could be reconciled with the ideals of the church. You can see this when you look at the attention to the human form in both of these epochs. Unlike the *Venus de Milo*,

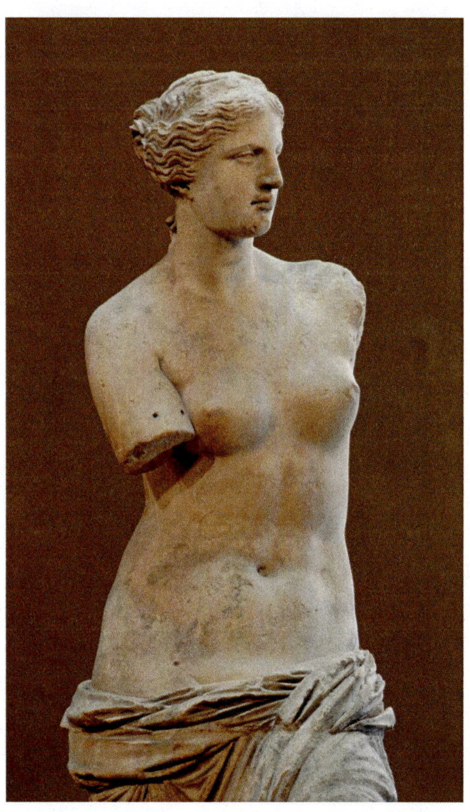

Venus de Milo 130-100 BC?

The human form became flattened and heavily covered in symbols. This is seen in the Byzantine icons and other works like, *Madonna Enthroned with Saints and Angels* by Agnolo Gaddi in the 1300's.

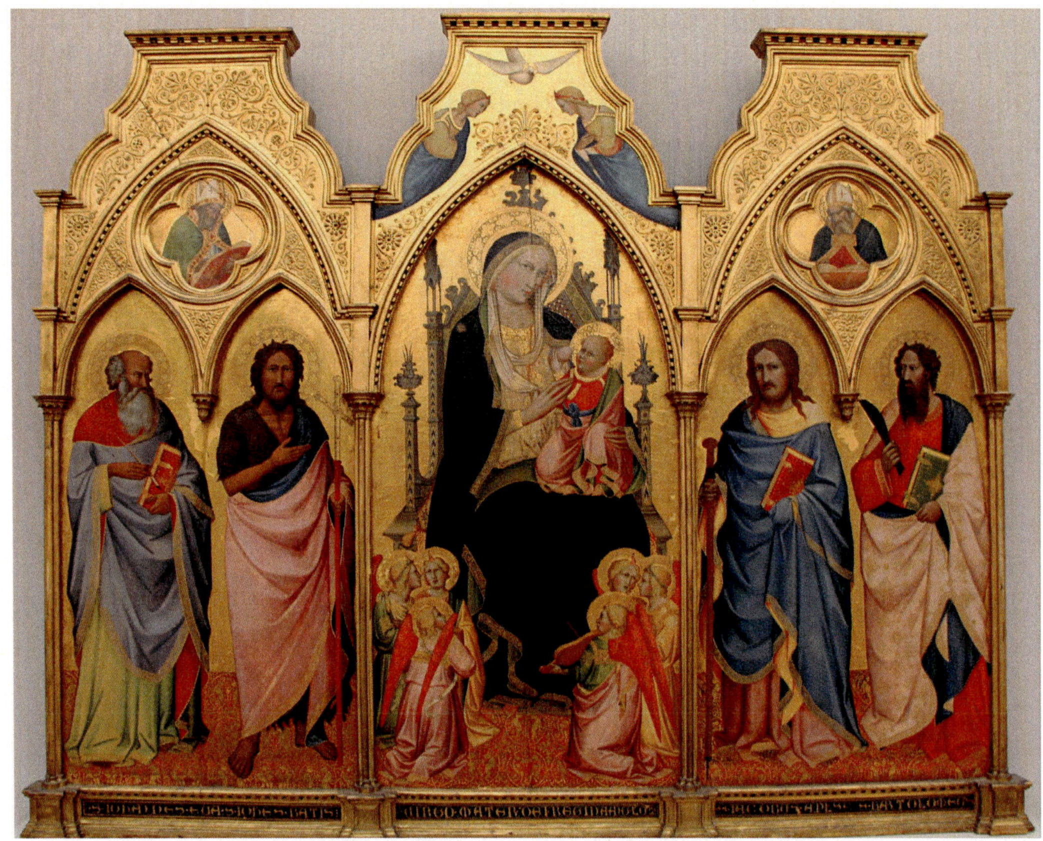

Madonna Enthroned with Saints and Angels by Agnolo Gaddi in the 1300's

While a discussion on the nature of the soul can be entertaining for an afternoon among scholars, the issue for the policy makers was to figure out who owned the right to declare what was good, evil, beautiful and ugly. Mathematics, as mentioned before was suspect at best in the 1300's for Europe. Past the utilitarian use for business, mathematics was on par with other divination practices in some circles (Conner, 2004).

However, Plato's Republic and the update of the psyche through the use of Freudian metaphors did not enter our world through a European vacuum. In fact, the cultural ethnocentric pride about the nature of morality and mathematics was not original. It must be said that every group that comes to a level of civilization where they start to explore higher elements of abstract reasoning comes to fear that they are the only ones in an exclusive group that are allowed to do so. Everyone thinks that their discovery of the divine must mean that the divine only shines on their fidelity to their faith. The bias toward who was intelligent enough to handle advanced mathematics is also not original. In fact, the early Islamic contribution to mathematics was an overt study of math and science to produce scholars that were an "imitation of God according to human capacity" (as cited in Baffioni, 2008). Like Pythagoras, a group of Islamic scholars called *Ikhwân al-Safâ'* or *Brethren of Purity* published a series of encyclopedias. These collected works ended up introducing algebra to Europe and were written from about 840 AD through 980 AD (Baffioni, 2008.)

In this text laid out in the format of letters, Epistles 35 and 47 state that best people, or religious elite were gifted with the legacy of being "most intelligent" (as cited in Baffioni, 2008). Approximately 200 years later in order to move Pythagoras and others forward, Medieval Spain placed Jewish, Islamic and Catholic scholars in *quadriviums* to work on translating these different mathematical texts (Baffioni, 2008; Devlin, 2002; Livio, 2002, 2005). The analogous graduate students of our era, advanced students would continue their studies from the *trivium* or "three roads" where the basics of grammar and rhetoric were covered. These *quadriviums* literally meaning "the four roads" (Devlin, 2002) and the advanced students and scholars translated texts and applied them in the arts, math and science of Catholic Spain and Italy.

Fibonacci, in fact, in studying in this system developed his ideas that ended up giving Europe his innovations around the Golden mean (Devlin, 2008). The Golden age of Islam gave rise to the Renaissance (Baffioni, 2008; McKeague, 2008). The scholars supported by two different religious cosmologies gave the modern era the tools of a technological revolution (Devlin, 2002; Livio, 2002, 2005). These tools helped Europe's commerce and science pull out of what was entitled the Dark Ages.

In Pre-Inquisition Spain, the Moors collaborated with Jewish and Catholic scholars by importing the mystical science and art of *Al-ge-bra* to Europe (Baffioni, 2008; Devlin, 2002; Jenkins, 2007; McKeague, 2008). The empiricist split between science and religion did not exist in its present severe form (Capra, 1976; Gould, 1999, 2003; Singh, 1997; Stewart, 1992). All subjects were studied in conjunction with each other giving rise to the current *liberal arts* university system (Baffioni, 2008; Devlin, 2002; Gould, 1999, 2003). *Al-ge-bra* is a transliteration into English of the Arabic word (Devlin, 2002; Smaller, 2001) or *Al-jbar* meaning *Allah restoring balance* (Livio, 2005). 200 years before this collaboration Islamic scholars thought abstract reasoning was reserved for the most intelligent (Biafonni, 2008). Islamic scholars also developed their system of mathematics in deference and honor to *Allah,* and all that was pure.

Al comes from the definite article in Arabic that mimics the Hebrew *el* when pointing to a noun (Jenkins, 2007; McKeague, 2008; Smaller: 2001). Both in Arabic, Aramaic and Hebrew the definite article is also a root for the name of their respective deities. In Hebrew, one name for a deity is *el-ah.* This transliterates into Arabic into *al ilah.* That gives the root to the name *Allah* (Jenkins, 2007). For these two language groups all nouns that imply an action supported by a deity can be implied with the use of the article. There is a debate as to how far that connection between the article and the intent of the mathematician goes, but it is beyond the scope of this discussion.

The linguistic origin of the *al* in Arabic forms the noun from the root verb *jabare* which means *unite what is broken* (Jenkins, 2007; Smaller, 2001). Mathematics and this uniting process was a holy cause with the inventors of this system along with the ideas of the Arabic based word *algorithm.* It was these religious underpinnings that led people to quote Mohammed in saying,

"The ink of scholars is worth the blood of a thousand martyrs." (Jenkins, 2007; McKeague, 2008; Smaller: 2001).

Mathematics at that juncture in history was an expression of a world view as much as a piece of sculpture or music. "Human culture arose from the material substrate of a complex brain: and science and art meld in continuity." (p. 82, Gould & Purcell, 2000). The modern empirical premise of objectivity and the severe divide between these mathematics, art and science has been criticized as arbitrary (Gould, 1996, 1999, 2003; Gould & Purcell, 2000, Searle, 1972). Historically, the Muslims came to Europe first by conquering what became Spain.

After the political climate changed and Catholic powers took over, scholars still stayed behind becoming part of the *quadrivium* system (Devlin, 2008). Through Jewish scholars, who understood Arabic, Hebrew and Latin, students began translating texts into Latin. Catholic scholars did not understand Arabic (McKeague, 2008) and needed the ideas represented in Latin. Latin was the network language of scholars (Conner, 2004; Posner, 1990) in Europe. These same Catholic scholars created the educational system that trained lawyers, teachers and physicians all over Europe (Conner, 2004). The influence of Islamic mathematics became subsumed in the height of the Renaissance and the artwork, as scene in Raphael' *School of Athens* suddenly became commandeered.

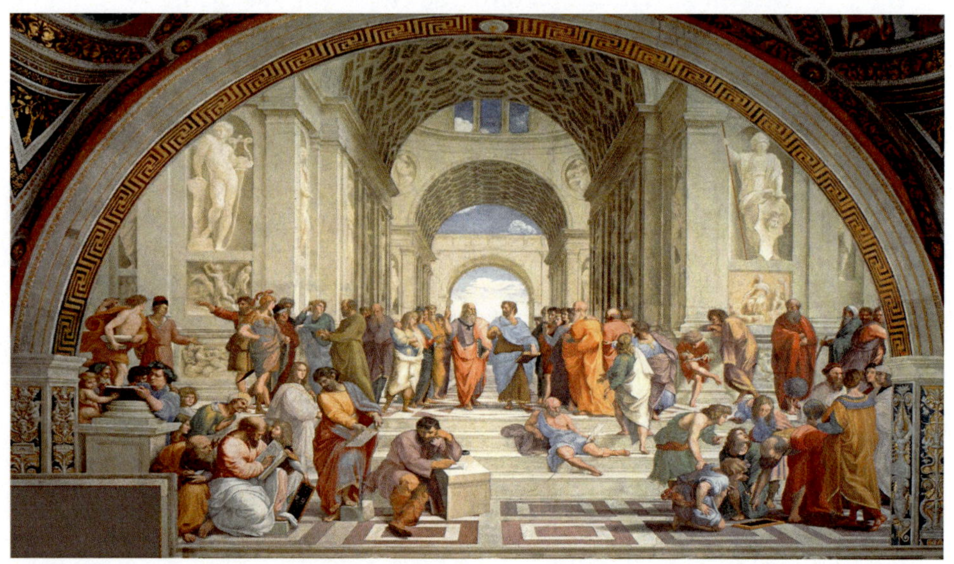

School of Athens (1511)—Raphael

Given the Inquisition, it becomes easy to see how cosmologies collide and even though mathematics continued to be studied, Plato's cosmology as transplanted in the Catholic Church ruled the day (Diamond, 1997). Plato, in *The Republic,* assumed mathematics as part of the ideal answer, not as part of the evil the lurked in the world. Remember that Plato's ideas function for politics, consciousness and geometric reasoning. Aristotle's ideas function for a taxonomy of nature, consciousness and geometric reasoning (Gould, 1996, 2003; Livio, 2005). Unlike Plato's theoretical Republic in the ideal, the ideas of the Catholic Church took on violent proportions (Conner, 2004; Gould, 2003) as the secular and sacred powers sought to eradicate their opposition with force. Johannes Kepler, discovering the heliocentric universe through mathematical proofs that used the ellipse, had to move many times from city to city throughout his lifetime. It all depended on who was his patron (Catholic or Protestant) and what faction was most violent in his region.

What led to violent revolts when thinkers expressed Plato and Aristotle through religion? The first part of the problem was in how much of Plato and Aristotle were adopted into the doctrine of the church. Aquinas, the most noted Aristotelian reconciled the notions of Aristotle with theological concepts (Bateson, 1987; McInerny, & O'Callaghan, 2013). Other followers of Plato were quick to adopt the idea that the soul was seeking perfection apart from the body (Conner, 2004). For both religious thinkers they were happy to place man as the pinnacle of the hierarchy of all beings (Gould, 1996). Further, with religious notions of Christ as a King figure, it was simple to transplant ideals out of *The Republic.* The sticking point became that while Plato and Aristotle insisted on logic locked into mathematical reasoning these thinkers supplanted that thinking with the biblical text (Conner, 2004; Gould, 1996, 2003; Livio, 2005, Ruse, 2003). Thus mixed into this political battle of good and evil was the notion of ultimate faith in the anthropomorphic God, apart from scientific enquiry. From this point forward it became a battle for who would corner the market on *Truth* in society. For the church it was reason tempered by faith in a Judeo Hebraic piece of literature. Very rarely did it reason out the solutions from a purely scientific basis (Conner, 2004; Gould, 1981, 1996, 2003; Quammen, 2003).

Descartes

Cogito ergo sum DesCartes declared in reaction (Livio, 2005). Reconciling another world view against the powerful political and religious groups became a challenge. Newton's discovery of the three laws of motion and his invention of calculus were all seen to be the revelation of God's handiwork (Livio, 2005). Newton's ideas were simply revealing that God gave the universe a mechanical nature that followed immutable laws and patterns. Again these were found in mathematics. DesCartes brought the issue up again, admiring Galileo's work and wanting to figure out a way to reconcile *truth* of things said around the soul with mathematical reasoning. Leonardo daVinci made the most intentional explorations of mathematics in his artwork, assigning the human form as the ultimate expression of that abstraction in *The Vetruvian Man.*

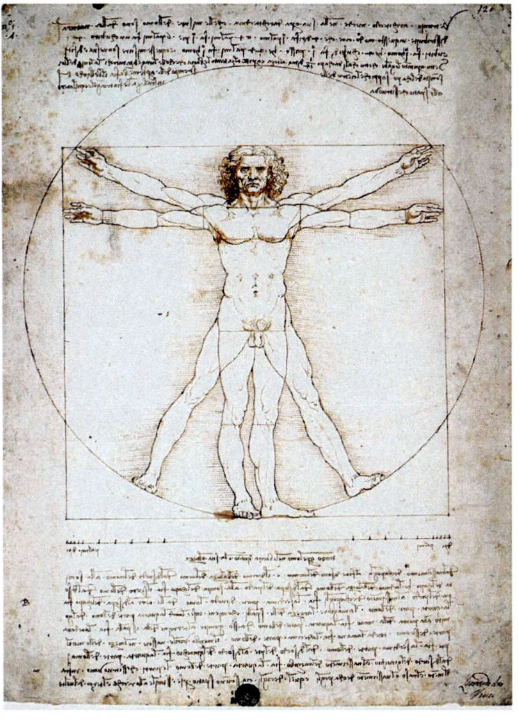

The Vetruvian Man (1490) Leonardo da Vinci

DesCartes took his approach from mathematics and created what is now termed *dualism.* He saw that the soul and body were distinct entities. Like Aristotle, however, he agreed that what comes through to our interior is a dynamic relationship of the inputs we get from our environment (Brook & Raymont, 2010). The difference was that he saw no hierarchy between the physical world (body) and the metaphysical world (mind, consciousness). Both of these were necessary to explain our idea of consciousness. The body was not the simple machine driven by the disembodied mind. They were integrated pieces that needed each other to demonstrate who a person is on the planet. His contributions to mathematics rival Newton and it was from his discoveries that he wanted to once again assert that the ability to seek out and develop these patterns was evidence of consciousness (Livio, 2005). He reasserted mathematical reasoning as a way for determining truth about the human interior. This is in sharp contrast to the earlier era where St. Augustine, a neoplatonist, who warned his flock against doing mathematics common in any fifth grade classroom today. He saw the process as divination and witchcraft (Conner, 2004).

Kant

These arguments raged back and forth as the Rationalists sought to reassert that examining the metaphysical should adhere to the strict dictums of reason, mathematics and physical laws apart from faith (Conner, 2004; Livio, 2005). As each generation of scholars sought to reassert themselves they would compromise either the tenets of their faith or the process of science. Regardless of the rhetoric, both parties continued reducing complex issues into polar opposites to fit their geopolitical agendas (Gould, 1981; 1996; 2003; Ruse, 2003; Quammen, 2003).

Brook (2013) asserts that Kant understood this dilemma. His objective was to 1) Establish that physics like mathematics held its own universal, necessary truth and 2) Establish that religion had its own prevue on immortality, leaving it outside the strictures of science.

Kant, like DesCartes agreed that consciousness necessitated both the mind and the interpretations of experiences coming in as inputs from the environment (Brook, 2013). Kant developed a *functionalist* model almost 200 years before it became popular among philosophers and his ideas were very influential among cognitive science community as they developed their own empirical branch of study (Brook, 2013). Accepting Kant's ideas for consciousness requires embracing his three foundational principles of cognitive architecture. 1) The mind is a group of complex functions and abilities. 2) Crucial to its function is the processing of a) spatio-temporal information and b) application of concepts to sensory inputs. 3) These functions are used in what Kant terms synthesis. At the core of what Kant is saying instead of pure reason outside the realm of the physical, as argued by Plato, Aristotle and even DesCartes, consciousness could best be described from observable inferences (Brook, 2013).

What is crucial to note here is the method by which Kant proceeded with his proof of consciousness. Before this time, introspection and reflection was the route to illumination in the metaphysical realm. That was how Plato framed his reasoning about beauty and the ideal, even if it was through mathematics like the Pythagoreans. Kant's ideas were hailed as a breakthrough for scholars looking for a way to take the idea of consciousness out of the realm of its root. *Psyche* from the Greek meant, *breath, life, soul* and everyone until Kant used the overtones of religion to generate their definition (Lorenz, 2009). Mystic introspection appealed even to St. Augustine, even if he was suspect of mathematics toward higher levels of consciousness (Brook, 2013; Conner, 2004). Even though Kant usedthe term *transcendental* as far as how the mind thinks about itself and the world around it, he put strict boundaries around that definition. Kant, instead, developed a system of using inference from different categories and systems that he deemed as functional. What he did was form the basis of how cognitive scientists researched consciousness well into the middle of the 20th century (Brook, 2013).

In fact he came upon this as an attempt to defend science, leaving faith outside of his system of logic (Brook, 2013). Part of the appeal of Kant to so many of his generation and later was that he brought up both elements of faith and reason, to the defense of reason. It is hard pressed to express to the modern reader how suspect physics and the sciences were in the eighteenth century. Beyond the violence, governments were not above full blown censure of ideas that did not align with biblical cosmologies holding faith as the ultimate route to truth. Criticism was vehement. Edward Stillingfleet, a conservative scholar and theologian wrote a treatise defending truth and reason only filtered through religion.

"What expressions of gratitude can be left to God for his goodness, if he interpose not in the affairs of the world? ... For if the world did of necessity exist, then God is no free agent; and if so, then all instituted Religion is to no purpose; nor can there be any expectation of reward, or fear of punishment from him who hath nothing else to do in the world but to set the great wheel of heavens going." (as cited in Gould, 2003 p. 33)

For all of the censure, however, the theories of Newton around planetary motion and optics were seen as beneficial (Livio, 2005). DesCartes advances were seen as beneficial and the ideas of empiricism and observed truth were taking hold. Kant, by offering his ideas on consciousness was trying create a bridge between rationalism and empiricism. One of the stronger elements of his theory was how meaning and perception in the world can be a constructed experience from what is formed in the mind. Kant acknowledged along with DesCartes that truth could be extrapolated through theoretical means before they were observed (Livio, 2005; Palmquist, 1993). This is the key debate keeps popping up around mathematical discoveries of any given phenomena (Livio, 2002, 2005).

He was also part of his generation and so he fell in line with the Neoclassicisst who took their cues from the resurgence of attention to Plato as the highest artistic standard, (Wincklemann, 1764/2006). Renewing the Hellenistic ideals that were lost in the penitent practices of the Catholic church, the Neoclassicist came back to exalting the human form as much as Kant exalted rational thinking. Note the content and styling of the *Apotheosis of Homer* by Jean-Auguste-Dominique Ingres.

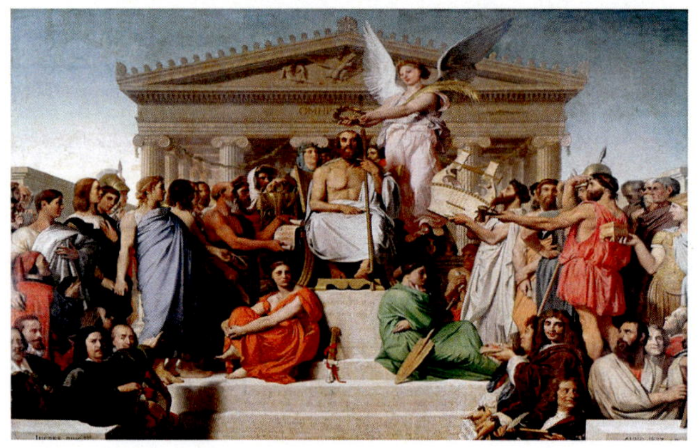

Apotheosis of Homer (1827) Dominique Ingres.

Schopenhauer

Kant sparked a reaction among scholars who became known as the German Idealists (Redding, 2014). Many of them were theology students when they started they wanted to adopt pieces of his rationalist underpinnings. They just thought that Kant went too far in restricting the arguments. They were termed Idealists, in that they followed Leibniz in that he ascribed to Plato's theories that consciousness follows *ideals* in the abstract versus strictly materials of observed behaviors such as with the Epicureans (Livio, 2002, 2005; Redding, 2014). What they reacted against with Kant was his strict limits on how the rational mind would be the standard of truth and experience. Although Kant wanted to insulate religion and maintain his faith, he also wanted to excise the ancient notions of soul from the arguments around consciousness (Brook, 2013). Schopenhauer also agreed with Kant, but reacted even more severely to the German Idealists and their insistence on a larger part of consciousness being allowed to be known from other sources such as from divinity (Wickes, 2011). Schopenhauer went as far as to declare the known world as chaotic and without meaning. He declared that a divine being should not enter the argument. Schopenhauer also ascribed to Leibniz and his sense of idealism. Leibniz was known to have independently discovered differential equations and calculus apart from Newton (Livio, 2002; 2005). Plato's ideals of abstract truth through mathematical reasoning were still very alive among the German Idealists following Leibniz. The grappling with the element of faith in a monistic god was a different challenge than Aquinas and St. Augustine had in centuries past. Rational thought was gaining more of a salient argument.

Schopenhauer took as his starting point one of Leibniz' tenets as to why the rationalist's cosmology was the best route to truth. For Leibniz, every operating mechanism and experience in the world had *sufficient reason* (Redding, 2014). Schopenhauer took this idea at it face value and took notes from DesCartes, demanding that for any process, event or experience there had to be a rational (sufficient) explanation (reason). Accidents, miracles or divine intervention were not explanations allowed into the system (Redding, 2014). He adamantly rejected any level of explanation that relied on traditions or the need to prove the existence of God, frequently attacking Hegel and other German Idealists (Redding, 2014).

When it came to his metaphysical conceptions of consciousness he agreed with DesCartes as far as positing that our self-revelation comes from our internal ability to think. However, he offered that each piece of knowledge humans have has a dual aspect. People can understand they have their own hand or foot as internal to their person. People can also see hands and feet as a piece of external knowledge (Redding, 2014). Although the German Idealists opposed Spinoza, Schopenhauer admired his system of defining consciousness and read the Upinashads, admiring the notion that there was an inner and outer experience as people interact in the world (Redding, 2014).

His most radical divergence from the Idealists was in declaring that the world in its present form is not something revealed in an orderly fashion from a divine being (Gould, 1999, 2003; Redding, 2014). He posited that the world, in contrast is a chaotic place devoid of meaning. The only meaning comes from Kant's epistemology of having the mind construct meaning through the sensory inputs. Meaning comes through the organization of rationale functions from sensory inputs and concepts. For Schopenhauer, the only order that exists occurs through a person's consciousness objectifying their experiences. Schopenhauer extrapolates Leibniz' process of sufficient reason placing it as the authority in the definition of the Platonic Ideals. Following his predilection toward Bhuddism, the world, thus, could be conceived as a dream with the sensory inputs creating reality for people when sufficient reason would arise to give the experience meaning (Redding, 2014).

He was also part of his generation and so he fell in line with the Neoclassicist who took their cues from the resurgence of attention to Plato as the highest artistic standard, (Wincklemann, 1764/2006). Renewing the Hellenistic ideals that were lost in the penitent practices of the Catholic Church, the Neoclassicist came back to exalting the human form.

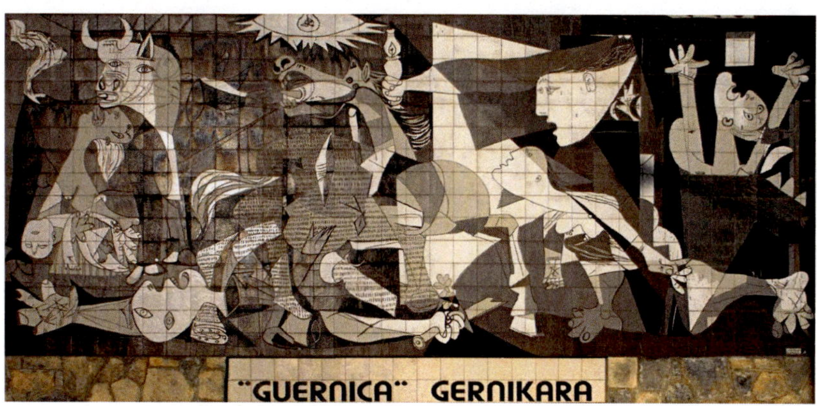

Guernica (1937) Pablo Picasso

All of this changed after WWI. Picasso and others started throwing out serene well-proportioned compositions. Primitive motifs erupted on the canvas. *Guernica* came reacted to what math, technology and war was doing in Europe. Abstract expressionists decided to fire bomb the image as the center of a composition. In the end, this generated a disturbing question. What defines reality? Mathematics had become the foundation and now artists, poets and other disciplines were calling the metrics into question. In the early 20th century, although equally disturbing to the notion of a letting go of a reality solely bound by the metrics of the cardinal number system, others took the middle ground in the visual arts. Surrealism became a way to explore Freud's newly accepted notions of the id. Taking cues from these painters, such as Salvador Dali, Latin American writers stretched the boundaries further becoming famous for cementing *magic realism* into as a way to offer answers to questions as to the nature of reality.

Magic Realism

The Golden Ratio *phi* Φ did not remain an overlord over all disciplines. Accepting that mathematical patterns could describe all beauty started to break down around the time of World War I. Alongside the rise of Freud's notion of the subconscious taking hold, rational mathematics also created the most potent and destructive weapons known to date. Thinkers discarded Plato's (mathematically based) desire for a unified notion of pursuing Truth, Beauty and Philosophy. Neruda (1966) said,

> *"...oh, muerte!, de ola en ola no vienes,*
> *Sino como un galope de claridad nocturna*
> *O como los totales números de la noche."*
>
> Neruda (in English) writes,
> *"the comprehensive mathematics of the dark."*

He personifies Death as a galloping, marauding predator. This is not the foundation of *Truth* and *Beauty.*

Neue Sachlichkeit

Magic Realism—Originally: a style of painting which depicts fantastic or bizarre images in a precise representationalist manner (first used in German to describe the work of members of the Neue Sachlichkeit movement). (*Oxford English Dictionary)* (as cited by Ríos, 2015).

Neue Sachlichkeit- or *New Objectivity* came out of Germany in the 1930's before Hitler took over and these artists, as the term was coined sought to take on Plato's ideal of truth and beauty from a with a different tactic. Turning the Venus de Milo, conceptually, on her head, they took the mundane and elevated the representations of reality into fantastic settings or manners. Scholars can debate as to if they were reacting to the growing abstraction erupting among painters, but what can be confirmed is that the etymology of the movement eventually termed *magic realism* was borne in their early efforts. Although, historically, this movement disappeared when Hitler rose to power, it wasn't the first time Latin America took something from an imperial dictator and bent it toward their own devices.

Since the imperialism of the *conquistadores* Latin America has long taken the strategy of surviving by adapting the European models to their own ends. Diamond (1997) notes that all complex civilizations need structured monolithic religion as a way to help streamline the base of political power and the *conquistadores* brought with them the Spanish mission system that ended offering trade routes across Mexico, up California and on toward the Philippines. This brought along with it the Catholic Church and all their administrative might and belief systems about God. The influence is still felt with 84% of residents in Latin America reporting as Catholic. Beyond that, a full 40% of the world's Catholic Church residing in Latin America. The Catholic trade routes established for Spain spread far and wide (Pew Research Center, 2014). The Spanish words that ended up in Tagalog offers proof of their lasting power. Like the substrates of African music that offered the United States and the African American the roots of spirituals and blues, Latin America chose adaptations that allowed them to survive the brutality of the political arena that continued to offer treaties with Europe and the emerging United States.

The most obvious example to the mainstream child of Mexico is the *Día de los Muertos* celebrations based out of the Catholic holiday for Hallowed Eve and All Soul's Day. However, more than a simple excuse for candy this speaks toward a deep and abiding split from the Aquinian-Platonic (and most recently, Empiricist) split of the soul around the River Styx. When you look at Mesoamerica long enough you realize that without the need to maintain this severe border, they didn't have to try as hard as the German painters of Neue Sachlichkeit. Quite simply, Latin American artists and writers are culturally more at home with their dreams than their European counterparts. Even the linguistic implications of the word *magic* speak to this comfort level. King (1981) notes, that in the modern mind, magic engenders an instant cultural value system centered in the Aquinian-Platonic soul of the occult. King (1981) cites Stoker's *Dracula* as an example of such a split. Dr. Van Helsing is a type of priest that when you strip away the mythologies of Europe he does not look much different than the supposed Mayan and Aztec priests offering a human sacrifices Yes, this practice seems abhorrent, but when is "demonized" by European scholars it ignores their own predilections toward violence, sexuality and the mystical (Quammen, 2003).

When you therefore, cross reference the Latin American writer's within their own cultural context to their European counterparts, it becomes apparent why scholars steeped in the Aquinian-Platonic soul of Freud and the Empiricists come to such vague confusion when trying to describe magic realism. Taking a glance at some of the surrealistic and magic realists of Latin American writers helps shed light on a later discussion of the reason Arreguín should be held in the canon with DaVinci.

Surrealism, Juan Rulfo and *Pedro Páramo*

Dali became the poster child for surrealism and one reason he was able to do so was that he stayed within the context of the newly minted Freudian conceptualization of the human interior. The other detail is that he manipulated space and foregrounds, but he gave us the stylings of Raphael and Velázquez with many of his figures. He just happened to not be interested in the traditional use of three dimensional space as you see in the *School of Athens.* Dali's surrealism is in lock step with the considerations of Europe needing to reconcile Freud's id with the Aquinian-Platonic soul. *Corpus Hypercubus* (1954) also takes it one step further, reaching back to the monuments to the human figure attributed to the Renaissance masters. The bottom line is that these ordinary representations are placed in magical spaces. Dali just figured out how to balance that line and offer the viewer a perception they would accept, which in this case is the crucified Christ. The Metropolitan Museum of Art (US) states:

> "Dali utilized his theory of "nuclear mysticism," a fusion of Catholocism, mathematics, and science to create this unusual interpretation of Christ's crucifixion. Levitating before a hypercube—a geometric, multidimensional form...." (metmuseum.org)

So surrealism gave magic realism its cue in making offering normal objects in magical spaces and this gave Juan Rulfo permission to create *Pedro Páramo.* The master stroke of this novella is that the reader is placed in the magical space without knowing it in the first three sentences.

"I came to Comala because I was told that my father, a certain Pedro Páramo, was living here. My mother told me so, and I promised her I would come to see him as soon as she died." (Rulfo, 1959, p. 1). The story moves on, and while the mood offers a centrality of the narrator that hearkens to Conrad's *Heart of Darkness,* there is no direct indication of the bizarre setting, like you notice in Dali's *Corpus Hypercubus*. Like Conrad's journey up the Congo looking for Kurtz, the narrator of this surrealistic journey takes us to Comala to look for an equally spooky mystery. Again, this is markedly different, however, than Dali's surrealism because it does not rely on the same assumptions of the object being central to the foreground and the dismissal of the background. Dali offers playful distortions of the *New Objectivity* of the Germans by testing the boundaries of the mundane placed in a fantastic space. No matter how mind bending, much of the space is obvious and epic.

In the visual arts the object in space necessitates the Aquinian-Platonic split in the psyche around the mystical. There needs to be a strict foreground and background because Western art worships the object. Likewise, in the novel format, the narrator offers the reader and assumption of the object (or objective) which goes unquestioned. What they define for the reader readily defines the reality. By Rulfo offering us an immediate scene of the narrator sitting by his dying mother's bedside, we click into an objective reality mode, assuming that we are being placed on a boat going down the Congo, like with Kurtz in *Heart of Darkness.* Snippets of memory and repeated dream sequences about the Miguel Páramo don't quite sink in to the reader. "No. You're not crazy, Miguel. You're dead." (Rulfo, 1959, p.20). The dialogues are so vivid that the reader can't believe they are actually dead. They also don't have Dali's space to use as a reference point as to what is pointing toward the surreal.

What this does is to blend the reality of the living and the dead into a glorious *Día de los Muertos* celebration of dialogue and reality. What has to be emphasized is that the Latino writer and artist have this as seamless cultural part of their aesthetic handed them down from their Mayan and Aztec ancestors in the exact same way that Dali inherited the paintings of Raphael in a structured Aquinian-Platonic space. One reason the European reader potentially misses so much of Pedro Páramo is that the only thing fantastic about the space, given all the dialogue, is that there is a distinct lack of detail about the specific buildings and geography from the narrator. Beyond that, there is still enough of a realistic sketch of the space, the reader doesn't always understand that they are talking about and to people who are dead in the novella.

It just makes perfect sense for the Latino artist and writer to blend the object in the foreground with the fantastic background with an equal weight. In a novel format the narrator ends up the object painted against a setting as a background. However, not steeped in the same occult markers as Stoker's *Dracula,* there is no need on the part of the Latin American writer to cue the reader much on who is dead or who is living.

Further, as far as the socio-political commentaries that become an emergent theme in Juan Rulfo and later *100 years of Solitude* by García Márquez, the fact that some of the ranchos were decimated by the Mexican Revolution wiping up much of Rulfo's family because an apropos jumping off point for Comala and Media Luna.

In short there is no need to worship the object (narrator) and its objective reality of foreground and background (setting) in Latin America. Their genius for blending the two worlds and handing us a plausible reality in a magical world comes exactly from the fact that they did not inherit much of Europe's overarching metaphor of a Platonic split of the human interior and the need to always delineate them in exterior works of art. Stoker's *Dracula* offers us the moralist play of the Catholic Church. Black. White. Right. Wrong. Living. Dead. Narrator. Setting. Magic Realism does not. Dali's surrealism plays off the same moralist play. Object. Center. Foreground. Background. Realistic Space. The narration of space in Dali still offers distance and worships the object. Magic Realism does not.

Gabriel García Márquez - *100 years of Solitude*

This Nobel Peace Prize winning novel transforms Comala into a symphony of magic realism by offering Macondo to the reader. Here García Márquez has muted the darker themes and woven them together with such subtlety the reader doesn't even notice that lullaby of his words and syntax putting you into a dream state.

Nevertheless, by generating a motif in the repeated names of the multigenerational family, he is able to offer a realistic space in which the characters move in and out of reality, as well as sometimes in and out of death. By offering us overarching metaphorical names like, *Buendía,* the irony continues to unfold as generation after generation moves in and out of rumors, politics, death and life. For instance, the name Melquiades comes from the Hebrew and biblical character Melchizedek. Instead of a mythical king living 475 years we are faced with irony of the king heading a traveling carnival. The irony rolls on and on throughout the work and detail after detail washes over the reader like some hypnotic wave from the ocean. García Márquez takes some pages from Salvador Dali in that he draws such a plausible space for these interactions to occur that it becomes impossible for the reader to become anything but mesmerized. If the reader allows it and does not attempt to dissect it into a Freudian metaphor, then they lose their own memories of how each novella unfolds in each generation as "time" moves on.

In this constructed hypnosis, then, the reader accepts this altered reality, without question. The reader is elevated or transported into this mystical space without noticing that they have ever left the planet. That is indeed the key to magic realism that can become disconcerting to the European viewing/reading the work. To people steeped in these traditions, life, death, heaven or hell are determined to be a location. Thus the necessity of art to reference or react to an object remains rehearsed over and over in these themes.

Borrowing from their polytheistic neighbors from other countries the European trained artist or writer maintains the assumption of heaven being part of a sky-god's realm and hell being part of Hades and Styx stays in place in some unknown *under*world (Diamond, 1997; Quammen, 2003). Thus the word *elevate* or *transport* to García Márquez' space ends up a misnomer. Unlike the object/ narrator in foreground which drives the viewer into an assigned role of distance, Garcia's characters blend in and out of the location.

How does he accomplish this in the novel? Macondo, as the magical place, is not Rowling's Hogwarts. Not only does he use dialogue (as seen in *Pedro Páramo*), he counts on the reader's poor memory of when and where a certain character may enter or leave the stage. Melquiades is dead at some point but then reappears. Unlike *Pedro Páramo* these characters are not snippets of memory and echoes of the dead. As they interact in Macondo novella upon novella is threaded together into an integrated unit by the end. There are generations that live and die. But the death of the patriarch José Arcadio Buendía demonstrates the blending as what would be interpreted as hallucinations with a non-entity are simply wrapped into the reader's reality. Of course he is carrying on conversations with people who are not there.

The title itself points toward eternity but under this hypnotic state the reader never calls into the question the implausibility of the fantastic sexual, or military feats. They may count it impossible, but that becomes tucked in the back of their mind after they meet Melquiades traveling show. In keeping with Allende's *House of Spirits* the implausibility found itself expressed in the reality of Latin American politics. While the rest of the world rehearsed Hitler's demise for two or three generations, García Márquez and Allende were writing about the dangerous state of current affairs in their areas of Columbia, Chile and Argentina.

For García Márquez and the other magic realists, and like their ancestors before, (who encountered the *conquistadores*) life and death can hang on a thread and meet a brutal end or beginning depending on where you live at the time. Thus, the fantastic or absurdities described by García Márquez are understood to document the harsh politics that any totalitarian state creates in the extreme (Diamond, 1997). By the end of the novel, there is no real beginning or ending to Macondo as the multi-layered story of a repeated José Arcadio Buendía echoing over and over for generations. The jungles of Latin America threaten to swallow up the story like it did Macchu Picchu.

Alfredo Arreguín- the visual counterpart

Arreguín has stomped, front and center, into magic realism for his generation and Latin America. By visually blending the foreground and background of his paintings, he became the counterpart to the Latin American writers of modern literature. To reiterate, he developed a style that worshiped neither the object, foreground, nor background. Although others demarcated magic realism as a way to differentiate the magical object in mundane space, Arreguín's paintings engage the viewer as an extension of Salvador Dali's surrealism and as the visual counterpart to Rulfo, Allende and García Márquez. It is in keeping with his other Latin American counterparts who are comfortable in a full blending of spaces for an interior mystical space. So while he takes cues from *Corpus Hypercubus* in blending elements of mathematics, Catholicism and the mystical, he has achieved similar effects without always worrying about the dimensionality of the composition.

Furthermore, the viewer is less interested in the Freudian analytical nature of surrealism when viewing Arreguín. Arreguín masters and yet branches out of Dali's world by infusing the mythology of Pre-Columbian influences from the Latin American intellectual world (Mayans and Aztecs) instead of a purely Western/Quixotic tradition.

Arreguín does this by constantly merging the disciplined, patterned geometry of Euclid with organic themes and forms. Thus, as mentioned above, his paintings and the ideas of Livio (2005, 2009) on theoretical mathematics and aesthetics collide with the modern body of Latino Literature with the works of Eduardo Galeano, Juan Rulfo,
Gabriel García Márquez, Isabel Allende, and Pablo Neruda (to name a few.) Arreguín is the consummate expression, in the visual arts, of magic realism found in this literature. Likewise, his work constantly proves Livio's premise of cultures using mathematics to express the divine. His triptychs of the Madonna with Mesoamerican folk motifs are key examples.

Ultimately, the vital need for the study of Arreguín is the fact that he masterfully advances and preserves the highest dignity of Latin American art proving that the use of mathematics in aesthetics is not bound by Euclid's geometry or even the Islamic "Allah restoring balance" with the Arabic word and practice of *Al-ge-bra* (Livio, 2005).

Mayans

This exploration remains necessary because a culture's documentation and manipulation of complex patterns infers abstracted paradigms. Livio (2009) argues that mathematics holds a strange preternatural place in cultures. These abstracted paradigms drive world views. It must be emphasized that formal abstraction of thought is a transcultural issue. It is not owned by a dominant culture's monopoly. However, quite often the *conquistador* of an era assumes they are given the edict of a god. Sometimes they even believe the *conquistador* has a larger brain—given by their gods above all other humans (Gould, 1981, 1996, 1999, 2000). It is not simply the modern West that assumes their proximity to the mystical and divine. Galleano quotes the ancient Aztecs as having said that there were be no greater civilization than their own. In the Post-Colonial and Post-Modern era the bias still exists but it warrants a closer examination from multiple cultures. One way to do that is to look at these cultures use of mathematics and more specifically, complex patterns documented into either theorems (Euclid) or databases of calendars for predicting seasons (Egyptians, Mayans and dynastic China).

Thus, there remains the need to study Alfredo Arreguín. Arreguín's work elevates the mathematical pursuit of beauty and truth within the bounds of Pre-Columbian Mesoamerican parameters. It elevates it without the domination of Euclid or Plato filtered through the colonization of the Americas. Aczel (2014) and Diamond (1997) both note that the development of zero for the base number of 20 system (also known as vigesimal) arose independently of other cultural influences since the Mayans are estimated to have been using this while Europe still struggled with the Roman numeric system. As stated before, it wasn't until the 13th century with Fibonacci that are current script for numerals was adopted. As seen below, the Mayans used a series of lines and dots instead of alphanumeric characters (Sharer & Traxler, 2006).

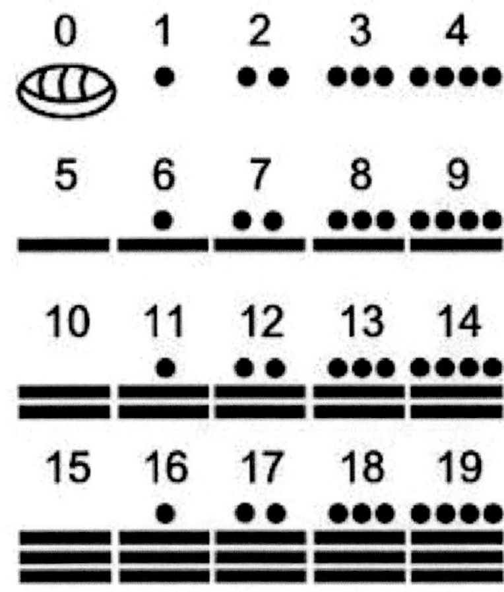

Some discussions about the dominance of Pre-Columbian artwork as "primitive" ignore the fact that the peoples of the larger Mexico area were astute mathematicians. With their documentation of astronomy through calendar making, they pursued the same goals as their counterparts in Europe.

> "Like the medieval alchemists of our own Western tradition, the ancient Maya pursued these realms for both mystical and practical purposes. In the Maya view, supernatural forces ruled over the numbers time, and the cosmos." (Sharer & Traxler, p. 100)

Morelia Mexico, Arreguín's birthplace, has constantly sought the same elevated culture as their ancient Mayan counterparts. To reiterate, for the most part in the Western traditions of art the mathematics were subsumed below the figure. The Golden Ratio *phi* Φ as was applied to architecture and even painting or sculpture but the figure, or the object covered the abstraction as if it were a blanket (object) over a sofa (mathematics). The viewer was always supposed to look at the blanket. While people in Western traditions were arguing over to what extent either of those ideas were separate, Latin American thinkers decidedly blended the boundaries of reality, leaving the demarcations fuzzy.

Arreguín's connection to the philosophical differences in Mexican thought with the blending of the figure and the geometry express the same mathematical precision. The key difference is that his blending the pattern is within the artwork. Like a Mayan calendar or pyramid, the mathematics holds as an equal or even servant to the philosopher who paints and points to the mystical. He points to the mystical just as his ancient counterparts did with their Day of the Dead rituals and other practices. Part of the blending of realities in the modern era was to again allow the Mexican psyche to explore their own unique Pre-Columbian world view in which the living and dead are not as deeply divided by either Hade's river Styx, Odin's Valhalla or the adopted sky god's cosmologies adopted by the Catholic church when they thought the world was flat and Plato and Aristotle were kings of the known, physical world.

To study Arreguín is to give honor to his ancestors. He portrays in paint what Neruda (1966) did about Macchu Picchu.

"veo el antiguo ser, servidor, el dormido
En los campos, veo un cuerpo, mil cuerpos, un hombre, mil mujeres,
Baja la racha negra, negros de lluvia y noche,
Con la piedra pesada de la estatua:
Juan Cortapiedras, hijo de Wiracocha,
Juan Comefrío, hijo de Estrella verde,
Juan Piesdescalzos, nieto de la turquesa,
Sube a nacer conmigo, hermano."

in English saying,

"I see the ancient being, the slave, the sleeping one,
Blanket his fields—a body, a thousand bodies, a man, a thousand
Women swept by the sable whirlwind, charred with rain and night,
Stoned with a lead weight of statuary:
Juan Splitstones, son of Wiracocha,
Juan Coldbelly, heir of the green star,
Juan Barefoot, grandson to the turquoise,
Rising to birth with me, as my own brother."

References

Aczel, A. (2014). The origin of the number zero. *Smithsonian magazine.* As retrieved from http://www.smithsonianmag.com/history/origin-number-zero-180953392/?no-ist

Al-Rasasi, I. (2005). *Plato's view on the importance of mathematics.* King Fahd University of Petroleum and Minerals. Retrieved from http://faculty.kfupm.edu.sa/math/irasasi/PlatosView.pdf

Baffioni, C. (2008). Ikhwân al-Safâ'. [Brethren of Purity]. Stanford Encyclopedia of Philosophy. Retrieved from http://plato.stanford.edu/entries/ikhwan-al-safa/

Bateson, G. (1987). *Steps to an ecology of the mind: collection of essays in anthropology, psychiatry, evolution, and epistemology.* Northvale, NJ: Jason Aronson Inc. Retrieved from http://www.edtechpost.ca/readings/Gregory%20Bateson%20-%20Ecology%20of%20Mind.pdf

Brook, A. (2013). Kant's View of the Mind and Consciousness of Self. *The Stanford Encyclopedia of Philosophy.* E. N. Zalta (Ed.). Retrieved from http://plato.stanford.edu/archives/fall2013/entries/kant-mind/

Darwin, C. (1874). *The descent of man.* (2nd ed.). Retrieved from http://psychclassics.asu.edu/Darwin/Descent/descent1.htm

Devlin, K. (2002). The mathematical legacy of Islam. Devlin's angle. Mathematical Association of America. Retrieved from http://www.maa.org/devlin/devlin_0708_02.html

Diamond, J. (1997). *Guns, germs and steel: The fates of human societies*, New York: W.W. Norton and Company.

Freddoso, A.J. (2014). *Aristotle.* University of Notre Dame. Retrieved from http://www3.nd.edu/~afreddos/courses/301/aristotl.htm

García Márquez, G. (1967). *100 years of solitude.* New York, NY: Harper Row.

Gould, S.J. (1981). *The Mismeasure of man.* New York: Bantam Books.

Gould, S.J. (1996). *Full House: The spread of excellence from Plato to Darwin.* New York: Three Rivers Press.

Gould, S.J. (1999). *Rock of ages: science and religion in the fullness of life.* New York: Ballantine Books.

Gould, S.J. (2003). *The hedgehog, the fox, and the magister's pox:* Mending the gap between science and the humanities. New York: Harmony Books.

Gould, S.J. & Purcell, R.W. (2000). *Crossing over: where art and science meet.* New York: Three Rivers Press.

Jenkins, O.B. (2007). Linguistic names of God. [Electronic version]. An outline introduction to Islam. Nairobi, Eygpt: Communications Press, 1991. Retrieved October 19, 2009 from http://www.orvillejenkins.com/outlineintro/namesofgod.htmlAlla

King, S. (1981). *Danse Macabre.* New York, NY: Berkley Books.

Lorenz, H. (2009). Ancient Theories of Soul. *The Stanford Encyclopedia of Philosophy.* E. N. Zalta (Ed.). Retrieved from http://plato.stanford.edu/archives/sum2009/entries/ancient-soul/

Livio, M. (2002). *The Golden Ratio: The story of PHI, the world's most astonishing number.* New York: Broadway Books.

Livio, M. (2005). *The equation that couldn't be solved: How mathematical genius discovered the language of symmetry.* New York: Simon & Schuster.

Livio, M. (2009). *Is God a Mathematician?* New York, NY: Simon and Schuster.

McInerny, R. & O'Callaghan. J. (2013). Saint Thomas Aquinas. *The Stanford Encyclopedia of Philosophy* E. N. Zalta (Ed.) Retrieved from http://plato.stanford.edu/archives/win2013/entries/aquinas/

McKeague, P. (2008). Reaching across curriculum and culture in developmental mathematics. Beyond Crossroads Workshops- transparencies. Retrieved from http://www.mckeague.com/Colorado08.pdf

Metropolotin Museum of Art (US) (n.d.) *Corpus Hypercubus Description.* Retrieved from https://metmuseum.org/art/collection/search/488880

Neruda, P. (1966). *The Heights of Macchu Picchu.* New York, NY: Farrar, Straus and Giroux.

Pew Research Report. (2014). Religion in Latin America: Widespread change in a historically Catholic Region. *Pew Research Center.* Retrieved from http://www.pewforum.org/2014/11/13/religion-in-latin-america/?utm_source=feedburner&utm_medium=feed&utm_campaign=-Feed%3A+pewresearch%2Fall+(PewResearch.org+%7C+All+Feeds)

Plato. (1932). *The Republic.* (P. Shorey Trans.). Cambridge, MA: Harvard University Press.

Posner, R.A (1990). *The problems of jurisprudence.* Cambridge, MA: Harvard University Press. Retrieved from http://ryanfb.github.io/loebolus-data/L237.pdf

Quammen, D. (2003). *Monster of God: The man-eating predator in the jungles of history and the mind.* New York, NY: Norton.

Redding, P. (2014). Georg Wilhelm Friedrich Hegel. *The Stanford Encyclopedia of Philosophy.* E N. Zalta (Ed.). Retrieved from http://plato.stanford.edu/archives/spr2014/entries/hegel/

Ríos, A.Á. (2015). *Magic Realism: Defining Terms.* Retrieved from http://www.public.asu.edu/~aarios/magicalrealism/index_files/Page278.htm

Rulfo, J. (1959). *Pedro Páramo.* New York, NY: Grove Press, Inc.

Ruse, M. (2003). Perceptions in science: Is Evolution a secular religion? *Science, 7,* 1523-1524. Retrieved from http://www.sciencemag.org/cgi/content/full/299/5612/1523

Shields, C. (2010). Aristotle's Psychology. *The Stanford Encyclopedia of Philosophy.* E. N. Zalta (Ed.). Retrieved from http://plato.stanford.edu/archives/spr2011/entries/aristotle-psychology/

Sharer, R.J. & Traxler, L.P.(2006). *The Ancient Maya* 6th ed. Stanford, CA: Stanford University Press.

Smaller, L.A. (2001). Definition of al jabar. *ULAR college of information science and systems engineering.* University of Little Rock Arkansas department of history. Retrieved from http://ualr.edu/lasmoller/aljabr.html

Van Gulick, R. (2014). Consciousness. *The Stanford Encyclopedia of Philosophy.* Retrieved from E.N. Zalta (Ed.) http://plato.stanford.edu/archives/spr2014/entries/consciousness/

Wickes, R. (2011). Arthur Schopenhauer. *The Stanford Encyclopedia of Philosophy.* E. N. Zalta (Ed.) Retrieved from http://plato.stanford.edu/archives/win2011/entries/schopenhauer/.

Winckelmann, J.J. (2006). *The history of art and antiquity. (trans.* Mallgrave, H.). (first published in1764). Los Angeles, CA: The Getty Research Institute.

Héctor González

Alfredo Arreguín: El pintor mexicano que conmovió a Carver

La anécdota es la siguiente: un mal día, Raymond Carver agarró una borrachera de notables proporciones. La consabida resaca fue en el mismo tenor. Alfredo Arreguín, su amigo mexicano y entonces joven pintor, le ofreció curar sus males con un buen plato de menudo. En agradecimiento, el narrador estadunidense dedicó un cuento al guiso.

Alfredo Arreguín vive en Seattle, rebasa los 80 años y es un pintor de considerable reconocimiento en la Unión Americana. Una de sus pinturas es parte de la colección del Smithsonian Institute. Como muchos, llegué a su nombre por la vía de Carver y su viuda, Tess Gallagher.

"Soy feliz pintando, continuamente me vienen oportunidades de Europa y Estados Unidos. Ya tuve la suerte de exponer en el Museo Smithsonian y en el Museo Nacional de Arte Norteamericano. Seguido dono obras a museos, porque me parece importante divulgar la cultura mexicana aquí", cuenta.

En México su nombre pasa casi inadvertido. Su tío, Enrique Arreguín, fue rector de la Universidad de Michoacán. "Es más fácil conseguir exposiciones en España que en México. Trabajo con una galería en San Antonio que se dedica a los maestros mexicanos: no han logrado demasiado".

Un paseo por el Bosque de Chapultepec cambió su vida, era 1956 o 1957. Mientras conducía su auto, encontró a una pareja de estadunidenses a quien ofreció llevar al Castillo de Chapultepec. "Me querían pagar, pero me negué a recibir su dinero. Les dije que estaba estudiando inglés y que su compañía me serviría para platicar. Hubo química y fuimos a bailar primero, después a Acapulco y finalmente me invitaron a Estados Unidos. Me trataron como a un hijo; creo que siempre habían querido tener un varón".

Gracias a ellos conseguiría entrar a la Universidad de Washington, años después.

Tiempos difíciles

Alfredo Arreguín creció con sus abuelos en Michoacán y empezó a dibujar casi por obligación. Los dibujos que a veces le hacía su madre los cambiaba por dibujos. Cuando ella lo descubrió prometió no darle ni uno más. "Mi mamá me dijo que necesitaba aprender a hacerlos yo mismo".

Al morir los abuelos se trasladó con su madre, pero con su padrastro no había química.

"Era un atleta, hacía pesas y me maltrataba. En una ocasión invité a un amigo a la casa para estudiar. Mis medios hermanos estaban haciendo demasiado ruido; entonces mi amigo tomó una pistola que me había regalado mi abuelo y la disparó; por error, el tiro rozó a uno de ellos. Mi madre me advirtió que mi padrastro me quería matar y que lo mejor sería que me escondiera. Me fui a la azotea de la casa de una tía en Morelia. Una vez me encontré a mi padrastro y se puso a perseguirme en su camioneta.".

u tía le aconsejó que se fuera a la Ciudad de México con otros familiares. Ahí tampoco encontró acomodo. A punto de migrar a una escuela para huérfanos en Veracruz, retomó el contacto con su padre. "Me sorprendí porque siempre había pensado que estaba muerto, pero una tía lo contactó".

Su padre lo llevó con su tío Enrique Arreguín, uno de los fundadores del Instituto Politécnico Nacional. Gracias a él consiguió un lugar en una secundaria del IPN por la Colonia Peralvillo y después entró a la preparatoria.

Inquieto, no dejó de tener problemas con el trago y su madrastra. Dio tumbos en casas de asistencia y las peleas eran algo cotidiano. "A los 18 años mi padre me dio dinero para que empezara un negocio. Pero en lugar de eso me compré un convertible, me fui a Acapulco y me gasté el dinero".

A su regreso conoció a la pareja de estadunidenses que cambiaría su vida. Mientras conducía su auto encontró a una familia. Los llevó al Castillo de Chapultepec. La química fue tal, que los llevó a Acapulco. Poco después lo invitaron a ir a Estados Unidos. Dados sus problemas, Alfredo aceptó. Su nueva familia le ayudó a conseguir trabajos de limpieza y a ingresar a la Universidad de Washington.

Cuando su vida parecía encontrar estabilidad fue reclutado para ir la guerra de Corea. Ahí pasó tres años. "Todos éramos extranjeros, solo había un norteamericano. Fue una experiencia muy fea, porque me discriminaron mucho y me hacían trabajar en cosas muy pesadas. Tenía que lavar platos y bandejas". A su regreso a la Unión Americana volvió a la universidad.

La presencia de Carver

Raymond Carver llegó a la vida de Alfredo Arreguín por conducto de Tess Gallagher, pareja del estadunidense. "Tess es mi amiga y un día lo trajo a casa; eran los setentas. A Ray le gustaba el alcohol, aunque ella trató de alejarlo del trago. Un día me puse a contarle todas mis historias y él no dejaba de apuntar. 'Este es muy buen material', decía. Se hizo famoso y viajó con Tess a Europa. Cada que podían pasaban por acá. Con una beca de 300 mil dólares se compró un Mercedes Benz al contado".

La amistad entre Carver y Arreguín echó cimientos. En una ocasión el escritor tomó senda borrachera en casa del mexicano. El mejor remedio para la cruda, advirtió el pintor, era su menudo: "Después de que pruebes mi guiso todos tus problemas se te olvidarán". Al otro día, "cuando desperté ya no había nada en la olla". Así nació el relato *Menudo*, de Raymond Carver.

El artista michoacano recuerda al narrador como un hombre atormentado. "Ray expresaba sus problemas a través de su arte. Nunca nos enfocamos en hablar de lo negativo. Intentábamos pasarlo bien. Le gustaba contarme sus aventuras de cuando viajaban, leer poesía... Una vez lo recogí de la quimioterapia y al entrar al carro empezó a llorar y abrazarme. Me decía que quería pescar. Yo le había prometido una pintura, quería hacerle una de mis selvas tropicales; pero preferí darle un cuadro de salmones. Poco después, en una conferencia de prensa, lo mostró a los periodistas. Para mí fue como un milagro porque los coleccionistas me comenzaron a llamar para pedirme pinturas de salmones".

Arte y redención

Alfredo Arreguín se alejó de los excesos de una manera súbita. Durante una fiesta alguien con unos tragos de más intentó meterse a la habitación de su hija. "Desde entonces dejé de tomar y fumar. Al principio me estaba volviendo loco, porque me parecían importantes para mi pintura. Cuando aquella energía se convirtió en algo creativo, mi vida cambió".

Ahora no pasa un día sin pintar. Con más de 80 años sobre su espalda, pasa entre ocho y diez horas en su estudio. Solo interrumpe su trabajo cuando va a caminar. "Tengo diabetes y el ejercicio es muy importante para bajarme el azúcar".

El estilo de su trabajo lo coloca entre dos aguas. En Estados Unidos lo ubican como un artista cercano al realismo mágico, mientras que en México lo etiquetan como un pintor chicano. "Cuando expuse en el Museo Mexicano de San Francisco, el director, Pedro Rodríguez, me preguntó si me colocaba en el área chicana o en la de los artistas mexicanos. Al final me pusieron con los primeros, pero la comunidad chicana se puso celosa. El actor Cheech Marin tiene una de las mayores colecciones de arte chicano y cuando vio una de mis obras en Chicago le comentó al director del museo que tenía interés en mi trabajo; sin embargo, cuando descubrió que era mexicano decidió no comprar nada. Otro curador que llevó mi trabajo a Francia, en representación de Estados Unidos, dijo que yo fui el fundador del movimiento *Pattern Painting*. Un especialista más de Los Ángeles escribió: 'Nadie pinta como Arreguín'. Creo que esto es más halagador".

Alfredo Arreguín se vale del color y elementos propios de la cultura mexicana para crear su discurso. "Soy una especie de puente entre el mexicano y el chicano. La pintura que exhibo en el Smithsonian se llama *El regreso a Aztlán*; tiene a Emiliano Zapata, a la Virgen de Guadalupe, Hidalgo, Morelos, César Chávez y Dolores Huerta. Me tienen en el museo porque represento un poco de ambas partes".

Pese al éxito en la Unión Americana, Arreguín no niega el resquemor que supone ser poco conocido en México. "No he tenido la oportunidad de exponer seriamente en la Ciudad de México. Me gustaría que alguien escribiera un libro sobre mí, porque aquí ponen cosas muy turísticas que no siempre coinciden con mis raíces. Probablemente me descubrirán cuando me haya ido de este mundo. En una ocasión iba a exponer con Francisco Toledo en Oaxaca, pero no se concretó. Alfredo Zalce también me respeta. Shinzaburo Takeda tiene buenos comentarios sobre mi trabajo e incluso ha reconocido mi influencia en su trabajo. Los museos y críticos están acostumbrados a ver solo lo que sucede en Nueva York o Inglaterra. Quiero regresar a México con mi obra, para mí sería un orgullo regresar al lugar de mi niñez".

Adriana Williams

Honoring Alfredo Arreguín

We salute and celebrate Alfredo Arreguín, this remarkable and unique artist, indeed one of our national treasures! I first met Alfredo when he had an exhibition at the Mexican Museum in San Francisco in 1977. Although, I was already an admirer of his work, I had not seen his paintings in person. I shall never forget my first impression. The intricate patterns and combination of colors were overwhelming. As I looked more closely fish, birds, butterflies, trees, and flowers began to emerge and, sometimes, even a recognizable face. Each painting drew you into the artist's magical world, where much was to be discovered.

In 1983, Alfredo had a second exhibition at the Mexican Museum, where I was also present. However, it wasn't until 1992 that I got to know Alfredo altogether. We were in Stockton, California for the retrospective exhibition at the Haggin Museum of Peter Rodriguez, founder of the Mexican Museum in San Francisco. This was the beginning of a warm and cherished friendship. Who could not love such a person as this warm-hearted man from Morelia, Michoacán?

Many summers my husband, Tom, and I traveled to Seattle, Washington to attend Wagner's "Ring Cycle" at the Seattle opera. We would call on Alfredo and his wife, Susan Lytle, also a painter. To see their house, to stand in the room where Alfredo's paintings were conceived, and to look at his canvasses lining the wall was always a thrill for us. Little did I know that one day I would be the proud owner of one of Alfredo's paintings.

During one of our trips, as I was walking around the house, I spotted a large clay sculpture standing on a shelf. It was a stern wolf depicted in judge's robe. Since my husband was a practicing lawyer and, enjoyed nothing better than arguing a case before the court, I purchased "Juez Canino" made by Alfredo in 1981 for Tom's upcoming birthday. We were thrilled because, now, we owned an 'Alfredo Arreguín!'

When my husband died in 2013, Alfredo wrote, thinking about you: "Susie and I re the tragic and sad news about Tom. I cannot imagine the suffering this horrible event has put you in. In situations such as this, I find myself lacking the right words to say, but my saddened heart, understands and shares in the sadness of losing a loved one. I am still mourning my dear, father's death. We send you our love, and we hope your beautiful face in my portrait of you, will give you some peace. I loved that picture with the scarf that is why I was inspired to paint it." Alfredo.

The photograph comes from a cruise Tom and I took from Athens, Greece to Dubai, Saudi Arabia through the Suez Canal in 2011. One of our stopovers was in Muscadet, Oman, a lovely white city. I spent the morning wandering around the bazaar. I was very much captivated by the many ways the men wore the headscarf wrapped around their head. I looked for a men's store and had the owner teach me to use one. Excited, I went back to the ship for lunch wearing my turban and causing a sensation in the dining room. Tom took many photographs, and I posted one on the internet where Alfredo discovered it.

Just before Christmas 2013, my portrait, "The Turban", arrived. Alfredo instinctively knew the painting would bring a smile to my face. It did indeed lift my sadness. I tried to send something for the painting but, he wrote, "No picture no money, or anything else." The painting is yours. You have already given me your beautiful friendship to continue admiring you. Alfredo."

What an extraordinary and generous gesture from my loving friend! I could only thank and convey to him that having your painting brings back wonderful memories and I will cherish it for the rest of my life.

The Mexican poet, Elías Nandino writes:

¡Nothing is more mine
than the sea
when I gaze on it!

This is how I feel when I gaze at my portrait. It brings forth all the emotion with regards to my Mexican heritage: The enormous pride I feel about Mexico's noteworthy traditions, the creativity and beauty of the people and, by far, the art which has shaped Arreguín, the artist.

It is also true of the imposing subjects of the portraits *Herencia*, (Zapata and Subcomandante Marcos), *The Return to Aztlán* (Emiliano Zapata, César Chávez and Dolores Huerta) in which historical legendary heroes of Mexican heritage, past and present, are depicted. Through Alfredo's vision, I recognize their sacrifices and struggles. Not only do I identify with their stance, but their principles unconditionally become mine.

What occurs when I allow myself to be immersed in a work such as the tryptic *Sueño (Dream: Eve before Adam)*? My gaze is engaged by the plants, flowers, toucans, monkeys, butterflies, even a fish. As my eyes move along, I discover the face of a beautiful woman and, gradually, six more appear and one lone man. Is he guided by the women? Who are these mysterious women? Are they the protectors of the jungle? Do they welcome us or shame us for what we have done to their world? I am lost in thought.

This work reminds me of Alfredo's Madonnas: *Nuestra Señora de la Selva*, *La Guadalupana*, *La Virgen de los Milagros*, *La Virgen de la Luz*, *La Virgen Negra*, *Madonna Afro-Latina*, *La Malinche* and the incommparable, *Trilogía de la Independencia* in which the devil of Ocumicho and Father Hidalgo are one with the Virgen of Guadalupe. These mystical and ethereal madonnas are imbued with feeling. The devotion with which Alfredo has painted them let us know they are forever here to love and protect all life.

My most recent discovery has been Alfredo's photographs taken on his daily walks. What his eye sees astonishes me. From the photographs of Green Lake and Rialto Beach beautiful paintings emerge. A photograph of salmon becomes a painting of salmon springing over the waves on their last run or a meditation as they leap into the waves; a flock of birds above the beach turns into a painting of birds that with the slow rise and fall of their wings seem to be attempting to join the enchanted moon.

A group of photographs, *Spring Sea*, *Carpet*, *Water Dance*, and *Frozen Leaves* are not just photographs of leaves or the movement of waves. They are much more. Alfredo sees patterns of great splendor that, most of us would overlook, later will be transformed into ornamental patterns and color forming the background or surrounding a figure in many paintings.

All of his work, including the photographs, demonstrates Alfredo's distinct and intimate relationship with Mother Nature. Speaking to his heart, she inspires and nourishes him and, in return, Alfredo creates work of immeasurable beauty. Philip James Bailey wrote "Art is Man's nature; nature is God's art." Alfredo Arreguín's work is poetry that fills my soul. I honor you and take great pride in your creation.

For several years, the Argentine poet and painter, Carlos Pillado and I have been celebrating our birthdays together at the end of October. In 2016, we had the extraordinary luck to have Susan and Alfredo attend the party. Carlos upon discovering Alfredo's work became an ardent admirer.

Homenaje a Alfredo Arreguín

Saludamos y celebramos a Alfredo Arreguín, un artista admirable y único, de hecho, ¡uno de nuestros tesoros nacionales!. Conocí a Alfredo en el año 1977 luego de una de sus muestras en el Museo Mexicano de Arte de San Francisco. Si bien yo admiraba su trabajo de arte, no había podido, aún, ver sus pinturas personalmente. Mi primera impresión al verlas fue "inolvidable".

Sus intrincados diseños y combinaciones de colores son apabullantes y al acercarme y contemplarlas con detenimiento y atención comencé a observar un sin número de peces, pájaros, mariposas, árboles y flores, como también, rostros reconocibles. Cada pintura me intruducía al mundo mágico de este artista con una infidad de temas y argumentos que me permitían dilucidar su historia de vida.

En el año 1983, Alfredo tuvo una segunda exhibición en el Museo Mexicano, donde también estuve presente pero no fue sino hasta el año 1992 que llegué a conocer a Alfredo personalmente, en Stockton, California, en el museo Haggin, durante una exhibición restrospectiva de nuestro querido Peter Rodriguez, quien fuera el fundador del Museo Mexicano en San Francisco. Desde ese momento, comenzamos una cálida y entrañable amistad que se ha ido fortaleciendo con el tiempo. ¿Cómo no querer a una persona como este hombre de Morelia, Michoacán, tan sincero y tan cariñoso?

Muchos veranos Tom, mi esposo, y yo, viajábamos a Seattle, Washington, para asistir al "Anillo del Nibelungo" de Richard Wagner, en la Opera de Seattle. Allí, nos encontrabamos con Alfredo y su esposa, Susan Lytle, también pintora. Era una experiencia bellísima ir a su casa y compartir con él el lugar donde sus pinturas eran concebidas, como también poder observar sus pinturas expuestas en las paredes de su casa. ¿Quién podría imaginarse que yo, sería una día, la poseedora argullosa de una de sus pinturas?

Durante uno de nuestros viajes a Seattle, mientras recorría su casa, vi una gran escultura de arcilla sobre una repisa. Era un lobo hosco y adusto que vestía una toga de juez. Mi esposo era abogado defensor y no había nada que él disfrutabara más que discutir un caso frente a un tribunal. Para su siguiente cumpleaños, adquirí esta pieza llamada "Juez Canino", realizada por Alfredo en el año 1981 y se la obsequié, como sorpresa, a mi esposo Tom. ¡Ambos quedamos encantados, porque ahora, éramos propietarios de un 'Alfredo Arrequín'!

Al morir mi esposo en el año 2013, Alfredo me escribió expresándo sus condolencias de la siguiente forma: "Estamos pensando en tí después que Susie y yo recibimos la triste y trágica noticia de la muerte de Tom. No puedo imaginarme el sufrimiento que este evento horrible te ha traído. No me alcanzan las palabras para expresar lo que siento, pero debo decirte, que mi triste corazón comprende y comparte la tristeza de perder a un ser querido, ya que estoy aún de luto, por la muerte de mi propio padre. Te enviamos nuestro cariño y espero que el retrato de tu bello rostro, que estoy ahora pintando, te traiga la paz que necesitas". Me encantó la fotografía tuya con la chalina sobre tu cabeza y me he inspirado para retratarla sobre una tela. Alfredo".

La fotografía proviene de un crucero que hicimos Tom y yo desde Atenas, Grecia hasta Dubái, Saudí Arabia, a través del Canal de Suez, en el año 2011. Una de nuestras paradas fue en Muscadet, Omán, una hermosa ciudad blanca. Yo me pasé la mañana recorriendo el bazar. Me cautivó ver las costumbres en que los hombres usaban una especie de tela enredada alrededor de la cabeza. Busqué una tienda para hombres y le pedí al dueño que me enseñara cómo usarla. Emocionada, regresé al barco para el almuerzo usando mi turbante y causando sensación en el comedor. Tom me tomó muchas fotografías, y puse una de ellas en el internet, donde Alfredo la descubrió.

Justo antes de la Navidad del año 2013, la pintura de Alfredo, mi retrato que él llamó "El turbante", llegó a mis manos. Alfredo, instintivamente, supo que la pintura me haría sonreír. Realmente, Alfredo consiguió aliviar mi pena. Yo intenté, de alguna manera, retribuir el obsequio

de Alfredo pero él me escribió diciendo: "Ningún dinero, ni ningún obsequio. La pintura es tuya. Tú ya me has dado tu hermosa amistad para continuar admirándote. Alfredo".

¡Qué extraordinario y generoso gesto de mi querido amigo! Sólo pude agradecérselo y dejarle saber que su cuadro me llenaba de alegría, me traía bellísimos recuerdos y que lo apreciaría por el resto de mi vida.

El poeta mexicano, Elías Nandino escribe:

"¡Nada hay más mío

como lo es el mar,

cuando lo miro!"

Así es como me siento cuando contemplo mi retrato, conectándome inmediatamente con mi herencia mexicana y sintiéndome orgullosa de nuestras nobles tradiciones, como también, de la belleza y la creatividad de su gente y el orgullo enorme que siento de las admirables tradiciones mexicanas y en este caso la creatividad el arte que ha distinguido a Arregín, el artista.

Lo mismo ocurre cuando contemplo otras pinturas que también encarnan estos temas, tales como, *Herencia*, (Zapata y el Subcomandante Marcos), *El Regreso a Aztlán* (Emiliano Zapata, César Chávez y Dolores Huerta) en los cuales se hallan retratados los legendarios héroes de la herencia mexicana. Es a través de la visión de Alfredo que logro admirar y respetar las luchas y sacrificios de nuestros compatriotas, no solamente por la manera en que me identifico con ellos, sino también, por la forma de hacerlos míos.

¿Qué es lo que ocurre cuando me permito conectarme con piezas tales como el tríptico *Sueño*? (*Sueño*: Eva antes de Adán). Mi mirada queda atraída por las plantas, flores, tucanes, monos, mariposas, inclusive un pez. A medida que observo la pintura, descubro el rostro de una hermosa mujer y luego, seis más, para más tarde observar a un hombre solitario. ¿Está este hombre conectado con estas mujeres? ¿Quiénes son estas mujeres misteriosas? ¿Serán las protectoras de la jungla? ¿Nos dan estas mujeres la bienvenida o nos culpan por lo que le hemos hecho a su mundo? Es así como quedo extraviada en mis pensamientos.

Este trabajo me recuerda a las Madonnas de Alfredo: *Nuestra Señora de la Selva, La Guadalupana, La Virgen de los Milagros, La Virgen de la Luz, La Virgen Negra, Madonna Afro-Latina, La Malinche* y la incomparable *Trilogía de la Independencia* en la que el demonio de Ocumicho y el Padre Hidalgo se funden con la Virgen de Guadalupe. Estas Madonnas, etéreas y místicas, están imbuidas de sentimiento. Con la devoción que Alfredo las ha pintado, sabemos que están aquí para proteger todo lo que es vida.

Mi descubrimiento más reciente han sido las fotografías que Alfredo toma durante sus paseos diarios. Me asombra lo que su ojos perciben. De sus propias fotografías de *Green Lake y de Rialto Beach* se originan bellas pinturas. De una fotografía de salmones deviene una pintura del salmón surgiendo de las olas en su última carrera, o una meditación cuando saltan sobre las olas; una parvada de pájaros sobre la playa se convierte en una pintura de pájaros que con el lento caer de sus alas, parecen estar intentando integrarse a la luna encantada.

Un grupo de fotografías, *Mar de Primavera, Tapete, Danza del Agua,* y *Hojas Heladas* no son sólo fotografías de hojas o del movimiento de las olas. Son mucho más que eso. Alfredo ve patrones ornamentales de gran esplendor que la mayoría de nosotros no captamos, y que más tarde formarán el fondo o el entorno de una figura en sus obras.

Todo su trabajo, incluyendo las fotografías, demuestra su relación distintiva e íntima con la Madre Naturaleza. Hablándole a su corazón, ella lo inspira y lo nutre, y a cambio, Alfredo crea obras de inconmensurable belleza. Philip James Bailey escribió "El arte es la naturaleza humana; la naturaleza es el arte de Dios."

El trabajo de Alfredo Arreguín es poesía que me llena el alma. Te estimo y me enorgullezco de tu extraordinaria creación.

Durante varios años, el poeta y pintor argentino, Carlos Pillado y yo hemos celebrado juntos nuestros cumpleaños al fin de octubre. En el 2016, tuvimos la gran fortuna de que Susan y Alfredo asistieran a la fiesta. Cuando Carlos descubrió el trabajo de Alfredo, se convirtió en un ferviente admirador.

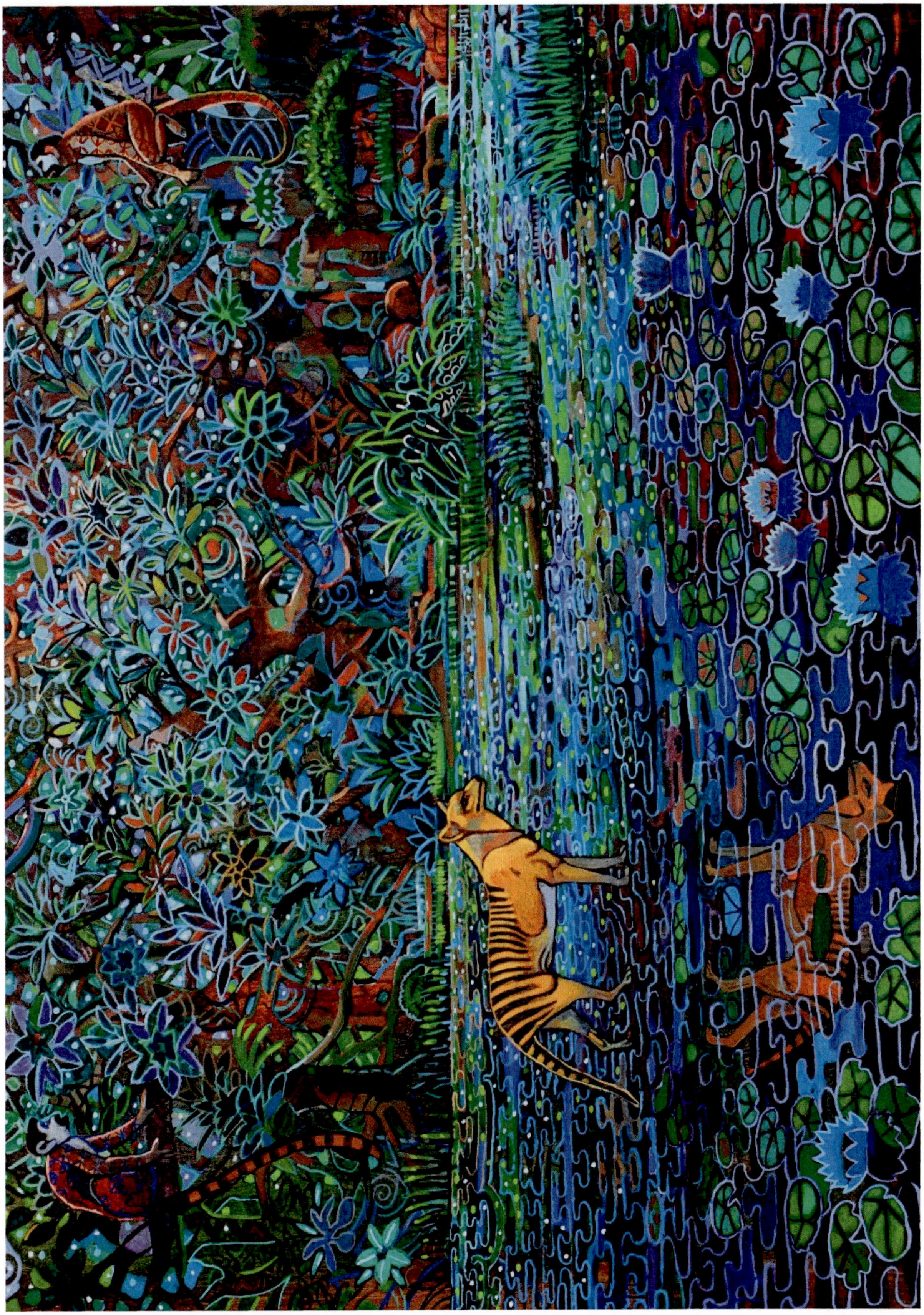

Rio Tasmano, 2017, 48 × 60, in., collection of the artist

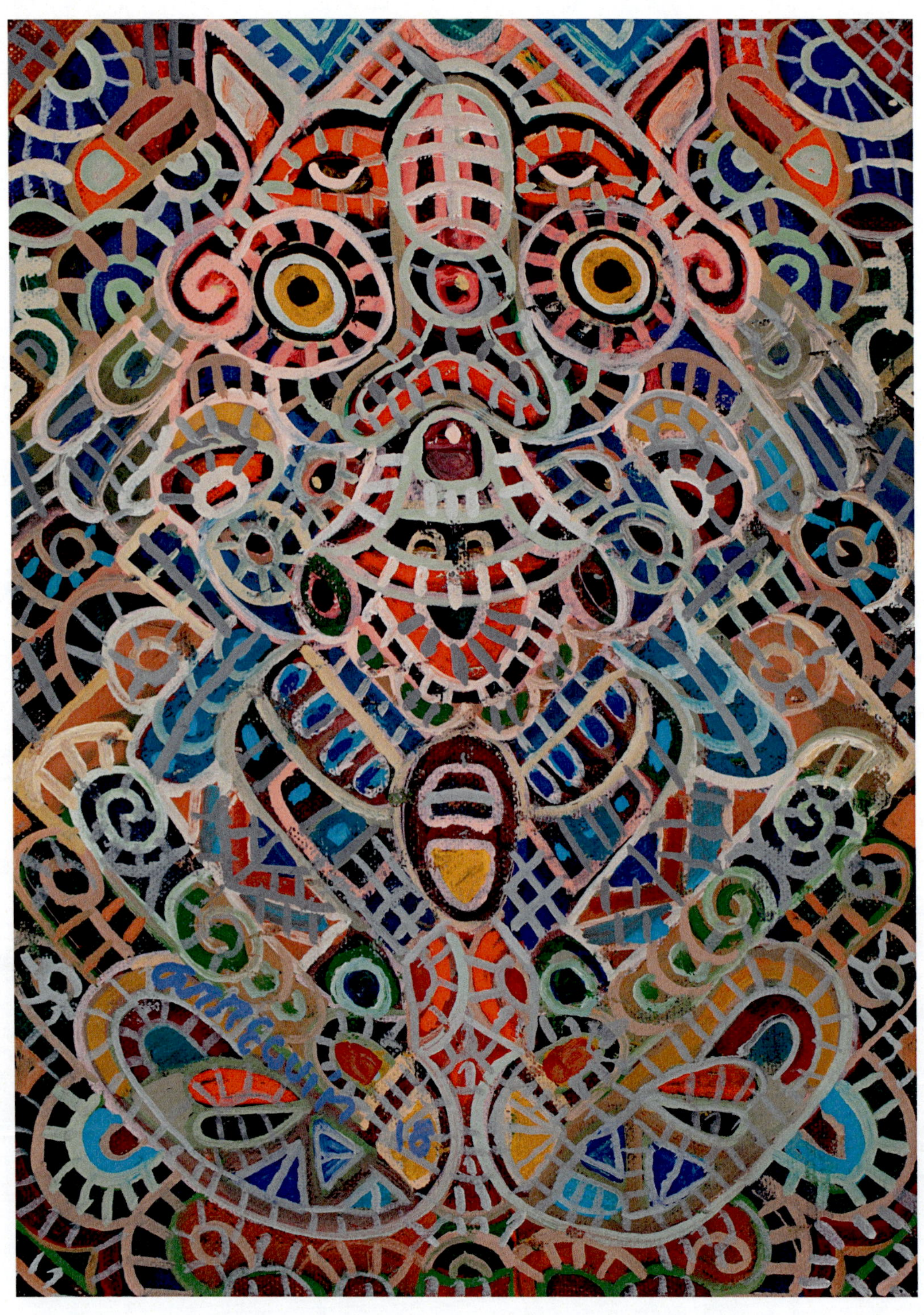

Cucu, 2018, 20 × 18 in., collection of the artist

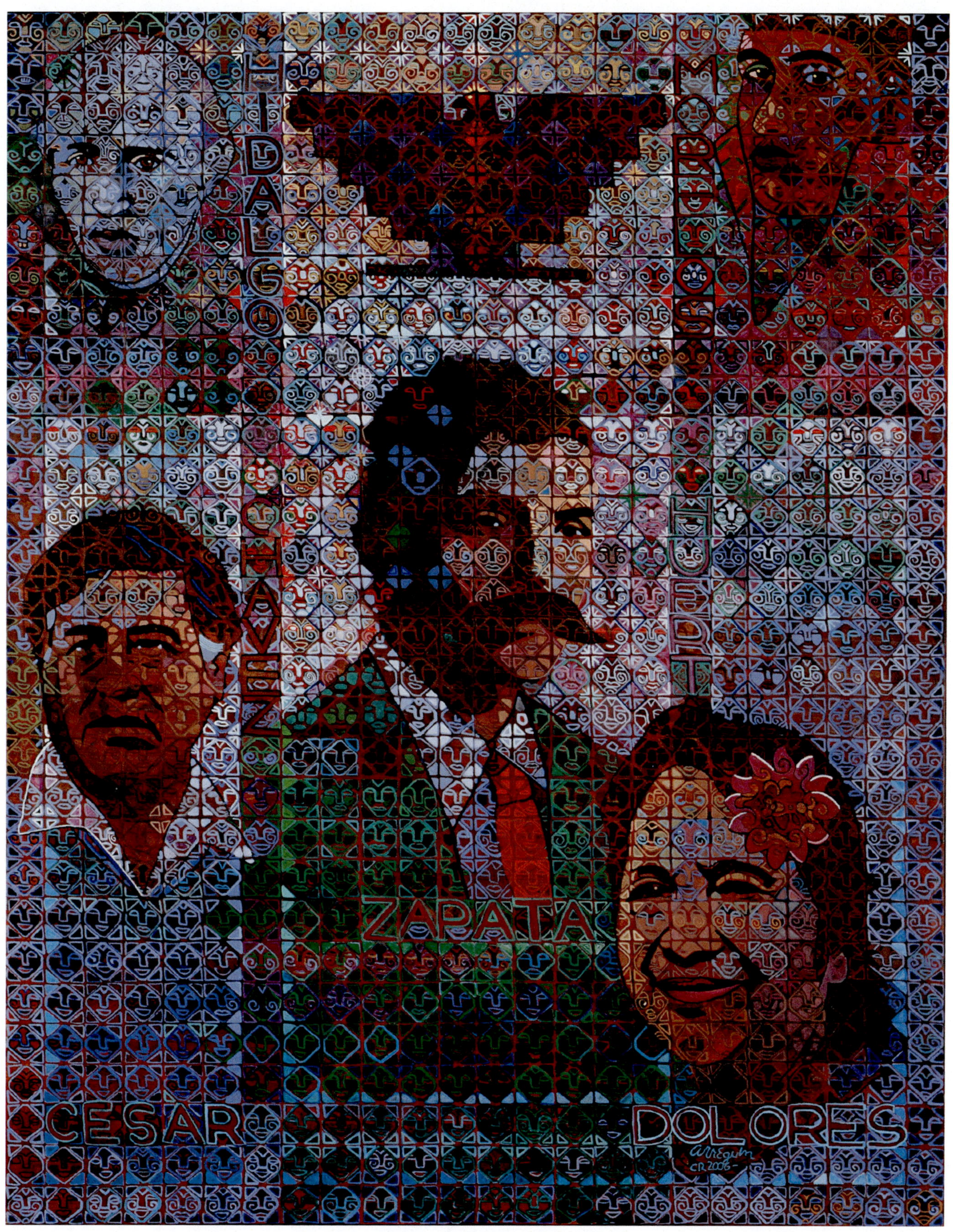

The Return to Aztlan, 2006, 60 × 48 in., National Portrait Gallery
Smithsonian Institute,
gift of Felix Arreguín Velez and Catalina Toledo de Arreguín

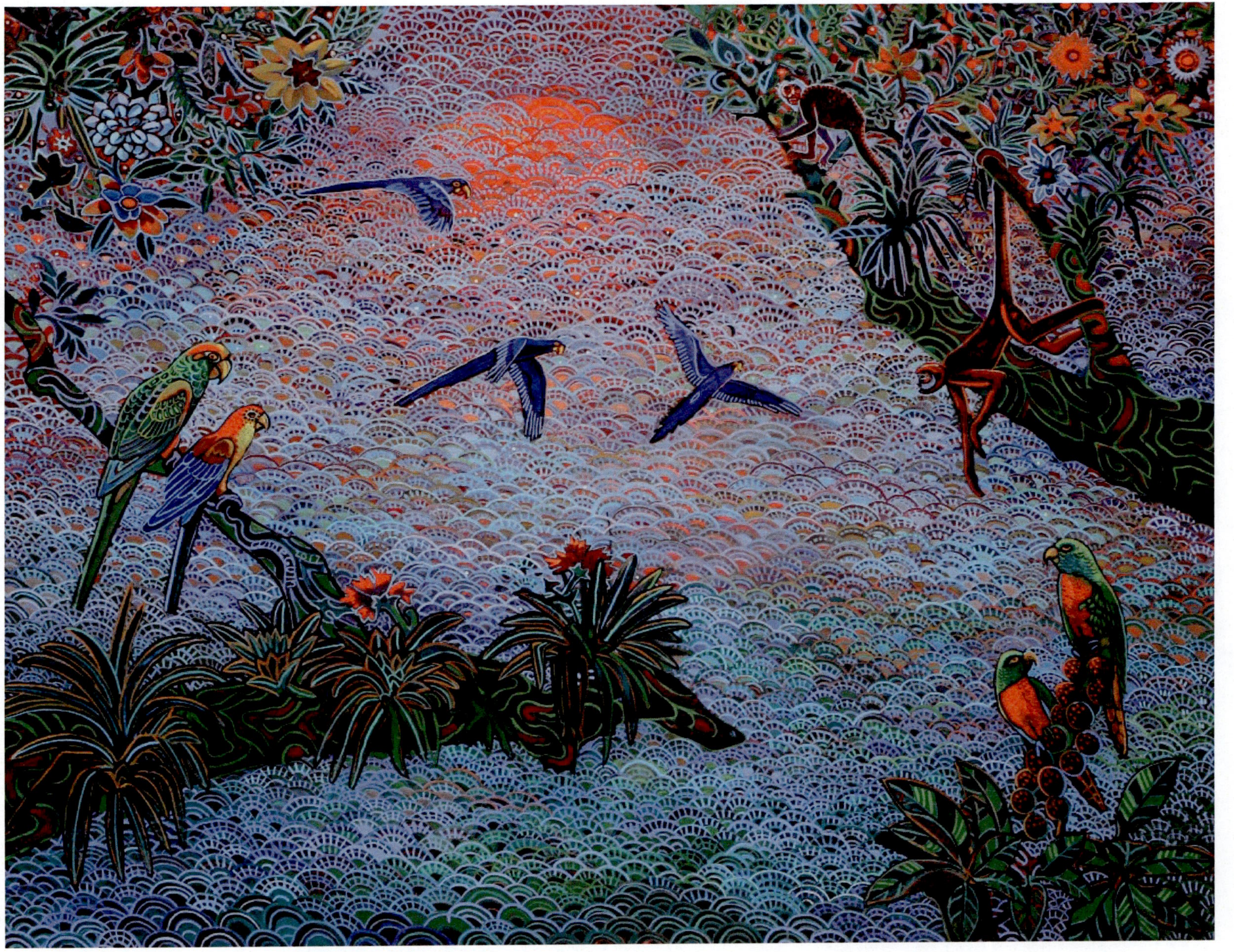

The Magic Garden 2017, 48 × 58 in., collection of the artist

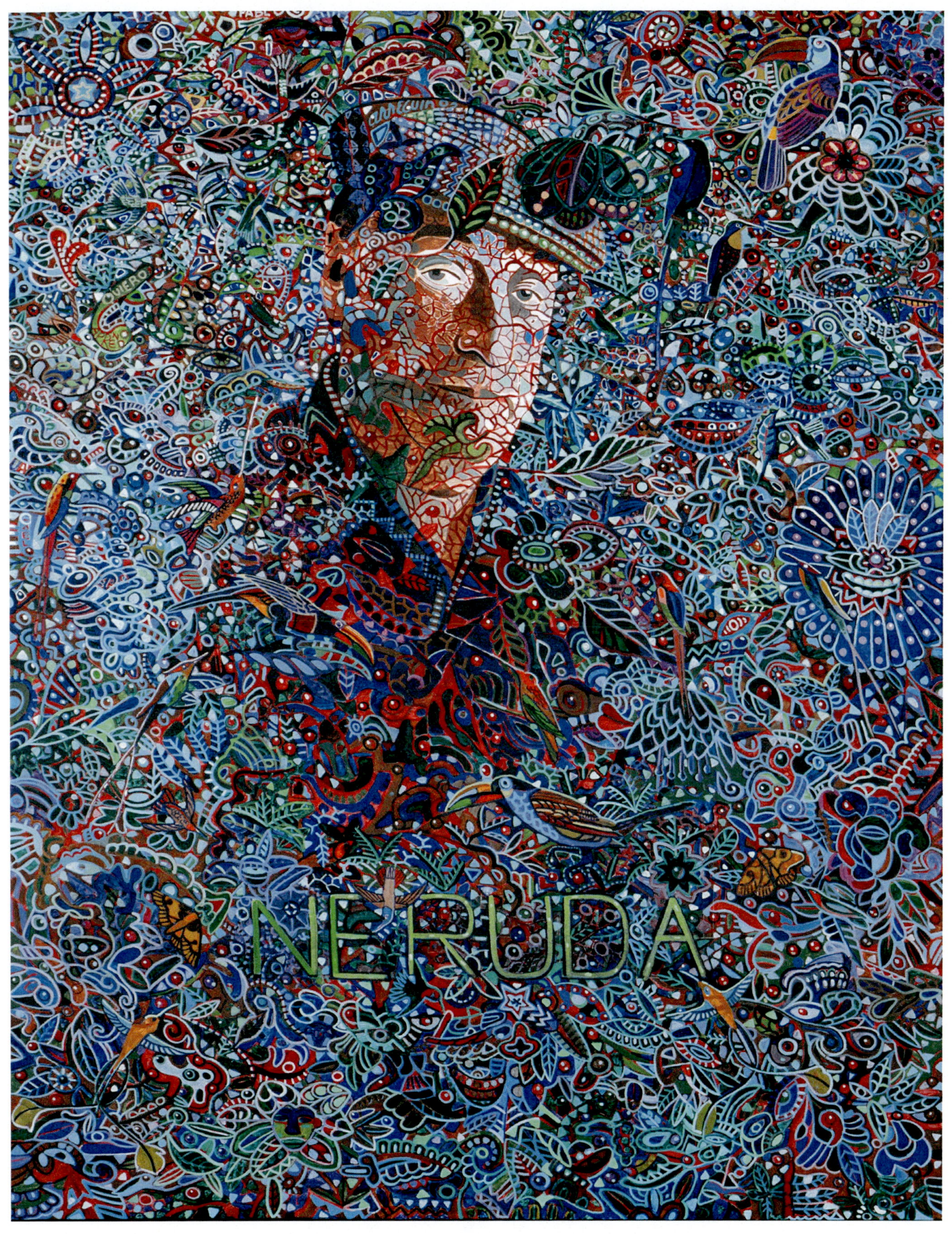

Isla Negra, 2003, 60 × 48 in., collection of the artist

Carlos Pillado

El artista de lo oculto.

Ocultos están tus sueños,
viejos, nuevos y futuros.
Escondida tu mirada,
libre, tersa, sosegada.
Ignorado eras el niño,
carente de algún cariño.
Secreto el dolor aullaba,
de pena aún bramabas.
Camuflada la esperanza,
sonriente, alerta, en danza.
Escondido en las miradas,
virtuosas, genuinas, osadas.
Encubiertos están tus ojos,
claros, amplios y brillantes.
Velado el amor de padre,
de hijo, de amigo amante.
Sabios los mensajes vivos,
ilustrados, percibidos.
Los colores son tus alas,
las formas son tus silbidos,
oculta queda tu alma,
detrás de tu lienzo niño.

Decir que la obra de Arreguín es exquisita, elegante y sobre todas las cosas enigmática. La mayoría de las veces sus mensajes están ocultos y el espectador debe, de alguna manera, descifrarlos. Creo que la vida de Alfredo está colmada de mensajes ocultos, recónditos e inexplicables que él mismo debió descifrar para volverlos inteligibles, penetrables, accesibles. El recorrido personal de este laberinto, muchas veces anárquico y caótico, ha definido el contenido de su vida y, por ende, ha sido el argumento y fondo de su arte. Mi poesía intenta definir, de alguna manera, de que esta hecho este extraordinario artista.

Contributor's Biographies

José Luis Alcubilla esta un narrador y poeta. Estudió Filosofía en la Facultdad de Filosofia y Letras de la Universidad Nacional Autónoma de México (UNAM). También estuve el Coordinador del Departamento de Bienes Artísticos y Culturales de la Dirección General de Patrimonio de la UNAM. Colaborador de El Fígaro, El Financiero, El Nacional, Gaceta UNAM y Unomásuno. Becario del Instituto de Investigaciones Estéticas, UNAM 1976, y del inba/fonapas, en Ensayo, 1982.

Lisa Alvarado is an educator, poet, novelist, and journalist, the founder of La Onda Negra Press. Her book of poetry, *Raw Silk Suture*, with a foreword by Juan Felipe Hererra, was released by Floricanto Press in 2008 and was positively reviewed by Rigoberto González. Lisa is the recipient of grants from the Department of Cultural Affairs, The NEA, and the Ragdale Foundation. In Fall, 2009, she was awarded Hispanic Author of the Year by the State of Illinois. In 2015, she curated and edited an anthology of on line jazz-inspired poetry, *Love You Madly.*

Raymond Carver was born in 1938 in Clatskanie, Oregon and grew up in Yakima, Washington. Known for helping to revitalize the American short story in the 1980's, he attended the Iowa Writer's Workshop and gained national attention for both his poetry and short fiction. He won a total five O. Henry Short Story awards. He was also nominated for the National Book Award and Pulitzer Prize for his third major collection *Cathedral*, (1984). After he discovered the "Bohemian group" (as Tess Gallagher writes), he became a close friend of Alfredo Arreguín. He died in Port Angeles, Washington in 1988.

Andrew Connors is Curator of Art at the Albuquerque Museum of Art and History. Previously, Dr. Connors served as Chair of the Visual Arts Department at Albuquerque Academy, as Senior Curator at the national Hispanic Cultural Center in Albuquerque and as Associate Curator at the Smithsonian American Art Museum where he developed collections and exhibitions on Hispanic, Latino, Native American, and Folk Art.

David J. de la Torre has served multiple museums as a curator, including the Smithsonian Institution. He currently serves on the US National Committee for the International Council of Museums (ICOM-US). In the 1980's, he served as the Executive Director for the Mexican Museum and was instrumental in securing the Nelson A. Rockefeller Collection of Mexican Folk Art as well as the Andy Williams Collection of pre-Hispanic Art, among other major gifts. De la Torre has organized numerous exhibitions on Mexican and Mexican American culture, including highly popular projects on Frida Kahlo, Diego Rivera and others.

Lauro Flores is Professor of Chicano and Latin American literatures and cultures at the University of Washington, Seattle. During his tenure at the University of Washington, he has been Chair of AES, Director of the Center for Chicano Studies, Chair of Latin American Studies, and Special Assistant to the Provost. Winner of a 2007 *UW Distinguished Teaching Award*, Dr. Flores has been visiting professor at Stanford University and UCLA.

Tess Gallagher was born in 1943 in Port Angeles, Washington, to a logging family. She earned degrees from the University of Washington, where she studied with Theodore Roethke, and the Iowa Writers' Workshop. Known for her poetry, Gallagher was inspired to take up writing short stories after her marriage to acclaimed Raymond Carver. She has won numerous awards, including fellowships from the Guggenheim Foundation, the National Endowment for the Arts, and a Maxine Cushing Gray Foundation Award.

Héctor González (Ciudad de México, 1974). Estudió la carrera de Comunicación y Periodismo en la Facultad de Ciencias Políticas y Sociales. Ha trabajado en Canal 22, ABC Radio y TV UNAM. Ha publicado crónicas, entrevistas y reportajes en los diarios Reforma, *Ovaciones Milenio, Crónica* y *El Universal.* Así como en las revistas *Etcétera, Época, Casa del tiempo* y *Siempre,* así como en medios de España, Cuba, Estados Unidos y Colombia. Además es coconductor del programa *Psicocinema* en la estación Circo Volador radio. Ha impartido pláticas y conferencias en diversas universidades y ferias del libro del país.

Rigoberto Gonzalez was born in Bakersfield, California, and raised in Michoacán, Mexico, he is the son of migrant farmworkers. His family returned Mexico in 1992, while González remained alone in the U.S. to complete his education.. He earned a B.A. in Humanities and Social Sciences Interdisciplinary Studies from the University of California, Riverside and graduate degrees from the University of California, Davis, and Arizona State University in Tempe

Juan Felipe Herrera was born in Fowler, California, on December 27, 1948. The son of migrant farmers, Herrera moved often, living in trailers or tents along the roads of Southern California. He was one of the first wave of Chicanos to receive an Educational Opportunity Program (EOP) scholarship to attend UCLA. He received a Masters in Social Anthropology from Stanford in 1980, and went on to earn an MFA from the University of Iowa Writers' Workshop in 1990. Hailed as a multi-faceted artist he served as the United States Poet Laureate from 2015-2017.

Doug Johnson is the founding editor of Cave Moon Press. His poems have appeared in multiple literary journals and he stays active as a composer. He is also an active visual artist, privileged to have a two-person show, *In the Shadow of a Master: the Art of Alfredo Arreguín and Doug Johnson.* Dr. Johnson utilizes his graduate degrees to help artists and poets connect to non-profits and community. Collaborate in print at cavemoonpress.com. Collaborate in the visual arts at pazarteproject.com.

Matthew Kangas is an independent art critic and curator, is the author of over 1,000 reviews, articles, and monographs including three volumes of his collected writings published by Midmarch Arts Press, New York. He is a fourth-generation Washington State resident, graduate of Reed College and The Queen's College, Oxford University, and taught English literature at University of Puget Sound/ Seattle. Winner of the Manufacturers Hanover/ART WORLD award for news paper art criticism, he has also received awards from the National Endowment for the Arts and was made an honorary professor at the Aesthetic Education Laboratory of Shanghai Teachers University in 1992. His latest book is *Julie Speidel: The Center Holds. Burning Forest: The Art of Maria Frank Abrams, a Holocaust survivor*, was a finalist for the Next Generation Indie Booksellers Award.

Lawrence Matsuda was born in the Minidoka, Idaho Concentration Camp during World War II. He and his family were among the approximately 120,000 Japanese Americans and Japanese held without due process for approximately three years or more. Currently he is a career educator/writer. In 2005, he and two Seattle University colleagues co-edited the book, *Community and difference: teaching, pluralism and social justice*, Peter Lang Publishing, New York. It won the 2006 National Association of Multicultural Education Phillip Chinn Book Award. Dr. Matsuda has received multiple awards. His book of poetry, *A Cold Wind from Idaho* was published by Black Lawrence Press in 2010.

Paul McVeigh's debut novel, The *Good Son*, won The Polari First Novel Prize. Born in Belfast, he began his award-winning career as a playwright before moving to London. His short stories have been read on BBC Radio and *Hollow* was shortlisted for Irish Short Story of the Year 2017. He has read his work at the International Conference on the Short Story in Vienna, twice at the Cork International Short Story Festival, among others. He is associate director of Word Factory, 'the UK's national organization for excellence in the short story', and co-founded the London Short Story Festival. Contact him at paulmcveighwriter.com

Amalia Mesa-Bains gained a Ph.D. in clinical psychology from the Wright Institute in Berkeley, California, Dr. Mesa-Bains worked for the San Francisco Unified School District as a psychologist. Between 1965–1985 she was the regional committee chair (Northern California) for the exhibition "Chicano Art: Resistance and Affirmation." Among other awards, she earned the INTAR-Hispanic Arts Center's Golden Palm Award in 1991, and the MacArthur Fellowship award in 1992.

Carlos Pillado was born in Salto, a province of Buenos Aires, Argentina in 1964. After mandatory military service, he completed a degree in political science from the University of El Salvador and then traveled extensively through Mexico until 1989, until he relocated to the United States. After marrying and having two children, his family moved to Mill Valley California. A successful restaurateur, he began painting in 2003, gaining rave reviews from luminaries such as Adriana Williams. View more of his work at carlospillado.com.

Peter Rodriguez was a well-known California painter who founded the Mexican Museum in San Francisco in 1975. He was appointed its first Director. He grew the collection to house 16,000 pieces and its new facility is being constructed in downtown San Francisco, and is an affiliate of the Smithsonian, largely due to his vision and passion.

Antonio Sanchez currently serves as an instructor of anthropology at Central Washington University. He also served in the Department of American Ethnic Studies at the University of Washington where he taught Hispanic studies. He specializes in the history and the heritage of Latinos in Washington State. He co-authored a K-12 curriculum called *Fruits of Our Labor*. He is the founder and director of Americas Institute of Art, History and Culture. Dr. Sanchez .has received numerous awards for his educational and international economic development accomplishments.

Jeffree Stewart is an oil painter and writer who keeps an indoor/outdoor studio north from Olympia. While working for the Department of Ecology, he served as an independent curator of Art In Ecology, focusing on northwest art.

J. D. Talasek is Director, Cultural Programs of the National Academy of Sciences (CPNAS) in Washington D.C. He creates and moderate events related to art and science. He is the art advisor for Issues in Science and Technology Magazine (jointly published by the National Academies, University of Texas at Dallas and Arizona State University). He has directed the planning curating, design, and installation of exhibits in three rotating gallery spaces and one permanent space. Exhibits that he has organized and also traveled including one that was supported by the Smithsonian Institution's Traveling Exhibit Program. He also serves one the Contemporary Art and Science Committee (CASC) for the Smithsonian's Museum of Natural History.

Adriana Williams wrote the definitive biography of Miguel and Rosa Covarrubias in 1994, *Covarrubias in Bali* in 2005, and *Miguel Covarrubias: Sketches: Bali – Shanghai.* Adriana has donated important Covarrubias collections of art and photography to the Library of Congress and to the Mexican Museum in San Francisco. Adriana lives in San Francisco. She and her husband were serious collectors of art nouveau, symbolism, contemporary art glass, and Mexican contemporary art and folk art. The author's grandfather was Plutarco Elias Calles, president of Mexico from 1924 to 1928. She enjoys close connections with Mexico and maintains ties with members of Mexico's most distinguished artistic circles.

Alfredo Arreguín- Biography

Seattle artist Alfredo Arreguin has exhibited his work internationally, most recently at the Museo de Cadiz in Spain (2015). He has exhibited solo shows at Linda Hodges Gallery since 2001. Arreguin has a long and distinguished list of accomplishments. In 1979 he was selected to represent the U.S. at the 11th International Festival of Painting at Cagnes-sur Mer, France, where he won the Palm of People Award. In 1980 he received a fellowship from the National Endowment for the arts. In 1988 in a competition that involved over 200 portfolios, Arreguin won the commission to design the poster for the Centennial Celebration of the State of Washington (the image was his painting Washingtonia); that same year he was invited to design the White House Easter Egg. Perhaps the climatic moment of his success came in 1994, when the Smithsonian Institution acquired his triptych, *Sueño (Dream: Eve Before Adam),* for inclusion in the collection of the national Museum of American Art. A year later, in 1995, Arreguin received an OHTLI Award, the highest recognition given by the Mexican government to the commitment of distinguished individuals who perform activities that contribute to promote Mexican culture abroad. More recently, success has been cemented by an invitation to show his work in the Framing Memory: Portraiture Now exhibition, at the Smithsonian National Portrait Gallery. One of his paintings included in this show, *The Return to Aztlan*, will remain in the permanent collection of the gallery. Thus, Arreguin's work is now in the permanent collections of two Smithsonian Museums: The National Museum of American Art and the National Portrait Gallery.

Index of Images